Florence Marryat

For Tanya, a Sensational Woman

Florence Marryat

Catherine Pope

EER
Edward Everett Root, Publishers, Brighton, 2020.

EER
Edward Everett Root, Publishers, Co. Ltd.,
30 New Road, Brighton, Sussex, BN1 1BN, England.
Full details of our overseas agents are given on our website.
www.eerpublishing.com

edwardeverettroot@yahoo.co.uk

Catherine Pope, *Florence Marryat*

Key Popular Women Writers series, Volume 2.

First published in Great Britain in 2020.

© Catherine Pope 2020.

This edition © Edward Everett Root 2020.

ISBN: 978-1-911454-63-2 Paperback
ISBN: 978-1-911454-66-3 Hardback
ISBN: 978-1-911454-70-0 eBook

Catherine Pope has asserted her right to be identified as the author of this Work in accordance with the Copyright, Designs and Patents Act 1988 as the owner of this Work.

All rights reserved. No part of this publication may be reproduced, stored in a retrieval system or transmitted in any form or by any means, electronic, mechanical, photocopying, recording or otherwise, without the prior permission of the copyright owner.

Cover designed by Pageset Limited, High Wycombe, Buckinghamshire.

Series editors:
Janine Hatter and Helena Ifill.

This innovative new series delivers original and transformative, peer reviewed, feminist research into the work of leading women writers who were widely read in their time, but who have been under-represented in the canon.

The series offers critical, historical and aesthetic contributions to current literary and theoretical work. Each volume concentrates on one writer.

The first five titles are available:

- *Geraldine Jewsbury* by Abigail Burnham Bloom.
- *Florence Marryat* by Catherine Pope.
- *Margaret Oliphant* by Valerie Sanders.
- *Mrs. Henry Wood* by Mariaconcetta Costantini.
- *Frances Trollope* by Carolyn Lambert.

These will be followed by volumes on:

- *Mary Braddon*
- *Rhoda Broughton*
- *Daphne Du Maurier*
- *Ouida*
- *Mary Shelley*
- *Marie Corelli*
- *Charlotte Riddell*
- *Edith Wharton*

We welcome suggestions for other titles.

The series volumes interrogate the ways in which women writers, their creative processes and published material can be considered feminist, and explore how recent developments in feminist theory can enrich our understanding of popular women writer's lives and literature.

The authors rethink established popular writers and their works, and rediscover and re-evaluate authors who have been largely neglected – often since their initial burst of success in their own historical period. This neglect is often due to the exclusivity and insular nature of the canon which has its roots in the Victorian critical drive to perpetuate a division between high and low culture.

In response, our definition of the "popular" is broadly interpreted to encompass women writers who were read by large sections of the public, and who wrote for the mass publishing market. The series therefore challenges this arbitrary divide, creating a new and dynamic dialogue regarding the canon's expansion by introducing readers to previously under-researched women writers who were nevertheless prolific, known and influential.

Studying the work of these authors can tell us much about women's writing, creativity and publishing practice, and about how popular fiction intervened in pressing political, social and cultural issues surrounding gender, history and women's roles in society.

This is an important and timely series that is inspired by, interrogates, and speaks to a new wave of feminism, new definitions of sex and gender, and new considerations of inter-sectionality. It also reflects growing interest in popular fiction, as well as a feminist desire to broaden and diversify the literary canon.

Ultimately the series sheds light on women writers whose work deserves greater recognition, facilitates and inspires further research, and paves the way for introducing these key women writers into the canon and modern-day studies.

SERIES EDITORS

The editors

DR. JANINE HATTER is an Early Career Researcher based at the University of Hull. With Nickianne Moody she has edited the volume *Fashion and Material Culture in Victorian Fiction and Periodicals,* already published by EER. Her research interests centre on nineteenth-century literature, art and culture, with particular emphasis on popular fiction. She has published on Mary Braddon, Bram Stoker, the theatre and identity, and Victorian women's life writing, as well as on her wider research interests of nineteenth to twenty-first century Science Fiction and the Gothic. She has also co-edited special issues for *Revenant, Supernatural Studies, Nineteenth-Century Gender Studies, Femspec* and the *Wilkie Collins Journal.* Janine is conference co-organiser for the Victorian Popular Fiction Association, and co-founded the Mary Elizabeth Braddon Association.

DR. HELENA IFILL is a Lecturer in English Studies at the University of Aberdeen where she is the Director of the Centre for the Novel. Her research focuses on the interactions between Victorian popular fiction, (pseudo)science and medicine. She is the Secretary of the Victorian Popular Fiction Association and a co-organiser of the Association's annual conference. As well as her monograph, *Creating Character: Theories of Nature and Nurture in Victorian Sensation Fiction* (2018), she has published work on Charlotte Riddell, Florence Marryat, Wilkie Collins, Bram Stoker, and Victorian mesmerism. She has also co-edited special issues for *Nineteenth-Century Gender Studies* and the *Wilkie Collins Journal.*

The author

CATHERINE POPE is a writer, publisher, and workshop facilitator. In 2014 she was awarded a PhD for her thesis on feminism in Florence Marryat's fiction. Since then, Catherine has contributed chapters on Marryat to a number of edited collections, including *For Better, For Worse: Marriage in Victorian Novels* (Routledge, 2017) and *British Women's Writing from Brontë to Bloomsbury, 1840–1940* (Palgrave, 2018).

Contents

Acknowledgements xi

Introduction 1
   "Questionable novels of the day": Women's Sensation Fiction 2
   A *Victorian* Feminist? 6

Chapter 1. A Notable Woman. 13

Chapter 2. "Entirely Different Creations": Marriage and the Sexual Double Standard 35
   "Civilised Monogamy" versus "the Disruptive Vortex": The Politics of Victorian Marriage. 36
   "Forever Defiled": The Wronged Wife in Victorian Fiction 40
   "Who made those laws?": Renegotiating the Marriage Contract 44
   "I've had enough of that sort of thing": Alternatives to Traditional Marriage 49
   Conclusion 56

Chapter 3. "An Entire Subversion of the Domestic Rule": Women and Property 59
   The Married Women's Property Acts in Fact and Fiction. 60
   "That blessed Property Act": Marryat's Political Fiction. 67
   "I don't like to see a woman do such unfeminine things": Women in Charge. 71
   The Majesty of Work. 74
   Conclusion 78

Chapter 4. In Bluebeard's Chamber: The Conflation of Medical and Patriarchal Authority. 81
   "the magnetic touch of his smooth palmed hands": The Doctor in Victorian Fiction 83

"it must be difficult to breathe there": *Nelly Brooke* 84
"You stand in the position of her father": *Petronel* 87
"Poked and prodded, hypnotised, all-but-anatomised": Mesmerism and
    Sexual Propriety...92
"A Bad Imitation of a Man": The Danger of Lady Doctors 95
Conclusion 103

Chapter 5. "Are you not a little prejudiced, dear Doctor?": The Pathologisation of Female Sexuality 105

A "gorgeous throbbing style": *For Ever and Ever* 107
"she is not a woman calculated to make a man happy": The Threat of
    the Racial 'Other'...109
"sbsurd fancies": The Masturbating Hysteric 114
"Are you going to cut me up?" The Rise of Gynaecology............119
Petronel..121
The Strange Transfiguration of Hannah Stubbs.....................123
Conclusion 125

Chapter 6. "Our Mother Who Art in Heaven: The Virgin Mary and Sacred Maternity......................127

"he shall rule over thee": The Biblical basis for male authority.........129
The "Divine Mother" in *My Own Child* 133
"A Bitter Penance": Neglected Spirituality in *The Dead Man's Message* ...144
Conclusion 149

Chapter 7. "Courageous Assertions": Spiritualism and Power 151

"Miss Marryat's Bogus Bogey"?................................152
"A scene of active frottage": Queerness in the Séance Room 155
"It isn't all jam to have a medium in the house": The authoritative
    female voice in *The Strange Transfiguration of Hannah Stubbs* 160
Vested Interests: Hyperfemininity and Homosexuality in *Open! Sesame!* .163
Conclusion 171

Woman of the Future: Conclusion 173

Notes 179

Bibliography 181

Index.. 195

Acknowledgements

It's over 10 years ago that I first encountered Florence Marryat. Since then, many people have aided my quest to discover more about this extraordinary woman. Thank you to the many Victorianists who have generously shared their ideas, questions, and resources – most notably Greta Depledge, Gina O'Brien Hill, Beth Palmer, and Tatiana Kontou. The late Sally Ledger expressed characteristic enthusiasm for my research plans, but sadly is not here to see the results.

During the research on which this book is based, I was supported by a number of people and institutions. Helen Webb from the Research Support Team in the University of Sussex Library helped get me started with my research; Gladstone's Library in Flintshire provided uninterrupted calm, without which I could never have conquered the thesis; the London Library kindly gave me a Thomas Carlyle membership and sent many really bad Victorian novels through the post; the staff at the Public Record Office helped me navigate Marryat's complicated life, and the assistance of the staff of the British Library's manuscript room, particularly Greg Buzwell, was greatly appreciated. My supervisor, Jenny Bourne Taylor, repeatedly reminded me this was a good idea and supplied invaluable critical insight and encouragement. Andrew Maunder and Lindsay Smith were generous and astute viva examiners.

Simone Hull, Florence Marryat's great-great-great-granddaughter illuminated some murky aspects of her ancestor's remarkable life, while Donald Bittner contributed useful information on Francis Lean. I am also grateful to the Beinecke Library at Yale University and the Harry Ransom Center for scanning and sending documents from the Marryat archives.

Thank you to John Spiers for publishing this book as part of the *Key Popular Women Writers* series, and to Helena Ifill and Janine Hatter both for their editorship and for their own contributions to our field. The peer reviewers also made many helpful suggestions.

My dear friend Juliana has been a wonderful cheerleader, providing unflagging encouragement over the last 25 years. Finally, my biggest thanks goes to my partner Tanya, who makes everything possible.

Introduction

When journalist Helen C. Black visited Florence Marryat's home in 1891, she was greeted by a scene of quiet domesticity. The tiny Kensington cottage in a newly-built *cul de sac* teemed with knick-knacks and family photos. The author herself was dressed with "graceful simplicity" (Black, 2011: 96). Missing from the picture was Marryat's lover, Herbert McPherson, an actor thirty-three years her junior. Marryat's two marriages had ended in divorce and separation, and she was shunned by polite society. Her fiction, too, was replete with glimpses of this unconventionality. All this colour is ignored by Black. Instead, we are given a lavish portrait of the author's "pretty, picturesque little house" (95), and invited to marvel at a shrine to her late father, Captain Marryat. Indeed, Florence's own achievements are completely overshadowed by this great man of literature and naval hero. Her novels — she had written over forty by this time — are barely discussed. Instead, Black lingers on the "courageous assertions" in *There is No Death* (101), Marryat's controversial recollections of the séance room.

This foregrounding of Marryat's spiritualist activities is one of the reasons, I propose, why her fiction is often ignored. Not only is Marryat perceived as having abandoned literature in favour of the spiritual realm, but also her beliefs apparently render her fiction unfit for critical attention. Janet Oppenheim in *The Other World* dismisses them all as "forgettable" (Oppenheim, 1985: 38), while John Sutherland categorises them, reductively, as "superheated domestic romances" (Sutherland, 2009: 415). Actually, the 1890s saw some of Marryat's most provocative and radical work, in which she confronted themes such as marital violence, religious doubt, terrorism, vivisection, and interracial marriage. Far from abandoning fiction, Marryat wrote twenty-three novels during this decade, alongside the pursuit of various business interests and a successful career on the stage. No wonder Marryat's daughter described her as exhausted, adding that "She never relaxed her labours, even for a day" (E. Church, 1899: 588).

It would be impossible to produce a study that embraced the breadth of Marryat's creative outputs or even attempt to address all her novels. Instead, by gathering evidence from across the range of her fiction, I seek to establish Marryat as an important (albeit complicated) feminist writer – one who consistently challenged prevailing ideas of femininity in both her life and her work. With a life (1833–99) neatly spanning the Victorian period, Marryat was well placed to experience and to observe how women's lives were transformed during the nineteenth century. At the time of her birth, a wife's legal identity was entirely subsumed into that of her husband; by her death in 1899, women had benefitted from momentous changes that granted them a separate identity and greater rights over their bodies and personal property. As we shall see, Marryat contributed to the debates that heralded these changes, partly through her ability to produce sensation novels at a prodigious rate, and also by pursuing a scandalous and thoroughly un-Victorian lifestyle.

"Questionable novels of the day": Women's Sensation Fiction

Florence Marryat began her writing career in 1865 when the sensation novel was at its zenith. This controversial genre administered "continual shocks by violating decorum" (Mitchell, 1981: 73), and presented "a turbulent universe far removed from mid-Victorian stodginess and respectability" (Hughes, 1980: 4).

Contemporary critics were keen to dismiss it as a fad, intent on limiting its appeal and durability. In an infamous diatribe, Margaret Oliphant complained that "all our minor novelists, almost without exception, are of the school called sensational" (Oliphant, 1867b: 258), quarantining these questionable novels from the work of canonical authors. Future Poet Laureate Alfred Austin remarked in 1870 that "the world may congratulate itself when the last sensational novel has been written and forgotten" (1870: 424). Austin's tirade appeared in the same issue as a serialised version of Marryat's *The Poison of Asps* (1870), a particularly gruesome novella in which a brutal husband disguises himself as an Indian to evade arrest for a crime – a vivid signal that the genre was still flourishing. Indeed, sensation fiction persisted into the 1890s, with Marryat adapting its tropes to make radical arguments about the position of women in Victorian society. It was this habit of subversion that provoked a hostile critical response, especially towards female authors.

In a review of Marryat's second novel *Woman Against Woman* (1865), Geraldine Jewsbury observed: "it is curious that the most questionable novels of the day should be written by women. To judge from their books the ideas of women on points of morals and ethics seem in a state of transition, and consequently of confusion" (1866: 233). This "state of transition" is clearly discernible in Marryat's fiction, and, while lamentable for Jewsbury, it characterises women's writing over the rest of the century. In *Temple Bar*, poet Robert Buchanan commented that: "The birth of the novel has given speech to many ladies who must otherwise have been silent. They have revealed to us hidden chords of the female heart, together with strange suggestions relative to woman's influence on modern society and manners; and they have given practical men some idea of the point of view from which women regard the ethics of the sterner sex" (1862: 135–36). For Buchanan, these "strange suggestions" are unwelcome. He resents the scrutiny to which men are subjected and regrets the inevitable judgement that follows. Denied a public voice in politics and established religion, popular fiction provided a vital platform on which women could voice their opinions – much to the chagrin of those who wished to maintain the *status quo*.

Yet, in the twentieth century, sensation fiction – particularly when written by women – was dismissed as tame and homogenous. As Janice Radway observes: "Most critics assume initially that because these popular genres appear to be formulaic, all differences and variations exhibited by particular examples of them are insignificant. As a result, it becomes possible to analyse a few randomly selected texts because they can be taken as representative of the generic type" (1984: 5–6). For instance, in Elaine Showalter's *A Literature of Their Own* (1977), Marryat is relegated to the 'feminine', rather than 'feminist', phase of women's writing ([1982]: 162). Lyn Pykett subsequently questioned this classification, arguing that some of Marryat's contemporaries made "interventions in the changing debate on the Woman Question" (1992: 6). Pykett nevertheless concludes that "Few (if any) of the female sensationalists could be regarded as either feminist or progressive" (49). Her study concentrates almost exclusively on Mrs Henry Wood and Mary Elizabeth Braddon, taking them as representative of the genre – exactly the approach against which Radway cautions. Nevertheless, Pykett's observation that Showalter's analysis "reveals the problem of concentrating too much on endings at the expense of the more complex middles of novels" is crucial to my study of Marryat (50). Pykett also goes on to call for research focused on individual writers, along with "informed historical analysis of the discursive contexts in which the sensation genre was produced" (78). Happily, this research is underway and significant progress has been made in recovering forgotten Victorian women writers.

Pamela K. Gilbert's *Disease, Desire and the Body in Victorian Women's Popular Novels* (1997) focuses on Mary Elizabeth Braddon, but also includes analyses of novels by Ouida and Rhoda

Broughton, then obscure authors, arguing convincingly that their categorisation as sensation novelists has restricted our willingness to see them as transgressive writers. Gilbert proposes that these authors "offer a rich complexity and intelligent commentary on the culture they represent and create" (7). Andrew Maunder's *Varieties of Women's Sensation Fiction* (2004) represented a landmark in the recovery project initiated by Pykett and Gilbert. Comprising six critical editions of novels by lesser-known authors, this collection challenged the misconception that these writers were simply "unadventurous imitators of their better-known contemporaries" (Maunder 2004, 1:23). It includes Marryat's first novel *Love's Conflict* (1865), Mrs Henry Wood's *St Martin's Eve* (1866), Felicia Skene's *Hidden Depths* (1866), Rhoda Broughton's *Cometh up as a Flower* (1867), Mary Cecil Hay's *Old Myddleton's Money* (1874), and Dora Russell's *Beneath the Wave* (1878). These novels are anything but homogenous, encompassing themes of detection, social commentary, eroticism, and the gothic. As Maunder explains, "sensation fiction by women is a crucial part of the literary history of the nineteenth century," and the increased availability of more obscure novels "enriches our understanding and interpretation of Victorian fiction generally" (2004, 1: xxvii, ix).

While some of these authors gradually became less sensational, Marryat retained her power to shock. As the following work shows, many of her later novels – engaging with controversial themes such as vivisection and female genital mutilation – were as provocative as her early fiction. Unlike her contemporaries, who were tamed by criticism and the passage of time, Marryat retained her impact. In the *Companion to Sensation Fiction* (2011), Greta Depledge explores Kate Newey's contention that Marryat's work is "ideologically challenging" (Newey, 2005: 181). Depledge acknowledges that Marryat "prefigure[s] and vocalise[s] the protests seen in … later feminist writers," yet ultimately agrees with Showalter that "Marryat clearly falls into the 'feminine phase' of women writers" (2011: 312). By evaluating Marryat's writing in relation to comparator authors, I argue that her work forms a uniquely radical protest, evincing the progressiveness often credited to New Woman authors such as Sarah Grand and Mona Caird.

Marryat is also significant in her use of autobiographical fiction, often appearing as a character in novels to share her experiences and opinions with readers. This direct relationship with her audience, often presenting overtly feminist ideas in a polemical style, makes her work distinctive and worthy of further consideration. Barbara Caine has argued that this willingness to create and articulate a shared female experience contributes to a "feminist consciousness" (1993: 9), and I use this concept below to justify my anachronistic use of the term "feminism" to describe Marryat's position.

A *Victorian* Feminist?

Applying the anachronistic label 'feminist' to a Victorian woman is, of course, problematic. As Karen Offen demonstrates, "The term 'feminism' can be endlessly qualified" (1988: 134), and is often used to discuss the women's rights movement before its invention in the 1890s and widespread use in the 1910s (Caine, 1993: 4). Surveying the use of 'feminist' to describe pre-twentieth-century campaigners, Offen identifies the shared characteristic as "the impetus to critique and improve the disadvantaged status of women relative to men within a particular cultural situation" (1988: 132). While Offen concludes that this approach is too simplistic to be effective (134), I nevertheless believe this "impetus" provides a useful model for establishing Marryat, and other campaigners, as nineteenth-century feminists. I agree with Caine's argument that "No other terms suggest adequately the extent or the intensity of their concern about the situation of women or their sense of need to remove the injustices, the obstacles, and the forms of oppression which women faced" (1993: 6). As Caine points out, the terms "liberalism" and "socialism" are used retrospectively (and no less problematically) to describe nineteenth-century political movements (6). Philippa Levine, too, insists that "women's positive identification with one another in a context of political struggle suggests that the use of the term feminism is not anachronistic" (1987: 14), and Denise Riley's argument that "both a concentration on and a refusal of the identity of 'women' are essential to feminism" proves the centrality of the idea to Marryat's fiction (1988: 1).

Through her novels and her non-fiction writing, Marryat campaigned on a wide range of women's issues, including property rights, employment, birth control, wife-beating, medical abuse, divorce, and education. In later life, she even questioned the need for marriage, portraying elective single motherhood in her fiction and lecturing on "The Mistakes of Marriage" (see Chapter 2). In some cases, Marryat actually makes an audacious claim for female supremacy, creating heroines who are physically stronger and more intelligent than their husbands.[1] There is no evidence that Marryat joined any political organisations, perhaps wanting to be seen primarily as a novelist rather than as a campaigner. However, as this book shows, she did engage with the writings of prominent activists such as Frances Power Cobbe, particularly on vivisection, an issue closely linked with the women's movement. Like many outspoken nineteenth-century women, Marryat was not an ardent supporter of female suffrage. While in a few of the more polemical novels, such as *Her World Against a Lie* (1878), heroines express their desire for the vote, Marryat makes no sustained argument in its favour. In *At Heart a Rake* (1895), a novel centred around a women's club, the issue is conspicuous by its absence. The reasons for Marryat's reticence are unclear but might be explained by apathy towards the political system, or a belief that women could control their own lives without governmental intervention once basic rights had been achieved. As will become apparent throughout this study, Victorian feminism was no less complicated than the twenty-first-century movement.

Marryat frequently appears ambivalent and often contradicts herself. While she appears a beacon of progressiveness in some novels, in others her views are repugnant to the modern reader, especially on issues of class and race. So, she is a feminist, but not one with whom twenty-first-century feminists would wish to wholeheartedly identify.

In her personal life Marryat challenged convention through openly adulterous behaviour, co-habiting in preference to marriage, and establishing a legal basis for her status as breadwinner. By also writing about these aspects of her life and adapting them for the stage, Marryat encouraged her readers to think about their own lives differently. If we see feminism as relative to its historical context, then Marryat's radicalism emphatically deserves that label. Riley identifies women as a "volatile collectivity in which female persons can be very differently positioned, so that apparent continuity of the subject of 'women' isn't to be relied on," concluding that "these instabilities of the category are the *sine qua non* of feminism" (1988: 2). I establish Marryat's heroines as a "volatile collectivity," with their instability indicative of the author's feminist agenda. Her heroines are often wives and mothers, but they are seldom confined to the domestic sphere. What emerges is a problematic female body that must be subjected to regulation to maintain social order, along with an inherent contradiction between the concept of femininity as innate and the need to reinforce it. Marryat does not show women as helpless victims of oppressive patriarchy, rather as cultural agents who resisted and redefined the identity imposed upon them during this crucial period of social change. As Mary Poovey observes:

> The epistemological term woman could guarantee men's identity only if difference were fixed – only if, that is, the binary opposition between the sexes was more important than any other kinds of difference that real women might experience. And this depended, among other things, on

INTRODUCTION

> limiting women's right to define or describe themselves.
> ... women were granted the authority to write and publish literature, but they were largely denied access to "masculine" discourses like medicine, law, and theology. (1988: 80–11)

By representing and then challenging the regulation that impeded women's participation in these discourses of medicine, law, and theology, Marryat's novels offer an important insight into how Victorian gender roles were constructed and resisted. As this book demonstrates, Marryat's work constitutes an effective protest against legal, medical, and religious regulation. As Ross Forman proposes, "Historicising sensation fiction and thinking historically about the culture in which it emerged gives us tools to access the secrets and stratagems the Victorians used in representing sex and gender" (2011: 416), an approach used here to argue that Marryat's work is far more ideologically challenging than previous critics have suggested.

Sally Mitchell makes the important point that it is "improper (as well as fruitless) to deal in wholly intellectual terms with novels which were written for an emotional – rather than an intellectual – response" (1977: 31). Most of Marryat's novels would collapse if interrogated in terms of artistic or literary quality, having been written hurriedly and for a largely undiscriminating audience. However, as Ann Cvetkovich concludes: "The sensation novel, and sensationalism more generally, makes events emotionally vivid by representing in tangible and specific terms social and historical structures that would otherwise remain abstract" (1992: 23). My theoretical approach is, therefore, primarily socio-historical, examining Marryat's novels within the context of contemporary discourses and making extensive use of associated primary sources. Arguing that history and fiction are effectively indistinguishable, Beverley Southgate concludes that "novelists, unconstrained by any pressure to disciplinary consensus might be more free than historians to look at the past in fresh ways – and so, as individual observers, catch sight of alternative people and events from alternative perspectives. Such writers can also foreground topics that have otherwise been ignored or sidelined" (2009: 10). It is these "alternative people" and "alternative perspectives" that Marryat presents in her novels, creating what Rosemary Bodenheimer calls "fictional paths through highly charged ideological territories" (1988: 3). They are not always neat paths. Many lead us through tangled and sometimes uncomfortable territories, and our guide is more interested in being provocative than in building allegiances.

In Chapter 1, I provide the context for Marryat's fiction by telling the story of her life. Using archival materials and her memoirs, I piece together the events that influenced the feminist ideas in her novels. Marryat's challenge to the institution of marriage forms the basis for Chapter 2. By exploring the ways in which she exposed the sexual double standard, I argue that Marryat undermined Victorian ideology and presented different possibilities for women. Moving on to the theme of money in Chapter 3, I show how the passing of the Married Women's Property Acts proved a crucial landmark for women like Marryat. I evaluate Marryat's engagement with the debates surrounding this legislation and her assertion of a wife's right to an independent existence.

The conflation of medical and patriarchal authority is a dominant theme in Marryat's fiction, evidenced in her repeated use of plots involving women married to doctors who abuse their position. I analyse those novels in Chapter 4, explaining how Marryat questioned men's supposedly unassailable moral authority. In Chapter 5, I consider the ways in which the diagnosis of hysteria was used to pathologise female sexuality and control 'deviant' behaviour such as lesbianism and masturbation. My close readings of Marryat's fiction reveal her argument that women's role was more than reproductive – for her, 'deviance' meant liberation.

Marryat's religious doubts were prompted partly by the ways in which the established church sought to uphold the subordinate

INTRODUCTION

position of women. In Chapter 6, I discuss her conversion to Roman Catholicism and espousal of Mariolatry – a practice that allowed her to create a strong yet feminine spiritual role model. Finally, in Chapter 7, I examine how and why Marryat came to embrace Spiritualism in her life and work, a bold move that allowed her to imagine a gynocentric faith that opposed the patriarchal hierarchy of the established church.

CHAPTER 1

A Notable Woman

"The great thing ... is to be bold. People take you so much for what you seem."

Mount Eden

Florence Marryat left no diary, few personal letters, and deliberately obfuscated some aspects of her life. She also suffered convenient memory lapses, and a tendency to cast herself as either the heroine or the victim in any situation. Much of what is known about her has been pieced together from fragmentary memoirs in her non-fiction works and accounts written by her contemporaries. Her daughter Ethel wrote a candid, yet affectionate, obituary – "The Real Florence Marryat" – that illuminates aspects of her character. Some gaps can be filled through official documents, such as marriage and death certificates, census returns, and court proceedings. We also have *The Nobler Sex* (1892), a novel that follows the documented events of Marryat's life closely with only a few details, mainly names and locations, changed. Written retrospectively in the first person as Molly Malmaison, it fulfils George P. Landow's criteria for the text to be classed as autobiographical: "a work must not only present a version, myth, or metaphor of the self, but it must also be retrospective and hence it must self-consciously contrast two selves, the writing "I" and the one located (or created) in the past" (Landow, 1979: xliii).

Every chapter heading in *The Nobler Sex* starts with "I", reinforcing that it is Marryat, rather than the heroine, who is addressing the reader. The narrative commences with the statement: "What I am about to write is the true history of my life" (Marryat, 1890b: 5–6), concluding: "I have told my story clumsily, perhaps, but I have told it truly" (313–4). Although interpreting autobiographical fiction is undoubtedly problematic, the intersections between known facts and dramatic versionings can offer an insight into the emotional turmoil behind the official documents. For example, Eliza Lynn Linton's *The Autobiography of Christopher Kirkland* is frequently accepted as an account of the author's life (Anderson, 2002: x), even though the central character is a man; this subterfuge allowing Linton to describe her sexual relationships with women. Marryat uses self-representation throughout her writing – telling Helen C. Black that "The most successful of my works are transcripts of my own experience" (2011: 101) – but *The Nobler Sex* is the only novel written in a clearly autobiographical style.

Florence Marryat was born on 9 July 1833,[2] the ninth child of Captain Frederick Marryat, distinguished mariner and popular novelist, and Catherine Shairp, daughter of the British Charge d'Affaires in St. Petersburg. Her parents legally separated in 1839, the young Florence dividing her time between their two homes: the Captain's Norfolk estate and her mother's small house at Southsea (E. Church, 1899: 588). Although she held her father in high esteem throughout her life, Florence was clearly perturbed by the way in which the separation affected her parents disproportionately, this forming a recurring theme in her fiction. As a middle-class woman born at the beginning of the nineteenth century, there was no possibility of Catherine Marryat earning her own living, so she spent the remainder of her life dependent on her daughters. In 1893, *The Idler* asked popular novelists "Is childhood the happiest or the most miserable period of one's existence?" Marryat responded candidly: "If I am to choose one, or the other extreme, I should say decidedly the most miserable, and made so by the folly, ignorance, or neglect of parents. Not one hundredth part of the men and women who marry are fit to become fathers and mothers" ("The Idlers Club", 1893: 234). This idea is perpetuated throughout her fiction, with heroines succeeding in spite of, rather than because of, their parentage. Later, Marryat spoke frequently on the need for alternatives to marriage and reproduction.

Marryat's biography of her father, *The Life and Letters of Captain Marryat* (1872), describes a benevolent and indulgent parent whose children received an erratic education. Florence and her sisters were taught by a succession of ineffectual governesses, their lessons supplemented by the Captain's language lessons (Marryat, 1872: 239–40). Given the sustained criticism of Marryat's French and grammar throughout her career, the Captain was an unsuccessful, if enthusiastic, pedagogue. Much of Marryat's later fiction calls for middle-class women to be formally educated,[3] either so they can seek fulfilling employment or become better wives to intelligent husbands. Captain Marryat was remembered with pride and affection by Florence; Catherine Marryat, conversely, is largely absent from her memoirs and there is no mention of her at all in the biography beyond the elliptical "His widow also survives him" (322). In a letter to the publisher Richard Bentley on 18 February 1866, Geraldine Jewsbury deplored the "cursory" manner in which the author treated her parents' marriage, concluding: "The impression made upon me by the biography is unpleasant" (Bentley Archives, Add. MSS 46657). Mrs Marryat was certainly a difficult character, and Florence perhaps thought silence preferable to either honesty or evasion. Recalling an encounter with the Marryats in Lausanne, Charles Dickens makes Catherine Marryat sound like one of his most ridiculous female characters: "Poor fellow! He seems to have had a hard time of it with his wife. She had no interest whatever in the children; and was such a fury, that, being dressed to go out to dinner, she would sometimes, on no other provocation than a pin out of place or some such thing, fall upon a little maid she had, beat her till she couldn't stand, then tumble into hysterics, and be carried to bed" (cited in Forster, 1873: 2: 269).

While she was discreet in her memoirs, Florence's various fictional portrayals of profoundly dysfunctional mother-daughter relationships indicate the sensitivity of the situation. Where mothers are present, they are at best ineffectual and at worst malevolent, conspiring to deny their daughters' right to self-determination. Most accounts of Catherine Marryat describe her as intensely pious, and the dedication in Florence's 1869 novel, *The Girls of Feversham*, indicates her mother's attitude towards her literary career: "My dearest mother, I dedicate to you this little story; the first, perhaps, from my pen, in which not a line is to be found which can be called 'sensational,' and trust you will accept it with the love of your daughter" (Marryat, 1869a). This dedication is either disingenuous or mischievous: the plot features murder, elopement, and two families functioning quite happily without a mother. Marryat makes a rare reference to Mrs Marryat in *The Spirit World* (1894), twelve years after her death, recounting her horror when her young son on his deathbed demanded beer instead of soothing descriptions of the afterlife (1894c: 28).

To escape the stultifying atmosphere of the family home, Florence married a man she hardly knew: "she naturally looked upon the prospect as one of emancipation from the muffin worries, tabby gatherings, and woolwork, which formed the only distractions of life at Southsea" (E. Church, 1899: 588). The wedding took place just a few weeks before her twenty-first birthday, although she later claimed to have been only sixteen (Dolman, 1891: 1–2; Black, 2011: 98) – perhaps to downplay her share of the responsibility for what proved to be an unfortunate match. Little is known of the courtship of Thomas Ross Church and Florence Marryat, beyond the fact that Church was a frequent visitor to Marryat's grandmother's house in Wimbledon (E.

Church, 1899: 588). After several years' engagement, she headed out to be married on the Malaysian island of Penang on 13 June 1854 (Public Record Office: Marriage Certificate). In the novella "A Lucky Disappointment", Laura Gray escapes a life that "had been monotonous in its dull tranquillity" (Marryat, 1876a: 13) by sailing for the Cape of Good Hope to marry her fiancé after a six-year separation. On arrival, she is bitterly disappointed by his sallow complexion and general air of seediness. Her dreams are shattered. Discovering that he has been pursuing a less-than-discreet affair with a mixed-race woman, Laura hops on the next ship home and rejoices in her escape. Perhaps this is what Marryat *wished* had happened to her. Writing after her mother's death, Marryat's daughter said of this marriage: "She was too young to realise the responsibility of entering into a life-long engagement with a man who was more or less a stranger to her" (E. Church, 1899: 588). As one of seven daughters in a genteel family, Marryat probably saw few options beyond marriage, not relishing the prospect of adding to the pool of 'surplus' women. Although the Marryats were relatively wealthy, Florence's inheritance comprised only a one-fifth share in an investment worth £15,804 – certainly not enough to lead the life she had been brought up to expect. While this money was meagre, it formed part of her marriage settlement, later becoming the subject of two legal battles.

Thus, Marryat became the wife of an Ensign in the 12th Madras Staff Corps and began her new life in the Raj. Describing the experience as "seven years passed in exile" (Marryat, 1868a: 1), Marryat grew frustrated with the expatriate community. In her wonderfully waspish and indiscreet memoir *Gup* (1868), she described them as "characteristically divided into three classes – the gay; the religious; and the inane" (Marryat, 1868a: 9). In an obituary of Marryat for *Womanhood*, C. J. Hamilton observed that these recollections "made enemies for the authoress" (1900: 3). In some respects, the environment was no more propitious than her former family home, but there were some distinct benefits.

Marryat recalls that married women were often left alone for long periods while their husbands were away on active duty; they were also allowed to receive male visitors without a chaperone. During a later posting to Burma, Marryat was free to ride through the Rangoon jungle with an unmarried man, intimating just how easy it was for wives to pursue extra-marital affairs when released from the strictures of English society. Commenting on the position of women, Marryat adds: "The Burmese laws are not much in favour of the weaker vessel, but in this again, I cannot see that in most respects our civilisation teaches us to outstrip them" (Marryat, 1868a: 282). Church, meanwhile, was not endearing himself to either his wife or his men. Marryat recalled that he was "considered a martinet". Such was his unpopularity, a Madras Sepoy fired at his back "with the intent to kill him". Unfortunately, the bullet instead hit his colleague, who subsequently died (Marryat, 1891c: 243).

Marryat returned home from India in December 1860, suffering from exhaustion and trauma. She was greatly shaken by the death of close friend John Powles eight months earlier, recalling that "His death and the manner of it caused me a great shock". This event and "other troubles combined" made it intolerable for her to remain with her husband. She was accompanied by three children and pregnant with a fourth, describing the five-month journey as a "terrible affair" (64). Church remained in India and they were effectively separated – his military records show that he progressed up the ranks and did not seek to join a regiment based in England (Public Record Office: Military Records). A fortnight after her arrival in England, Marryat gave birth to her fourth child, also called Florence. She was born with a cleft palate and had to be fed by artificial means during her ten-day existence. Her death certificate cites the causes as "inanition" (General Register Office: Death Certificate for Florence Church), or what became known as failure to thrive. Essentially, she was unable to feed and there was no reliable surgical procedure for cleft palate at the time. Marryat claims the baby's condition was considered so unusual that it was reported in *The Lancet*, although under assumed names,[4] adding: "I was closely catechised as to whether I had suffered any physical or mental shock that could account for the injury to my child, and it was decided that the trouble I had experienced was sufficient to produce it" (73).

In Marryat's short story "The Box with the Iron Clamps", published in *London Society* in May-June 1868, Blanche Damer gives birth to a deformed baby after an extra-marital affair. She carries its tiny skeleton around in a sealed box as a symbol of her guilt. In *A Fatal Silence* (1891), Paula Bjørnson's son is born with severe learning difficulties as a result of her husband kicking her in the stomach during pregnancy. Perhaps most notably, in Marryat's first novel, *Love's Conflict* (1865), Elfrida Treherne's sickly baby survives only a few hours. Thanks to censorship by Geraldine Jewsbury, Elfrida blames herself for thinking of a man other than her husband and sees it as God's punishment.[5] Significantly, in a later novel, *A Harvest of Wild Oats* (1877), Elfrida reappears to ascribe the baby's death to the stress of living with a violent husband. One possible interpretation is that Marryat became pregnant after an extra-marital affair, causing her husband to react violently. Certainly, the latitude she was given in India and Burma, along with repeated references in memoirs to a friendship she was obliged to end, make this plausible. The most likely candidate is John Powles, whose death in India contributed to Marryat's breakdown. Although Marryat insisted they never had any physical contact, the episodes in which his spirit visits her in *There is No Death* suggest intimacy beyond that which might be expected from a platonic friendship at the time.

Alone in England with three children to support, and receiving only limited financial assistance from Church, Marryat was encouraged to start writing by her childhood friend, Annie Thomas, herself a successful author. Marryat initially exploited her father's illustrious network, asking Charles Dickens for help in establishing her literary career. Although her original letter has disappeared, his withering response (described by the *Metro* as a "sassy reply to a wannabe writer" ["Charles Dickens Sent This Sassy Reply to Writer Florence Marryat"; online]) recently came up for auction at Bonham's. In the sale catalogue, the auctioneer describes it as "wonderfully rude". Annoyed that Marryat had the temerity to solicit feedback on an article she had offered to *All the Year Round*, Dickens denounced her request as "scarcely reasonable": "To read professed contributions honestly, and communicate a perfectly unprejudiced decision respecting every one of them to its author or authoress, is a task of the magnitude of which you evidently have no conception" (Bonhams, nd: online). Undaunted, Marryat would go on to edit her own journal, and to enjoy a personal life just as complicated as Dickens's. She later described him as "highly strung, nervous, and imaginative" (Marryat, 1891b: 7).

Marryat submitted her first novel, *Love's Conflict*, to Richard Bentley in November 1864. It was published the following year, although only after extensive revision by his reader, Geraldine Jewsbury. This work earned Marryat a relatively modest fee of £100, but she quickly followed it up with two further novels in the same year, *Woman Against Woman* and *Too Good for Him*, in which Isobel Reverdon turns to novel-writing to support her baby after her husband absconds. The plot, title, and emetic dedication suggest a jibe at Thomas Ross Church: "To Him whose life is one with mine, and for whom every effort of my own is made" (Marryat, 1865b). There appears to have been an uneasy truce between Marryat and Church during the remainder of the decade. They corresponded regularly (the letters have been since destroyed) and he visited "3–4 times" ("A Military Divorce Case", 1878: 5) (there were four more children, so four is the more likely figure, assuming he was the father). He is recorded as present in the family home at the 1871 census, but this coincides with their more formal separation, so he had probably returned temporarily to settle his affairs. In this year the first Married Women's Property

Act came into effect, allowing Marryat to control her own earnings and live more independently (see Chapter 2). Church's brother, Edward, was a frequent visitor and seems to have helped Marryat through this difficult time ("A Military Divorce Case", 1878: 5). She dedicated her 1866 novel *For Ever and Ever* to him. Notably, it is the story of an adulterous army captain in India who physically and mentally abuses his wife and child.

Matters had come to a head in 1870 when Marryat converted to Roman Catholicism. Her daughter Ethel later commented that "The emotional character of that faith was peculiarly adapted to a temperament like hers" (E. Church, 1899: 589). Church strongly disapproved, fearing his children would be brought up as papists. He threatened to divorce her unless she converted back to Anglicanism, and she dutifully obliged. This rapprochement swiftly gave way to an irrevocable breach, and the couple resolved to separate. Marryat was now effectively an independent woman. In 1872 she assumed the editorship of *London Society*, a monthly shilling magazine that regularly published her work. Through her regular unsigned opinion pieces, she assumed a male identity and lent support to her favoured causes, such as the status of the theatrical profession and, later on, Spiritualism. She was an imposing figure, both physically and professionally, and letters from her male contributors show deference and respect (Palmer, 2009: 148, 147). Edmund Downey, assistant to Marryat's publisher William Tinsley, was warned: "She is a tall, striking-looking woman, and she'll talk to you just like a man" (Downey, 1905: 38–9). As an editor, Marryat inhabited the public sphere, but she became an even more prominent figure when she entered the theatrical world.

Marryat's first play, *Miss Chester*, opened at the Holborn Theatre on 6 October 1872, and has been described as "the searing dramatisation of the pain of an older woman" (Newey, 2001: 157). Although Newey categorises the play as a "full-blooded domestic melodrama ... in the mould of *East Lynne* and *Lady Audley's Secret*," she also views it as "more subversive than the overt critiques by later Victorian feminists" in terms of challenging the relegation of emotion to the private, and therefore feminine, sphere (157–8). Although most reviews were unfavourable, all critics noted the force, passion and emotion of the title character. Marryat took a bow on the opening night, thereby publicly associating herself with the piece ("Holborn Theatre", 1872: 72).

The following year Marryat was encouraged by a fellow journalist to attend a séance at the home of Mrs Holmes, a celebrated American medium. So began a life-long belief in Spiritualism, which made her even more conspicuous. Marryat again converted to Roman Catholicism in 1874 and managed to reconcile it with her spiritualistic beliefs, creating her own gynocentric faith (see Chapters 6 and 7). This return to Rome infuriated Thomas Ross Church, who asserted his masculine privilege by claiming sole custody of the children and making another attempt to claim his wife's marriage settlement. Marryat recalled this episode through her heroine Mollie in *The Nobler Sex*:

> It was to the Court of Chancery, therefore, that, by my solicitor's advice, I presently appealed, to afford me some redress against the man who had benefited by the use of my earnings for so long, and then actually robbed me of the possessions I had acquired with them. The [Second] Married Woman's Property Act had not then passed, but had it done so, my marriage had taken place too soon for me to take advantage of it, so that an appeal to the Lord Chancellor for protection was the only remedy open to me. (1890b: 133)

The Bill of Complaint (Public Records Office) filed against Church shows that the investment he claimed should have been passed down to their children, and, in any case, only after the death of Marryat's mother, Catherine. Church had already tried to declare his (still living) mother-in-law dead in order to access the funds through probate. As coverture still operated and husband and wife were indivisible in law, Marryat and Church were cited as the defendant, and their infant children were the plaintiffs. The legal files show that Marryat's earnings were covering two-thirds of the household expenditure, and her statement that she had "largely provided towards the support of herself and her children for several years" weakened Church's position. The court decided that the money should be retained for the children and that they were sufficiently well cared for by their mother. Marryat's public protest belied the idea of the husband as breadwinner. As she later wrote, "it would not need much perspicuity ... to guess from whom the butter that spread the bread came" (1894c: 95). This was a bold and very public challenge to patriarchy.

In return for her partial freedom, Marryat agreed to largely support herself and the children, this point marking her transformation from wife to businesswoman. She became more aware of her earning capacity, demanding larger advances from her publishers and licensing her copyrights, rather than selling them outright. This allowed her to support a household of seven children and four servants (Marryat, 1891c: 68). Marryat's contracts in the Bentley Archives show that she stipulated better terms and was more commercially astute than some of her literary contemporaries (Bassett, 2010: 60–6). Through his research in the Tillotson archives, Graham Law notes that Marryat could earn up to £360 for the serialisation of a novel (2000: 68). Not afraid to capitalise on her famous name, Marryat used her father's contacts and kept pestering Dickens for endorsements. When she sent him a copy of *The Confessions of Gerald Estcourt* (1867), Dickens recoiled from her portrayal of extra-marital sex and prostitution, complaining of a "certain coarseness" (Marryat Family Papers).[6] His discomfort was compounded when Marryat dedicated her bigamy novel *Veronique* (1869) to him.

Marryat subsequently made a complete break with her previous life, undertaking a theatrical tour with the celebrated actor and satirist George Grossmith (Joseph, 1982: 61). The tour lasted much of 1876–77, taking them all over the United Kingdom and Ireland. The show was called *Entre Nous* and comprised piano sketches and recitations in historical costume, concluding with a short play entitled *Cups and Saucers*. Although the performance received mixed reviews, the attendant publicity raised their respective profiles, establishing them both as public performers (62). While performing in Chatham, Marryat met Francis Lean, a retired colonel with eight children. He had already filed a petition for divorce from his wife, Lettice Anne Cumming, on the grounds of her adultery with two men and her "habits of intemperance and drunkenness" (Public Record Office: Divorce Court Proceedings, J77/186/4810). The illustrator Harry Furniss, who worked with Marryat on *London Society*, recalled in his memoirs that "she sent all her friends and acquaintances, myself included, a statement in cold printer's ink, informing us that she was not divorced, but that in future she wished to be known as Mrs. Lean. This little piece of eccentricity fell into her husband's solicitor's hands and thus ended the Church business" (1923: 11).

Thomas Ross Church sued for divorce, citing his wife's adultery with Lean. Both denied the charge, but a *decree nisi* was granted to Church, with costs. Counsel for the prosecution spoke of the difficulties caused by Marryat's religious conversion, resulting in "unpleasantness," probably a euphemism for violence. A letter to her daughter Ethel was read in which she described taking the seemingly foolhardy step of living with Lean owing to all the unhappiness she had endured during her married life: "However surprised and shocked you may be at the intelligence, do not leave off loving me when I tell you that Colonel Lean and I have determined for the future to live together as man and wife. My darling, you do not know half of what I have suffered, and I pray God you may never know" ("Sad Immorality", 1878: 3).

After the decree absolute was issued, Church again (unsuccessfully) claimed Marryat's inheritance through a variation of settlement. Marryat responded: "I further say in answer to the said Petition that the Petitioner has sufficient means of his own for his own maintenance and that he has no occasion to resort to my property for the purpose of obtaining a settlement out of the same for his own benefit but that I am willing upon my death that my 1/5 share of the said sum be divided amongst my children" (Public Record Office: Divorce Court Proceedings, J77/209/5660). Although now free, Marryat had suffered the unedifying experience of divorce and found herself ostracised from polite society. While divorce became easier after the 1857 Matrimonial Causes Act, there were only around 250 petitions filed each year, compared with 170,000 marriages. A divorced woman remained an anomaly. Marryat felt solidarity with George Eliot, writing her a heartfelt letter of sympathy on the death of George Henry Lewes, with whom she had co-habited while his wife was still living.[7]

Marryat and Lean were married on 5 June 1879, a week after the final decree was granted – the bride admitting to only thirty-nine of her forty-five years on the marriage certificate. Curiously, Lean's journal makes no mention of his marriage to Marryat, whereas he includes full details of the guest list and gifts for his first wedding (Bittner, 2013: email). Cumming was reluctant to relinquish her husband, apparently exerting a malign influence over his second marriage. A medium told Marryat: "She would go any lengths to take that you value from you, even to compassing your death. She is madly in love with what is yours" (Marryat, 1891c: 176). There is no record of Cumming's antics, but this marriage was no happier than the first. The violence and humiliation endured by Marryat is painfully chronicled in both *The Nobler Sex* and *Miss Harrington's Husband* (1886). *With Cupid's Eyes* (1881) is a bitter tale of a talented and hard-working artist whose dissipated husband fritters away all her earnings. A clairvoyant helpfully pointed out where Marryat had gone wrong: "You tell him too often that you love him ... He is not the only man in the world. Why should you deceive him by saying so? You are much to blame" (179). Lean's infidelities were legion, and Marryat later recalled suffering a number of stillbirths during their marriage (158). This was the model of an unhappy marriage.

After spending a week alone in Brighton in July 1880 (48), Marryat distanced herself from Lean, again taking to the stage. Shortly before their marriage, she had written to the actor-manager Henry Irving, informing him of her dramatic talent and requesting that he consider her for Shakespearean parts (Marryat, 1879: online). There is no record of his response or of Marryat having assumed the role she craved. It seems unlikely that a distinguished actor would have taken a risk on an untrained forty-five-year-old actress. In 1881 she took matters into her own hands by adapting her novel *Her World Against a Lie*, securing for herself the lead role of Hephzibah Horton, a crusading feminist who encourages a young friend to leave her violent husband. The novel discusses both the Matrimonial Causes and Married Women's Property Acts, a programme of legislation that gradually improved the legal position of women (see Chapters 2 and 3). As with her earlier play *Miss Chester*, Marryat portrayed the wrongs of woman on the public stage.

Having received excellent reviews, she was invited to join the D'Oyly Carte company, touring Britain and Ireland for twelve months as Lady Jane in *Patience*. Due to the illness of her predecessor, Marryat had less than a day to rehearse for her first performance. Unsure of the timings, she made an unscheduled appearance on stage and belted out the wrong note, throwing the chorus into utter confusion (Marryat, 1891c: 37). How Marryat secured such a prestigious role is unclear, given there is no evidence of formal training. What she lacked in experience, though, was countervailed by her tenacity, appetite for hard work, and willingness to exploit her father's name. Although her performance schedule was demanding, she nevertheless managed to write three novels during this period, all of them concerned with elevating the position of actresses, describing the stage as a respectable career for an independent woman. Marryat also published a pamphlet entitled "The Majesty of Work" (1882), in which she argued forcefully that women should be encouraged to train for gainful employment, as they would be then less likely to enter into unhappy marriages (see Chapter 2).

The 1880s also saw several unauthorised stage adaptations of Marryat's novels, the letters page of theatrical newspaper *The Era* broadcasting her annoyance with the worst offenders, Augustus Daly, C. H. Hazelwood and J. S. Blythe (Marryat, 1886b: 11). She felt particularly strongly about the versions of *Her World Against a Lie* that heightened the sensation and abandoned the political message regarding women's rights. It is ironic that a novel that espoused a woman's entitlement to her own income should have been so ruthlessly exploited by men. As Kerry Powell writes, adaptations of women's novels by male playwrights "represent a massive assault against women writers that is both textual and sexual in nature" (1997: 101). Marryat was also obliged to defend her literary reputation five years later, when Charles Ogilvie published a serialised novella *The Lost Diamonds*, claiming that it had been co-authored by Marryat. In fact, she had contributed only one scene, which Ogilvie expanded into four chapters (Marryat, 1891d: 3). Marryat's name was highly marketable. Finding herself single again after formally separating from Lean, Marryat needed to control her literary assets carefully. This time, however, the law was on Marryat's side and she could extricate herself from her husband without sacrificing her wealth or future earnings. The 1882 Married Women's Property Act ensured that both her money and her home belonged to her, rather than to him.

Marryat celebrated her liberty with a one-woman show, *Love Letters* – described as an "immediate and undeniable success" – which won her a role in W. S. Gilbert's *The Palace of Truth* (Marryat, 1891c: 161). In Spring 1884, a Boston-based impresario invited her to tour the USA with *Love Letters*, an opportunity she immediately grasped. Marryat recounted her experiences in a memoir, *Tom Tiddler's Ground* (1886), including an investigation of the American divorce laws:

> A judge in New York sent me the Code of Divorce, and I was astonished to see the penalties attached to any breach of the marriage contract. A man cannot strike his wife, nor call her a bad name, nor use any violence towards her, without running the risk of being had up in court for the offence. In the State of New York, divorce is obtainable only on the grounds of adultery. No cruelty is needed to be proved against the man in addition to the first offence, for it is a thing almost unknown that a man should treat his wife as men do in England. (Marryat, 1886c: 199)

This anecdote suggests that Marryat was considering divorcing Lean, but she opted instead for a legal separation. Her reasons are unclear, but if she had no intention of remarrying, then there was no compelling reason to suffer the expense and humiliation of a second court case. As Marryat wrote when still married to her first husband: "No single life, however lonely and unblest, can be so cursed, as that of a woman unhappily married" (Marryat, 1865b: 3:257). Thanks to a transformation in the legal position of wives, she was financially independent and also protected from the man who had abused her.

On her return from the tour, Marryat established the School of Literary Art, instituted for the "instruction of both sexes desirous of entering the Literary Profession, in the Arts of Composing and writing Fiction, Journalism, and the construction of Drama" (British Library, 1885: np). As an entrepreneur, Marryat was looking for other ways to profit from the ever-growing demand for novels. In his memoirs, novelist Francis Gribble claims she addressed her first pupil, a shy and timorous youth, thus: "Are you in love? No? Have you ever been in love? No? Then go away and fall in love at once, and when you have done so, come back and tell me about it. No one can possibly write fiction until he has fallen in love" (Gribble, 1929: 122). The youth was said to have run away from the school and never dared return. In *The Private Papers of Henry Ryecroft* (1903), George Gissing's protagonist recalls: "I heard not long ago, of an eminent lawyer, who had paid a couple of hundred per annum for his son's instruction in the art of fiction — yea, the art of fiction — by a not very brilliant professor of that art" (Gissing, 1904: 211). Admittedly Marryat was not a "not very brilliant professor," but one who was more astute than Gissing in surviving the late-Victorian literary marketplace. These anecdotes aside, there is no evidence to indicate the success or otherwise of this venture.

In 1887 Marryat was devastated by the death of her beloved eldest daughter, Eva. Although the death certificate records the cause as "Premature Labour Septicaemia 8 days" (General Register Office: Death Certificate for Eva Florence Stevens), her great-granddaughter believes it was the result of a botched abortion, as no record exists of a baby having been born (Hull, 2010: email). As a touring actress with five children and married to a fellow actor, another addition to Eva's family was perhaps unwelcome. Marryat supervised the posthumous publication of Eva's only novel, *An Actress's Love Story*, writing a moving preface in which she implored critics to treat this literary début gently, as the author had no opportunity to learn from her mistakes (E. R. Church, 1888). Characteristically, Marryat used work as a distraction from her grief, producing and appearing in her son's play *The Golden Goblin*, the first woman to claim this distinction (Dolman, 1891: 2). Her writing and performances also became increasingly feminist in tone, including talks and articles on "What to Do with the Men" and "The Mistakes of Marriage". While this might suggest a renunciation of the sterner sex, Marryat had not abandoned men altogether.

The 1891 census shows she was living with Herbert McPherson, an actor thirty-three years her junior. Marryat artfully closed the gap by claiming to be only forty-five (she was actually fifty-seven). Papers in the Harry Ransom Archive suggest they met in 1885 while Marryat was touring the USA, and an extract of a poem by Marryat reveals the nature of their relationship:

> You in the bloom of Spring,
> And I, in the fading year;
> What magic wrought this wondrous thing,
> What made you love me, Dear? (Mayes Family Papers).

Two of her novels during this period show women in relationships with much younger men. In *Gentleman and Courtier* (1888), Elsa Carden breaks off her engagement to Jocelyn Yorke after friends presume he is her son. Reviewers were relieved by this narrative twist, believing the nine-year age gap to be insupportable. The fact that the teenaged Elsa's first suitor, the family doctor, was a quarter of a century her senior was not mentioned ("New Novels", 1896a: 382). Through the narrator, Marryat ponders:

> It is said that there is no love like that of a woman for a man younger than herself, and it is not improbable, since it unites the connubial and maternal love with the knowledge of being necessary in a double sense to the object of her affection – that is, as friend and counsellor as well as a wife. How many marriages between young people turn out miserably, because the woman is led to expect she can look up to and lean upon a man whose moral strength snaps like a rotten reed at the first strain; and the husband, who has married for companionship and assistance in his domestic life as well as love, finds himself closeted evening after evening with a girl who has no power to amuse him by her conversation. (Marryat, 1888: 2: 214)

Marryat is more confident in her next depiction of a May-December relationship, *The Beautiful Soul* (1895), allowing her plain middle-aged heroine, Felicia Hetherington, to marry handsome young journalist Archibald Nasmyth.

The Nobler Sex (1890) marks a watershed between her unhappy marriages and this new phase of her life. Closely modelled on Marryat's own experiences, heroine Mollie Malmaison endures two disastrous marriages, during which she supports her family through writing novels and appearing on the stage. Most reviewers identified the novel as autobiographical and were united in their disapproval. The *Westminster Review* wondered "how far ... it may be a sort of romance of the author's own life," concluding that it was a "hateful book" in which Marryat "goes out of her way to fall foul of Mrs Lynn Linton" ("Belles Lettres", 1892: 382). This was almost certainly Marryat's intention. Marryat's 1891 interview with Helen C. Black for the *Lady's Pictorial*, later published in *Notable Women Authors of the Day*, was carefully designed to resurrect her reputation and distract attention from the ghastliness of reality. Emphasising her femininity, Black refers to Marryat's "exceeding softness," describing her literary career as having been motivated by a love of telling stories, rather than economic necessity (2011: 96, 104). Marryat showed her gratitude for this portrait by dedicating her 1896 novel *The Dream that Stayed* to Black. Conversely, the obituary of Marryat by her daughter portrays her as a weary (and unfeminine) workhorse, driven to her physical limits by the need to support her extended family (E. Church, 1899).

Still producing novels at an astonishing rate, Marryat became more famous for her Spiritualism during the 1890s. *There is No Death* (1891), her best-selling account of her early séance experiences, was praised and castigated in equal measure. She received hundreds of letters of gratitude from bereaved parents around the world, but the press ridiculed her. Undaunted, in 1893 she helped celebrated medium Bessie Williams write her memoirs and also presented a more sustained and scholarly defence of her own beliefs in *The Spirit World* (1894), in which she criticises the hegemony and dogmatism of established religions. Another tour brought her new admirers, and she became better known for her unorthodox views than her novels. One regional newspaper noted: "Florence Marryat is being drawn more and more into the realms of Spiritualism, and now devotes a great deal of her time to the study of that occult science. Miss Marryat is really Mrs Frances Lean, and is now a grandmother. Despite her years she is not yet grey, and retains much of that masculinity of manner which has always distinguished her" ("Purely Personal", 1894: 9). Appropriately entitled "Purely Personal", in this piece the author attempts to domesticate Marryat, referring to her by her married name (even though she had been separated from Lean for over a decade) and drawing attention to her status as a grandmother (her first grandchild was born almost twenty years earlier). There is a suggestion here that, given her status, Marryat should have by now lost that "masculinity of manner" that characterised her professional persona.

Although her literary star seemed to be in the descendant (her later novels were barely noticed by the British press), Marryat's final decade was partly devoted to the professionalisation of writing. Marryat became active in the Society of Authors, attending their annual dinner in 1895, along with Sarah Grand and Mathilde Blind ("The Society of Authors", 1897: 7). Marryat also campaigned vigorously for the passing and subsequent extension of the International Copyright law. Despite being the self-styled most popular writer in the United States of America, her transatlantic earnings had been minimal, thanks to "pirates" such as the Seaside Library (Marryat, 1886b: 119, 121). In defiance of poor health, Marryat was still touring the country. In 1898 she collaborated with Herbert McPherson on an adaptation of her first novel, *Love's Conflict*, taking for herself the lead comedy role.

Marryat died on 27 October 1899, the cause of death given

as diabetes and pneumonia (General Register Office: Death Certificate for Florence Lean). She had been working until the very end, propping up her ulcerated leg on a chair while hammering away on a typewriter (E. Church, 1899: 588). The funeral, which took place at a small Catholic church in St. John's Wood, celebrated her life and varied career. The mourners spanned the worlds of literature and the stage, including George Grossmith, Arthur A'Beckett and Annie Thomas, who were accompanied by members of Marryat's family – those who were still speaking to her ("The Late Miss Florence Marryat", 1899: 13). She was buried at Kensal Green Cemetery, sharing a grave with her beloved daughter Eva. *The Era* praised Marryat's career, but most other obituaries commended her industry while condemning her output. *The Times*'s obituarist wrote that her novels were "certainly not all of equal merit; but their author had imagination and dramatic instinct, and many of them enjoyed a good deal of popularity" ("Obituary", 1899: 8). Her estate at death was valued at £1,479 16s 8d – surprisingly little given her sustained success. Referring to her fortune, Marryat commented: "Others have spent it for me … and I do not grudge it to them" (Black, 2011: 99) Marryat left two houses to her son Frederick and a third to her daughter Ethel. She bequeathed her main home, 26 Abercorn Place in St John's Wood, to Herbert McPherson "in token of many year's [sic] unbroken affection,"[8] with all other possessions and literary royalties divided between him and her son Francis. Thomas Ross Church, who had tried to claim a share of Marryat's literary earnings after their divorce, later left a considerably larger estate of £16,769 15s 9d.[9]

Marryat's sixty-eight novels[10] were undeniably popular, their author a household name throughout the Anglophone world, but were largely forgotten after the so-called "Great Divide" of 1914. She stuck resolutely to her sensational plots, making few concessions to the stylistic shift of the New Woman novel. However, she did enjoy an unexpected afterlife in Stella Gibbons's *Cold Comfort Farm* (1932), where Marryat's *How They Loved Him* is included in Flora Poste's list of novels one can read while eating an apple (Gibbons, 1998: 53). Michael Sadleir later categorised Marryat, along with Annie Thomas, as a "purveyor of dangerously inflammatory fiction, unsuitable for reading by young ladies, but much to their taste" (1951: 1:229). It is partly this reputation that has led to the dismissal of her work. Superficial and often inaccurate accounts of her life and career have also caused her to be overlooked in favour of some of the more famous authors she influenced. However, an evaluation of her prolific and varied body of writing alongside an appreciation of her struggles as a woman reveals an important neglected Victorian feminist who questioned and disrupted the institution of marriage.

CHAPTER 2

"Entirely Different Creations": Marriage and the Sexual Double Standard

> "You were born to rule, and you have sat down a slave."
> *There is No Death*

In his 1901 lecture on the development of women's rights during the nineteenth century, eminent lawyer Montague Lush referred to the previous thirty years as a "revolution in the law" (342). Concluding that the married state for the mid-Victorian woman was one of "almost absolute subjection," Lush expresses surprise that one finds "no trace in the ordinary literature of the time of their occupying any such subordinate position, or of marriage making the woman the mere nonentity in point of law which she actually became" (349). It is certainly true that few authors made overt challenges to the status quo. However, as I show, many sensation novelists, most notably Mary Elizabeth Braddon and Wilkie Collins, did examine, and sometimes protest against, the inequitable position of wives, but they often stopped short of making radical arguments, frequently opting for conventional conclusions where outspoken heroines are ostracised, tamed, or otherwise silenced. As Ian Ward observes, the common choice for the literary heroine was to "put up with it, or run away" (2007: 151).

As we saw in the Introduction, Marryat was well placed both to witness and to benefit from the momentous social changes that took place, particularly those affecting the position of women. Through her fiction Marryat also participated in this process, contributing to debates that triggered a programme of transformative legislation, using her novels to articulate the wrongs of woman, and depicting through her heroines the possibilities that emancipation might bring. By subverting the traditional courtship plot, Marryat challenged the institution of marriage, disputing its centrality to women's lives and imagining a radically different role for them. This chapter considers the 1857 Matrimonial Causes Act, ostensibly designed to make divorce more accessible, but in reality legislation that enshrined the sexual double standard in law. The following analysis of Marryat's fiction shows how she portrayed marriage as a carceral institution for many women, campaigning instead for a more equal union. Challenging the image of the submissive and forgiving wife that emerged from Parliamentary debates, Marryat presented heroines who successfully insisted on a single sexual standard. By comparing Marryat's novels with those of more conservative authors, I demonstrate how she made potent arguments that undermined dominant ideology.

"Civilised Monogamy" versus "the Disruptive Vortex": The Politics of Victorian Marriage

In the mid-nineteenth century, matrimonial practices were seen as an indicator of civilisation with "civilised monogamy" believed to make Britain superior to those countries that either allowed easy access to divorce or practised polygamy (Gill, 2004: 66). The significance of marriage brought it under increased regulation, although with very different implications for men and women. The concept of coverture, originally described in Blackstone's *Legal Commentaries* (1756) and based on common law, decreed that the very being or legal existence of the wife was suspended during marriage. A single woman was known as a *feme sole* and a married woman as a *feme covert*, signifying that her identity was subsumed into that of her husband (Steinbach, 2004: 250). This is vividly illustrated by Marryat's experience of appearing as the defendant in the court case she pursued against her husband (see Chapter 1).

Leonore Davidoff and Catherine Hall, in their influential examination of gender differences during this period, propose that "marriage became both institution and symbol of women's containment" (2002: 451), seeing the middle classes as divided into separate public and private spheres delineating the appropriate realms of masculine and feminine activity. However, the diversity of the lives they describe belies their argument, and subsequent critics have shown that these spheres represented a retrospectively-applied conservative ideology, rather than a fundamental organising characteristic. Amanda Vickery, for example, perceives the separate spheres ideology as a "defensive and impotent reaction to public freedoms already won," arguing that the perpetuation of the model ignores the "unpredictable variety of private experience" (1993: 414, 390). Linda Colley concludes that women largely accepted their role in the domestic sphere, but saw this arrangement as "profoundly contractual" (1996: 277), assuming this subordinate position in return for (often non-existent) financial support and protection. The notion of separate spheres was, therefore, subject to challenge and negotiation from within the institution that was its embodiment: marriage.

Furthermore, the findings of the 1851 Census disputed the existence of the domestic ideal of middle-class marriage, instead identifying what Lynda Nead terms a "clear hierarchy of sexual behaviour" (Nead, 1988: 35), with married couples at the top and unmarried mothers languishing at the bottom. As Karen Chase and Michael Levenson explain, the need for this classification "exploded the myth of neat family units" (2000: 3). Although marriage was supposed to be central to a woman's life, the

Census showed that there were nearly two million unmarried women – single, divorced, or widowed – who had collected into a "disruptive vortex" (183). This epiphany placed gender at the centre of Parliamentary debates and subsequent legislation can be seen as a series of attempts to regulate this area of such vital national importance and suppress the "disruptive vortex".

Marryat was exposed to the inequities of marriage at a formative age when in 1839 her parents decided upon an irrevocable separation. At the time, a divorce would have involved a prohibitively expensive Act of Parliament – an option open to only the wealthiest members of society. Captain Marryat granted his wife Catherine an annual allowance of £500, a small sum for maintaining their seven surviving children in the comfort befitting their upper-middle-class status, and also miserly given he had inherited a large share of his father's £250,000 fortune (Pocock, 2000: 162). The Captain had no obligation to support his family and could have withdrawn payments at any point. Fortunately for Florence, legal changes and a successful literary career meant that she fared better when her own marriages broke down.

The 1857 Matrimonial Causes Act, popularly known as the Divorce Act, was part of a wider programme of reform initiated by Lord Brougham, with the intention of gradually removing legal authority from the Church and placing it in the hands of the state. This move gave Parliament greater latitude, enabling them to privilege national interest above Christian doctrine. Under the terms of the Act, men could divorce their wives on grounds of adultery alone, whereas a wronged wife had to prove that her husband's adultery had been 'aggravated' by bigamy, incest, sodomy, or cruelty (Shanley, 1993: 42). The Act, therefore, established and formalised the sexual double standard: female infidelity was a more serious crime and should be more easily punishable. During the debate, Lord Cranworth declared that it would be harsh to punish a husband for being "a little profligate" (3 Hansard 134 (13 June 1854): 7). Although at odds with the seventh commandment, which states that adultery is equally sinful for both parties, Cranworth's view was shared by many. Women were believed to be innately chaste, whereas men struggled to contain their animal instincts. The consequences of a wife's adultery were also perceived to be more serious, as she might potentially palm "spurious offspring upon the husband" (Hansard); the core of this Act was, therefore, as much concerned with the control of property and inheritance as it was with allowing spouses to extricate themselves from unhappy marriages.

The Act established a London-based Divorce Court, presided over by the "incarnate omnipotence" of the impressively-named Sir Cresswell Cresswell (Leckie, 1999: 77). In theory, this made divorce more readily obtainable through a judicial process, as hitherto a final and irrevocable separation could be achieved only by means of a lengthy and expensive Parliamentary Bill. Although *The Times* described the reform as "one of the greatest social revolutions of our time" ("The Suitors in Our Courts", 1867: 11) there was only a small increase in the subsequent divorce rate in the following decade, and this remained fairly constant as a proportion of the population until the late-1870s (Horstman, 1985: 85). *The Times* felt duty-bound to report divorce cases in full, subscribing to Jeremy Bentham's view that "publicity is the very soul of justice" (Humpherys, 1999: 227) and the repeal of the stamp duty on printed material in 1855 meant there was a proliferation of weekly newspapers preying on the more sensational cases. Consequently, rather than serving to release the unhappily married, the Divorce Court simply made marital problems more visible by holding them up to public scrutiny. As F. M. L. Thompson concludes, "The immediate effect of forensic divorce was to expose the sanctity of the middle-class hearth to the public gaze" (1988: 455). Desperate to avoid such exposure, the middle classes faced a domestic crisis as the institution of marriage itself was effectively placed on trial. Mary Poovey identifies the Act as "the first major piece of British legislation to focus attention on the anomalous position of married women under the law" (1988: 51). They emerged from debates as subordinate creatures, whose identities were bound up in those of their husbands. As Jane Jordan observes: "Given Parliament's failure to provide greater protection to wronged wives, it is unsurprising that the literature of the period took up the question, or that a new genre of sensation literature emerged" (Jordan, 2011b: 509).

"Forever Defiled": The Wronged Wife in Victorian Fiction

Indeed, novelists seized upon this rich new source of material, and marital conflict became a popular theme in the sensation novels of the 1860s. While marriage had formed the basis of many a novel, "divorce erupted into imaginative life without any coherent metaphors" (Chase and Levenson, 2000: 187). The fictional response, however, was not an outpouring of divorce plots, rather a flurry of bigamy novels. Literature was articulating the confusion of a population coming to terms with the fact that marriage was no longer indissoluble. Furthermore, bigamy was more palatable than divorce, with Margaret Oliphant acknowledging that it did at least show a "certain deference to the British relish for law and order" (1863: 169). Novelists also became preoccupied with the 'irregular' marriage, an informal ceremony often taking place in Scotland or Ireland, where the lack of proof could mean either spouse getting away with bigamy. The most famous example was the 1861 Yelverton Case, in which Theresa Longworth undertook a lengthy legal battle to prove that her husband Major Charles Yelverton had married her bigamously. This exposure of a problematic area of the law was explored most notably by Wilkie Collins in *Man and Wife* (1870).

One of the few novels to deal directly with divorce during the 1860s was Mrs Henry Wood's *East Lynne* (1861). After conniving Afy Hallijohn convinces Lady Isobel Carlyle of her husband Archibald's infidelity, Isobel elopes to the continent with the rakish Captain Levison, only to find herself swiftly abandoned and subsequently divorced. Whereas Archibald Carlyle is free to marry the importunate Barbara Hare, his ex-wife becomes a shadow of her former self, forced to endure demotion to the rank of governess, and to watch impotently as her young son dies. In *East Lynne*, divorce means liberation for the husband but humiliation for the wife. Rather than lamenting the double standard, Wood issues a warning to her women readers, and the message is salutary rather than subversive. The conservative tone of Wood's novel is confirmed by Geraldine Jewsbury's approving reader's report, contrasting starkly with her views on Marryat's manuscripts (Bentley Archives, Add. MSS 46656).[11]

The anonymously published novel *My Lady* (1858) is a more sympathetic portrayal of the wronged woman. When Lady Umphraville's husband, Sir Philip, elopes with another man's wife, she suffers the ignominy of the case being discussed at length in the press. After the failure of his affair, Sir Philip returns to the family home, resuming his position at its head. When Lady Umphraville refuses to countenance this final insult, Sir Philip invokes the custody laws to deny her access to their children, subsequently obtaining a court order to sue her for restitution of conjugal rights. Lady Umphraville has no case for divorce, as her husband's adultery has not been compounded by another 'aggravating' factor, and her only release is through the expedient of his untimely death. This novel shows that the Matrimonial Causes Act had done little to protect wives, showcasing – but never really challenging – the implications of the sexual double standard.

Ouida's *Moths* (1880) showed a divorced woman happy and enjoying a new life, an outcome never before attempted in fiction. Earlier writers, like Wood, had bowed to social convention, ensuring that divorcées were both repentant and ruined. Although nominally radical, *Moths*, with its sparkling narrative sweep across the glamorous capitals of Europe to the snowy outposts of the

Russian empire, embodies a fairy-tale quality, removing the action from the reality of readers' lives. Jordan argues that "in dealing with the heroine's ... legal incapacity to extricate herself from marriage, it engages very seriously with contemporary debates concerning anomalies in legislation relating to marital separation and divorce" (2011a: 49). This is true to an extent, but, by setting the action overseas and making her heroine Vere subject to Russian laws, Ouida ensures that she is rendered passive in the divorce (only husbands can issue proceedings) even though in England she would have substantial grounds for divorcing him, on account of his serial adultery and cruelty. Vere is liberated only when Prince Zouroff tires of her, and she is denied the agency necessary to release herself. Indeed, Vere believes that "The woman who can wish for a divorce and drag her wrongs into public—such wrongs!—is already wanton herself ... A woman who divorces her husband is a prostitute legalised by a form, that is all" (Ouida, 1880 [2005]: 422–3) Ouida does allow her heroine a second, more fulfilling marriage, but she remains "forever defiled" (451). Her happiness is tempered by shame.

Wilkie Collins's *The Evil Genius* (1886) was, in many ways, ahead of its time, featuring a partly sympathetic portrayal of a mistress, and also of Catherine Linley, a woman who refuses to forgive her husband's adultery. Collins's initially radical treatment of the marriage question suddenly recoils, however, as though terrified of its own subversion. By the end of the novel, the sexual double standard is firmly upheld, with Catherine denied a divorce. To strengthen his morally conservative message, Collins devotes a paragraph to the authorial voice in which he declares that a husband's "sexual frailty" should not be deemed sufficient grounds for divorce (Collins, 1886 [1994]: 347). Although divorce is shown to be Catherine's only means of recourse, Collins advises that she should have exercised forgiveness, by allowing her daughter to live with her estranged husband and his mistress. Perversely, Catherine's initial forbearance is criticised by the divorce court judge, who accuses her of being "impulsively ready to forgive" (214), and ultimately she is held to be equally responsible for the marital breakdown. This imbrication of patriarchy and the law places Catherine in a double bind, thereby epitomising the powerlessness of women. What begins as a tentatively disruptive text resolves itself into a morally conservative conclusion. Collins argues that male sexual urges render monogamy impossible and that a husband's adultery should be accommodated within marriage. While tacitly acknowledging that this situation is unfair to wives, he finds himself unable to suggest a viable alternative. As Pat Barker astutely observed in *The Guardian*, Collins has a "trademark ability to create powerful female characters who then make him so nervous he can't wait to put them back in their box" (2018: online).

In a review of Marryat's *The Fair-Haired Alda* (1880), the author complains that the heroine "takes the marriage law into her own hands, finds it prickly, rages against it, and finally tramples it under foot" ("Miss Florence Marryat's New Novel", 1880: 11). Marryat herself is described as a "carping novelist ... with a certain rebellious and hostile attitude ... towards the world and its social institutions" (11). The *Athenaeum*, meanwhile, described it as a "farrago of vulgarity" ("The Fair-Haired Alda", 1880a: 788). Anyone familiar with Marryat's writing might now imagine a lurid tale of unwifely outrages, yet the ferocity of this review is perplexing. Alda's transgression is to elope with a husband of her choice, rather than marry the dissipated valetudinarian favoured by her parents. She remains loyal to her husband through the most trying of circumstances, and it is her family who behave badly in trying to force her into a bigamous marriage. When this plot fails, her father stabs her husband to death in a frenzied attack. For the reviewer, Alda's failure to observe the fifth commandment remains the cardinal sin, while the murder goes unremarked. Alda is certainly prepared to break the rules in the interests of autonomy, but she is no Lady Audley. Nevertheless, she is held up as an irredeemable villainess. The *Spectator* deemed Alda "distinctly of the order of evil-doers who ought not to escape a whipping," and one of a long series of young women who ought to be, and no doubt would be, carefully avoided by respectable, God-fearing people, in real life, and who are not even amusing acquaintances in the flimsiest of novels." ("The Fair-Haired Alda", 1880b: 1044) Alda has done nothing legally wrong, so her detractors invoke religion, or at least their interpretation of it. Marryat's novel is about a woman's right to choose her own husband, rather than an argument for marriage reform, yet many reviewers opted to interpret it as an attack on a sacred institution.

"Who made those laws?": Renegotiating the Marriage Contract

Unlike many of her sensational peers, Marryat uses bigamy as a narrative device in only a handful of novels, preferring instead to challenge the institution of marriage from within, or to present alternatives for women. Rather than indulge in handwringing, Marryat prefers practical solutions. Divorce is seldom invoked directly, Marryat aware from her own experience that life as a divorcée or separated woman was a difficult one. The eponymous young hero of *The Confessions of Gerald Estcourt* (1867) is, like the six-year-old Marryat, caught up in his parents' divorce, receiving an early education in the disparity of the sexes: "I lay awake pondering on the account which I had heard of my parents' separation, and the reason of the great inequality in their establishments. The question puzzled me; it was my first insight to the law of England as exhibited in favour of men versus women" (Marryat, 1867: 1:67).

Estcourt's father is a successful novelist who retains his fortune and makes his estranged wife live on a pittance. The 1857 Matrimonial Causes Act made no provision for alimony, this situation remaining unaddressed until the 1878 Act. The young Estcourts enjoy a much better life with their father, resenting the periods they must spend in Croydon with their bitter and impecunious mother – a situation likely to have been based on Marryat's own peripatetic childhood. Gerald is confused by the inequitable dissolution of his parents' marriage, asking: "When people marry, don't they promise to share everything together; why should there be a difference between them?" His sister Emmeline responds: "Oh! Don't ask such things, Gerald; it's the law of the land, dear; beyond your understanding or mine" (1:65).

As an adult, Gerald enjoys his masculine privilege, forgetting his earlier introduction to sexual inequality. As eldest son he has inherited a fortune and is able to move freely between his London *pied à terre* and the family estate. Believing his status places him beyond reproach, he moves a young woman into his house, even though they are unconnected. His actions are challenged only when he attempts to woo Ada Rivers, a "thinking woman" (1:206). Imagining her preoccupations to be as frivolous as his own, he is astonished to discover that she is pondering the "vast difference with which the same actions are judged in men and women," continuing: "We are made by the same Hand; endowed with the same feelings, impulses, and affections: and yet the world judges us as if we were entirely different creations." Gerald replies that it is the laws of society that are responsible, to which she retorts: "The laws of society – yes! but who made those laws? Were they not laid down by men for their own advantage and against ours? And yet they call us the weaker vessels, and profess to cherish and protect us!" (1:204) Ada draws the reader's attention to the fact that women's subordination is literally man-made, rather than the result of biological determinism.

Already unnerved by Ada's outburst, Gerald's enthusiasm is further dampened by the discovery that she has a child by a deceased husband. His pride struggles with living proof of Ada's sexual experience and he wishes the baby dead. The novel ends not with Gerald taming this independent-minded woman, but with her delivering an ultimatum that he must prove himself worthy of her love by renouncing his earlier chauvinism. Their marriage is by no means inevitable and is subject to negotiation before Ada will consent. The parliamentary debates might have dwelt on the implications of a wife's adultery, but they were implicitly also denying a woman's right to a sexual past, whether within or beyond marriage.

In *The Prey of the Gods* (1871) Marryat depicts a woman deploying similar tactics to Ada. Trapped in a loveless marriage with the sepulchral Sir Lyster Gwynne, Lady Gwendoline falls for the dubious charms of Auberon Slade, a notorious poet based on Algernon Swinburne. Their plans to elope are abandoned when Lady Gwendoline's daughter Daisy sustains a serious injury and she resolves to perform her maternal duty by remaining in the marital home to care for her. Disgusted by his lover's decision to put the needs of her child before him, Slade quickly agrees to a hasty and improvident marriage to a dull young woman. He soon comes to regret his haste when Sir Lyster dies of apoplexy on Slade's wedding day. Although Marryat releases Lady Gwendoline from her marriage through the expedient of her husband's death, rather than through divorce, she does not merely use it as a device to unite her star-crossed lovers. Instead, Marryat makes Slade suffer as a single father who comes to realise the responsibility of parenthood after his wife dies in childbirth. A decade passes before Lady Gwendoline decides he has achieved a greater understanding of women. Only then does she agree to marry him. By this stage, they are both past their prime and their union will be based on a true meeting of minds, rather than on sexual excitement. Like Gerald Estcourt, Slade must prove himself worthy of a woman's love, rather than unashamedly expecting her devotion as his right. Having already experienced the carceral state of marriage, Lady Gwendoline is keen to stipulate her terms.

In this novel, Marryat subverts the traditional plot trajectory — the wicked (or morally questionable) prosper, whereas the virtuous (but dull) meet with an untimely end. Lady Gwendoline is presented sympathetically and is by far the most appealing character in the novel. Furthermore, as the story is told in the present tense, the reader is invited into her consciousness, thereby creating a sense of vicarious participation in her actions. Her ten years of living independently is also presented positively: she is financially secure and has no need of a husband, unless she decides to marry for love. She rejects a marriage proposal from a retired army major, privileging her autonomy over security and convention. Lady Gwendoline is also shown to be an excellent mother — Daisy flourishes under her care and does not miss the dead father who neglected her.

Marryat's portrayal of this heroine is in many respects a riposte to the downfall of *East Lynne*'s Lady Isobel Carlyle. Rather than punishing her for her adultery, Marryat rewards Lady Gwendoline with the death of her rebarbative husband and by a fulfilling relationship with her daughter. She is even reunited with her lover once he has undergone a teleological experience that divests him of his arrogance. The characters of Sir Lyster and Lady Gwendoline are also evocative of Sir Lester and Lady Dedlock in Dickens's *Bleak House* (1853), with Marryat creating a similar sense of ennui and marital dissatisfaction. Rather than prostrate herself with impotent longing for her lost lover, however, Lady Gwendoline embraces independence. Although Marryat avoids portraying her heroine as a divorcée, she is radical in portraying elective single motherhood and suggesting that a child could be happier without a father. In this novel, Marryat manages to be radical, but is also careful to avoid criticism that proponents of women's rights shunned the responsibilities of motherhood, showing that what is right for the mother also benefits the child. Unsurprisingly, the *Athenaeum* was appalled by *The Prey of the Gods*, describing Sir Lyster as "the whipping-boy whereon Mrs Church exercises her lash against husbands in general" ("The Prey of the Gods", 1871: 397–8).[12] The fact that Marryat provoked such a strong reaction shows that her writing was challenging deep-held beliefs and the prevailing domestic ideology. Marriage is shown as requiring compromise on both sides, rather than as an institution that succeeds by subjugating women.

In *The Dream that Stayed* (1896), Marryat returns to the plot of *East Lynne*, having condemned elsewhere its timidity and unoriginality and criticised Wood's decision to have Lady Isobel elope with an unworthy man. Marryat argues that authors like Wood are "so terribly afraid of outraging the sensibility of their readers, that they try to make an improper thing as proper as possible, and render it (to my mind) far worse than it would otherwise have been" (Marryat, 1890b: 187). This time, Marryat's aim seems to have been to outrage the sensibility of her critics. In *The Dream that Stayed*, Mary Raynham abandons her husband and daughter for an old lover with whom she goes on to have another child. When her lover dies, Mrs Raynham returns to her husband, who is prepared to put the affair behind them. Still in love with his wife, he withstands the taunts of the local community. Here Marryat transposes traditional gender roles, with the wife succumbing to carnal desires and the husband exercising compassion and forgiveness. Marryat argues that an adulterous woman should not be condemned and ruined for a mistake as Lady Isobel was in *East Lynne*. The reference to Mrs Henry Wood's novel is made mischievously clear when one of the children refers to Mrs Raynham as "muvver," recalling the famous line from the stage adaptation: "Dead! Dead! And never called me mother!" or sometimes "Gone! And never called me mother!" (Wood, 1861 [2000]: 774). Again, the critics were incredulous, the *Academy* decreeing: "If a woman plays battledore and shuttlecock with the seventh commandment in the irresponsible, motiveless way that she does, she ought to take the consequences" ("The Dream that Stayed", 1896: 528). Marryat's attempt to establish in fiction a single standard for sexual behaviour was roundly condemned. Whereas men could be "a little profligate," women – in both life and fiction – should be beyond reproach.

"I've had enough of that sort of thing": Alternatives to Traditional Marriage

The critics' frustration with Marryat was matched by her own frustration with the institution of marriage. Increasingly, she presented alternatives to traditional relationships and questioned conventional gender roles. She again addresses and promotes the idea of elective single motherhood in *How They Loved Him* (1882). This time she reworks elements of Elizabeth Gaskell's *Ruth* (1853) and Ouida's *Moths* (1880) to realise one of her most radical messages, challenging both marriage and heteronormativity. Fenella Barrington spends her adolescence in a Belgian convent, abandoned by a mother more interested in securing a rich husband than in caring for her daughter. Fenella emerges aged sixteen "a white innocent lily" (Marryat, 1882a: 1:17), with little knowledge of the outside world. When informed that she must leave and find a husband, Fenella professes that she loves her friend Honorée St. Just and would like to marry her instead, imagining them living a happy life together (1:30). The setting of the scene in a homosocial environment carries more than a suggestion of lesbianism. This same-sex desire is mirrored by Mrs Barrington's lady's maid, Eliza Bennet, who finds herself "magnetised" by her mistress' presence and "thrills" at her touch (1:104); in her presence her face "glowed with ardour" (2:92). Advised that female marriage is both impossible and undesirable, Fenella is banished to Eliza's brother's farm in a remote area of Wales (a clear parallel with Gaskell's *Ruth*). Upon arrival, Eliza promptly breaks her leg, leaving Fenella to move around unchaperoned, "a child in experience, and a woman in feeling" (2:5). She is easy prey for the handsome and urbane Geoffrey Doyne, who persuades her to enjoy a series of secret trysts with him. The nature of these meetings is suggested by the name of the local man who enjoys watching them: Mr Tugwell. When his family force him to marry a woman he does not love, Doyne abandons Fenella. By this point she has told him, blushingly, "you have made me a woman" (2:18).

Fenella is obliged to return to London and live with her mother. When Mrs Barrington discovers that her daughter is pregnant, she strikes her hard across the face, the first of many blows. They move to Belgium to avoid scandal, where the local community comments on the screams emanating daily from the Barringtons' cottage. Mrs Barrington is determined to induce a miscarriage through regular beatings and kickings. After one particularly brutal episode, Fenella throws herself half-naked into an icy stream. Her baby girl is born soon afterwards, mute and without the use of her legs. She is placed immediately with foster parents and Mrs Barrington and Eliza collude to convince Fenella that she died. Determined to recover the family reputation, Mrs Barrington forces Fenella into a loveless marriage with the respectable Sir Gilbert Conroy. Although himself a Lothario, Sir Gilbert is appalled to discover that the new Lady Conroy has a 'past,' and one evidenced by her newly-discovered daughter, Valeria. Exercising the full gamut of masculine privilege, he declares himself free of the marriage, while dictating that Fenella must remain in the marital home and subject to his financial and moral control. Instead, Fenella instigates a legal separation, insisting on maintaining herself and Valeria. Reverting to her maiden name, she cultivates her singing voice and pursues a career on the stage, ignoring the gossip that inevitably follows her.

When Doyne's wife dies, leaving him with four young sons, he seeks out Fenella, asking her to marry him so he can become her "protector and guardian" (3:267). Fenella accuses him of hypocrisy, having maintained a façade of respectability for so long when she was obliged to deal alone with the consequences of their affair. A cynical reader might also suspect that he is more interested in securing a stepmother for his children, rather than making amends for the wrong he has done her. When Doyne explains the importance of having a man in her life, she retorts "I have had enough of that sort of thing to last me a lifetime," also impugning his masculinity (3:291). Marriage for Fenella is irrelevant; Doyne failed to provide either emotional or financial support, forcing her to become both mother and father to Valeria, and she has no need of a protector or guardian. Marryat illustrates that the notion of separate spheres that limits women is entirely specious if men fail to fulfil their self-appointed role as provider and protector.

Ruth and *Moths* both attracted opprobrium, but Marryat artfully pushed those themes even further than either Gaskell or Ouida had done. Whereas Ruth must do penance and eventually die for her 'sin,' Fenella embraces the opportunity to live beyond the realms of respectable society. Marryat makes clear "this is not the history of a saint" (2:290), establishing her heroine as a real woman, rather than a virtuous cypher. The critical response was one of outrage. *The Spectator* referred to *How They Loved Him* as a "powerful and unpleasant novel" and an "utter mistake" ("How they Loved Him", 1882: 1234). The *Westminster Review*, meanwhile, thought it an "unsavoury book" with "no redeeming quality," their exasperated critic imploring Marryat to cease writing altogether ("Belles Lettres", 1882: 580–1). The vehemence of these reviews demonstrates the provocative nature of Marryat's work. The 1851 Census had placed single mothers firmly at the bottom of the pile, but Marryat elevates them, making them heroic rather than shameful figures, and showing marriage to be an unattractive prospect for some women.

While Fenella shuns the idea of marriage altogether, elsewhere Marryat's heroines attempt to overhaul the institution. Having catalogued the problems with husbands, in her penultimate novel *A Rational Marriage* (1899), Marryat effectively sets out her manifesto for a successful marriage. Joan Trevor, a secretary and aspiring novelist, agrees to marry Larry O'Donnell only on the understanding that she retains her independence: "If people want to be married, to have a license for being the closest of friends, well, let them — but why in the name of goodness should they alter all their lives on that account — give up their ambitions, their fancies, their friends, and settle down in the same house to bore each other from morning till night!" (Marryat, 1899: 23) Larry, who thinks his wife "must be all his own; as much his property as his hair-brush or his razor" (28), but desperately in love with Joan, finally agrees to her draft contract. The terms stipulate that they must have separate finances and apartments, and also keep their marriage secret. Furthermore, there is a spoken agreement that she will only wear a wedding ring on a watch chain; and "as for being called by your name, of course that is out of the question; but I shall be your wife all the same, so that doesn't signify" (64).

By the novel's conclusion, Joan has relented on the need for a written agreement, but there is no sign of concession on the other points. Joan's cousin is shocked by her modern approach, citing examples of happy marriages in literature where initial difficulties are overcome by a "lovely wedding". Joan responds: "Yes, that's the mistake of novels ... the lovely wedding comes at the end, just where the misery beings. The surgeon stops dead there – smiling at you with the knife concealed in his hand – he won't let you see any further, for fear you should shrink from the operation" (122–3). Marryat's sinister image recalls Émile Zola's preface to *Thérèse Raquin* (1867), in which he explains "I simply carried out on two living bodies the same analytical examination that surgeons perform on corpses" (Zola, 1998: 2). Throughout her literary career, Marryat performed a similar "analytical examination" on marriage, demonstrating that the legal regulation of wives that simultaneously sanctioned husbands' unreasonable behaviour was the cause of much unhappiness. As A. James Hammerton notes, the idea of female subordination "was premised on assumptions about male perfection which were bound to strain credibility" (1992: 75). In both her life and her fiction, Marryat exposed these assumptions as a myth.

Indeed, Marryat often portrays feminine strength juxtaposed with masculine weakness. Throughout *A Rational Marriage*, Joan is shown to be the superior partner. As the narrator comments: "Miss Trevor was not like other young women of her time." She was "wearing a tailor-made suit of pale gray, with a white waistcoat and tie, and an Alpine hat upon her head adorned with an eagle's feather" (9). Lawrence, in contrast, is "little man" with a "sweet disposition" and "blue eyes as clear and honest as a child's, and a sensitive mouth that was ready to sympathize with all human trouble" (10). Furthermore, he is a journalist for *Queen* magazine, and in the opening scene we see him discussing fabrics with Joan for an article he is writing. Wanting to keep their relationship secret, Joan patronises Larry by offering to hide him in a pink-trimmed dog basket if anyone comes to her flat (73). Joan is also compared favourably with her own family. Her grandfather, once powerful, is described as "a thin, acidulated-looking old man ... with an eagle eye, a hooked nose, and a beardless chin, which had been the *bête noir* of his life – being moreover endowed with a squeaky voice, and a general want of muscle, he was compelled in order to cover the deficiencies in his sex, to talk as if through a speaking trumpet, and generally to bully on the slightest occasion" (45). She also corrects her male employer's Latin, much to his annoyance (78). Larry's friend laments: "oh, these girls of the *fin de siècle!* What will they do next?" (227).

In *Mount Eden* (1889), Evelyn Rayne is compared favourably with her cousin, Will. While she is "tall, womanly, and commanding" (Marryat, 1889 [nd]: 123), he is "slight, with lovely blue eyes ... and such beautiful hands and feet" (129). Will is keen to marry her, fearing himself unable to manage the family's estate alone. He requires her strength to sustain and protect him. The narrator observes: "There is such a strong tide of maternal feeling welling up in every female breast, and ready to cast a cloak of protection over the creature that has proved himself to be weaker than herself ... It is only men who have named women 'the weaker sex'. In love and hate they are incomparably the stronger vessels of the two" (55–6). Will, desperate to escape the consequences of having committed a fraud, dresses in Evelyn's clothes, making "a very personable girl" (77). When Evelyn meets him again, some years later, she finds him "not manly enough to suit her taste. He looked more like a poet or a troubadour than a gentleman of the nineteenth century" (159). She describes herself "as hard as nails" (202), and denounces him as an "effeminate sham" (228).

Now she has inherited the estate, visiting misogynist Jack Vernon says of Evelyn: "Mount Eden is rightly named. It is a paradise, and she is its Eve. But a solitary unmated Eve is an anomaly. Adam should, by rights, have been here to meet her" (122). Her loyal bailiff responds: "Well, he isn't here, and, what's more, we don't want him" (120). Evelyn certainly doesn't want him – she is far more interested in Agnes Featherstone, a young woman who lives on a neighbouring estate. Aware of the unconventional relationship, he declares: "Well, it is incredible to me, one woman being so fond of another. ... Your description of Miss Rayne's excitement at their return home sounds so much more like the anticipation of meeting a lover than a female friend" (121). Indeed it does: "As soon as the young women met, they flew into each other's arms, and for a few minutes nothing was to be heard but the sound of their repeated kissing, and a few low sobs of pleasure from Agnes" (123–4).

Evelyn is distraught when Agnes announces her engagement to a foppish poet (in fact, it is Will in disguise). Having been brought up in a conventional environment, Agnes comments that "It's the usual thing for girls to marry" (129). She is simply fulfilling her destiny as a young woman, adding "Don't you like men? ... Mamma says you ought to have married years ago" (130). Evelyn responds: "Your mamma judges me from the usual feminine standpoint, Agnes, and I am not much like other women. Sometimes I think I have much more the mind and feelings of a man" (130). Although Agnes has apparently embraced heteronormativity, she confesses to her future husband "I should not feel married at all if Evelyn were not there," prompting the terse response that "She appears to be more necessary to your happiness than the bridegroom" (219). Agnes can only tolerate marriage if it still involves the woman she loves. For Evelyn, this is not enough: she must be a partner, rather than an adjunct. Of course, Marryat stops short of portraying a female marriage, but she does imply bisexual polyamory. Her alternatives are not always fully realised, yet her examination of the institution and exploration of unorthodox relationships remain an important part of the debate on women's role in Victorian society.

Marryat's growing cynicism – or, perhaps, misogamy – culminated in "The Mistakes of Marriage", a lecture tour that took her all around the United Kingdom, often performing before small and bewildered audiences. The text was also published in the *Belgravia* holiday number for August 1892, which must have had a sobering effect on many family excursions. A journalist for the *Daily News* reported:

> Sad to relate, the speaker took an exceedingly gloomy view of the average status of connubial happiness, and emphatically pronounced that the majority of united couples found marriage to be a failure "worse even than penal servitude, since the convict was at least sometimes left to himself." This alarming state of domestic felicity was, Miss Marryat considered, due to the fact that young couples saw too little of one another before the ceremony in church, and too much afterwards. ("Florence Marryat on Marriage", 1898: 6)

While the men in the audience applauded Marryat's plea for greater independence within marriage, the ladies "manifested a polite sign of distinct disapproval". Surprisingly, given its twenty-first-century reputation, the *Daily Mail* provided a non-judgmental account of the lecture, confining itself to a summary of Marryat's demands: "[Marryat] would advocate greater care in the choice of life-partner, more individual privacy … and a limitation of the number of children. … she was not sorry that women no longer considered marriage as a profession, but were striking out for themselves" ("Mistakes of Marriage", 1898: 3). When the heroine of *Driven to Bay* (1887) is consoled on the death of her violent husband, she responds: "I am not weeping for the loss of *him*. I am weeping for the loss of my self-respect" (Marryat, 1887b: 2:40). For Marryat, marriage was not the destiny of all women, and their status was not always elevated by the acquisition of a husband.

Conclusion

The need to regulate the supposedly immutable separate spheres through legislation demonstrated that they did not reflect biological determinism, a concept discussed further in Chapters 3 and 4. Their tacitly contractual foundation was shown to be unworkable, necessitating state intervention to police the boundaries. This regulation in turn prompted a discourse concerning gender roles, with the novel providing a space in which concerns and experiences could be articulated. The gender binary that emerged from the dominant ideology relied on imposing on women an acceptably feminine identity that Marryat rejected. Instead she asserted a feminine subjectivity through her portrayal of strong heroines who were prepared to transcend their designated role. Poovey has argued that such narratives transformed women "from silent sufferer of private wrongs into an articulate spokesperson in the public sphere" (1988: 64), and by also taking to the stage, Marryat widened this sphere considerably.

The law was unable to impose its ideology on women's lives and eventually it realised that they were resisting their containment. The 1857 Matrimonial Causes Act, while theoretically making divorce easier, actually did little to help wronged wives. Unless they were willing to admit to their own adultery in a public court, or to accuse their husbands of worse crimes, there was no option for release. As Marryat reflected in *The Nobler Sex*: "Let them attempt to rend the chains that gall them, and they will find how little justice there is in England for the woman, however innocent, who is separated from her husband. It is divorce without freedom – loss without hope of gain – the pulling down of a domestic hearth, without any chance of building it again" (1890b: 141).

Although she did rebuild the domestic hearth with Herbert McPherson, it was a clandestine relationship and meant ostracism from polite society. And as Marryat's first marriage showed, prescribed gender roles were not necessarily reflected in reality. In her case, the wife was the breadwinner and the husband a dependent. As I discuss in the next chapter, the Married Women's Property Acts transformed the position of wives such as Marryat. She believed firmly that women needed an alternative role in society, one in which they could pursue a profession and control their own property. Only then would marriage mean happiness, not something merely to be endured.

Rather than simply grant her heroines second, happier marriages through bigamy or the death of an inconvenient spouse, Marryat often directly challenged the institution of marriage itself, questioning its centrality to a woman's life. Lady Gwendoline and Ada Rivers negotiate the contract of the separate spheres before they will agree to its terms; Fenella Barrington rejects it altogether; and Mary Raynham manages to find within the institution the latitude usually enjoyed only by men. Whereas her contemporaries were subtly reworking the marriage plot, Marryat was redefining it by imagining new possibilities for her heroines, both within and outside marriage.

CHAPTER 3

'An Entire Subversion of the Domestic Rule': Women and Property

"A married woman cannot be too independent. It serves to keep her husband in order."

A Harvest of Wild Oats

When the Married Women's Property Bill was debated in Parliament in 1870, MP George Shaw-Lefevre quipped that the marriage service ought to be changed: the husband said that he endowed his wife with all his earthly goods, but in reality it was the other way around (Holcombe, 1983: 154). Upon marriage, a wife effectively ceded all control of her financial assets to her husband. Except for her clothing and personal ornaments, known as 'paraphernalia,' a husband could dispose of his wife's wealth as he saw fit and without her permission – a situation exemplified by Thomas Ross Church's attempts to seize Marryat's inheritance. Even gifts from husband to wife remained the former's property and could be revoked (a situation examined at length in Trollope's *The Eustace Diamonds*). If a husband deserted his wife, he was still entitled to control her earnings and property, even to support another household and common-law family. When her husband did exactly that, novelist Mrs Alexander Fraser was on two occasions denied a judicial separation, thereby obliging her to subsidise his adultery (Black, 2011: 344). Such outrages were not confined to the wealthy. In 1858, a working-class Devon wife was forced to support her husband, even after he entered into a bigamous marriage with another woman. The magistrate – appropriately named Mr Bastard – ruled that the notion of wifely duty still applied ("Exeter Guildhall", 1858: 5).[13] Although women were supposedly supported financially by male relatives, the 1851 Census showed that a quarter of married women were employed outside the home (Holcombe, 1983: 8). As with marriage itself, it became apparent that reality was rapidly diverging from ideology.

For Marryat, the ability of a wife to control her own finances was vital, more so than the right to vote. Women's property is a recurring theme in her fiction, which she frequently used as a medium to lobby for legal change. As this chapter shows, she repeatedly illustrated the need for women to be recognised as responsible and independent citizens, also arguing vigorously for their right to meaningful work outside the home.

First, this chapter examines the debates surrounding the Married Women's Property Acts and how they were addressed in fiction, usually by conservative writers. Then it focusses in detail on Marryat's polemical novel *Her World Against a Lie* (1878), in which she seeks to advise female readers of their property rights. I also explore some of Marryat's other novels that include positive portrayals of independent women. In the final section I consider Marryat's strong belief in the importance of work for women as an alternative to marriage. For Marryat, legal independence and meaningful employment opportunities were the two most important steps towards equality.

The Married Women's Property Acts in Fact and Fiction

In his influential *Legal Commentaries*, Blackstone decreed: "There is nothing which so generally strikes the imagination, and engages the affections of mankind, as the right of property;

or that sole and despotic dominion which *one man* claims and exercises over the external things of the world" (Blackstone and Lewis, 1922: 2:1, emphasis added). The 1850s saw the beginning of the campaign to grant woman dominion too, with a petition presented to Parliament on 14 March 1856. Among the signatories were Elizabeth Gaskell, Geraldine Jewsbury, Jane Welsh Carlyle, Marian Evans, and Elizabeth Barrett Browning. None of these women was an outspoken advocate of women's rights (quite the reverse in the case of Jewsbury and Gaskell), yet they recognised the importance of retaining their own earnings. Marryat would have been in India at the time and possibly unaware of events back home. However, the progress of this long-fought campaign was to have a profound effect on her life. Although a resolution was subsequently moved and seconded to reform the law, traditionalists on all sides succeeded in replacing the Bill with the 1857 Matrimonial Causes Act, legislation that, as discussed in Chapter 2, enshrined the sexual double standard in law and did little to protect wives. Following a sustained campaign by the Married Women's Property Committee, fourteen years later the Bill passed through the Commons intact, only to be eviscerated by the Lords, who thought its further passage would herald "an entire subversion of domestic rule" (Holcombe, 1983: 174). Its chief enemy was Lord Penzance, who would later preside over Marryat's divorce proceedings.

The Married Women's Property Act of 1870 satisfied few of its supporters' demands, but did at least recognise that in some circumstances married women should control their own earnings and inherit property. Montague Lush described it, with the benefit of hindsight, as a "curiously tentative and partial measure" (Lush, 1901: 353); one MP at the time thought it "a feeble compromise" (quoted in Holcombe, 1983: 179). Significantly for Marryat and the literary signatories of the original petition, a married woman who wrote a book after 1 January 1871 would herself hold the copyright, rather than it belonging automatically to her husband.

For example, Millicent Garrett Fawcett's husband Henry had to bequeath to her in his will the copyright of one of her early books (Rubinstein, 1991: 53), and Charlotte Elizabeth Tonna changed her name so that her estranged husband could not claim her literary earnings (Peterson, 2009: 44). Margaret Oliphant thought it "a mere trick of words to say that the woman loses her existence and is absorbed in her husband" (1856: 381), but Mr Oliphant died before she enjoyed most of her literary success. She changed her tune twenty-five years later in "The Grievances of Woman" (1880) for *Fraser's Magazine*, complaining about taxation without representation. Now acutely aware of her own earning capacity, Oliphant's perspective had shifted.

Having come so close to victory, campaigners redoubled their efforts, finally achieving their demands in the Act of 1882, described by Mary Lyndon Shanley as "arguably the single most important change in the legal status of women in the nineteenth century" (1993: 103). Married women were at last granted the same rights over property as unmarried women and were treated as a separate legal entity. They were now *femes soles* rather than *femes couverts* – husbands and wives were no longer one person under law. Women would never again find themselves in the anomalous position of taking legal action against their husband, but finding themselves a defendant, as Marryat did in 1875. Opponents damned the Act as a "social revolution" (Holcombe, 1983: 201) as its effect was to "sweep away for all practical purposes the old common law disabilities of a married woman" (Lush, 1901: 354). Conservatives feared that this power shift would turn the wife into a "domestic tyrant," the final debates punctuated with cries of "No, no!" (Holcombe, 1983: 201) As John Tosh observes, "To be head of a household, and to be visibly head of it, was essential to masculine status" (2007: 60–61), and this Act suggested the possibility of two heads, with equal authority. As Deborah Wynne explains: "If wives were autonomous property owners they would 'exist as reason' and enter society to assert their individuality, an idea which threatened the conservative view of marriage as a union of unequal partners, with wives as dependents on husbands and legally disabled for their own protection." (2011: 23)

It was this "individuality", rather than property ownership *per se* that bothered some politicians. Alexander Beresford Hope, Tory backbencher and vocal opponent of women's rights, challenged the Married Women's Property Bill on the grounds that "it was written in scripture that the husband was head of his household" (quoted in Griffin, 2012: 180). As with the sexual double standard, where it proved difficult to make a legal case, the Bible was invoked to defend the subordination of women. Beresford Hope's stance is intriguing given his personal circumstances. At home, he was completely subservient to his wife, Lady Mary Cecil (180). This contradiction manifests in what is mercifully his only work of fiction, *Strictly Tied Up* (1880), a novel far less exciting than its title would suggest. Here he explores his own claim that wealthy women were already protected by settlements, so there was no need for legislation: "[Lucy Curteis] was just able to grasp a pleasant idea that she would have a great deal of money, and that her child, if she had one, would have a great deal after her; but that all was 'strictly tied up' – an awful condition of matters, which she hazily connected with some form of imprisonment as the punishment for the transgression of unknown and incomprehensible laws" (Beresford Hope, 1880: 1:198). Yet, her perfidious husband is confident of his ability to circumvent this protection, imagining money "pouring into his lap, year by year" (220). As the father of seven daughters, Beresford Hope was perhaps mindful as to the vulnerability of his own wealth.

Such contradictory attitudes – or the ability to separate the personal and the political – were not confined to Beresford Hope. Anthony Trollope includes several portrayals of exploited women in his fiction, yet always presents the problem without a solution. In *An Old Man's Love* (1884), housekeeper Mrs Baggett is pestered by her disreputable husband, who regularly importunes her for money. Although they have been estranged for some time, he urges her to perform her wifely duty by providing him with gin and shelter. The politically aware reader might assume that Mrs Baggett is able to invoke the recently-passed 1882 Married Women's Property Act, but she repeatedly submits to her fate in melodramatic fashion, insisting on doing her "dooty". (Trollope 1884, 1:190) Trollope suggests that even the law cannot deny a woman's responsibility to her husband. The authorial voice – usually prominent in his novels – remains silent. Biographer Victoria Glendinning concludes that Trollope thought marriage good for women, and good for the world. His association with prominent feminists such as Kate Field and Emily Faithfull opened his mind, but "this horror of women abandoning the domesticity which sustained men overruled his intelligent sympathy" (1993: 328). Ultimately, he believed the best right of a woman was "the right to a husband" (321).

Male authors like Trollope had much to lose through legal change, yet the property debate is noticeably absent from women's fiction of the mid-Victorian period, even though some writers had given their support during the initial campaign. For example, in addition to signing the original petition, Elizabeth Gaskell in her letters made two references to the fact that her husband pocketed her earnings, yet there is no consideration of this law in her fiction. She remained unconvinced that it would "do much good," adding "a husband can coax, wheedle, beat or tyrannize his wife out of something and no law whatever will help this that I can see. (Mr Gaskell begs Mr Fox to draw up a bill for the protection of <u>husbands</u> against wives who will spend all their earnings)" (quoted in Dolin, 1997: 12, original underlining).[14]

One of the novels that dealt most explicitly with the theme of married women's property was Dinah Mulock Craik's *A Brave Lady* (1870). Serialised between May 1869 and April 1870, the story unfolded as the Bill was debated in Parliament. In her polemical novel, Craik invokes powerful maternal imagery to argue that wives' financial assets should be protected for the sake of their children. Josephine Scanlan is struggling to bring up her six children with little help from her spendthrift husband. Edward Scanlan puts his own needs first, purloining the housekeeping money to ensure he never wants for anything and encouraging their eldest son to beg. Appalled and frustrated by this behaviour, Josephine leaves him, taking the children with her. With the help of a kindly lawyer, she discovers that she has no right to retain her own earnings, even to support her family. Initially, Josephine resolves to move to France, beyond the reach of her husband, but takes pity on his newly-diagnosed heart condition and returns to care for him. In a gloomy denouement worthy of George Gissing, all six children die and Josephine is left with a husband suffering from early-onset dementia.

The overwrought emotion of the narrative shows the potentially devastating consequences of mothers' continuing lack of financial autonomy. However, the relentless misery heaped on her heroine distracts the reader from Craik's political message. Josephine Scanlan is presented as a victim of male solipsism, rather than as a strong woman capable of managing her own financial affairs. In her non-fiction, Craik is unequivocally opposed to the women's rights movement, arguing that her sex is inferior due to "our frivolity, irrationality, and incapacity to seize on more than one idea at the same time" (Craik, 1870 [nd]: 166). Craik's impassioned argument for legal change in *A Brave Lady* went no further than a wife's right to control the housekeeping money.

Charlotte Riddell's short story collection *Weird Stories* was published in 1882, just as the Second Married Women's Property Bill was debated in Parliament. In contrast to both Marryat and Craik, Riddell's stories depict the unfortunate consequences of women gaining financial independence. In "The Old House on Vauxhall Walk", the ghost of Miss Tynan, a woman who refused to share her fortune during life, is condemned to eternal Scrooge-like lamentation over her miserliness. She finds peace only by relinquishing her wealth to a male heir. The living "ghost" in "The Open Door" is a malevolent woman seeking a lost will, who is prepared to poison or shoot anyone who attempts to thwart her search. As Vanessa Dickerson observes, "the desire for money has transformed the demure angel into a fury the male can barely control" (1996: 139). Her barely controllable fury is Riddell's prophecy of the havoc that legal change might wreak. The character of Miss Gostock in "Nut Bush Farm" is an even less subtle warning. An astute businesswoman, she wears men's clothes and keeps her hair short. Shockingly, her house does "not contain a single feminine belonging – not even a thimble" (Riddell, 1882 [2010]: 67), and she prefers brandy to housework. She is described in summary as "some monstrous figure in a story of giants and hobgoblins" (68). Riddell is vulnerable to John Stuart Mill's criticism of "those who find it easier to draw a ludicrous picture of what they do not like, than to answer the arguments for it" (Mill, 1859 [2006]: 241).

Riddell presents this character as the corollary of women controlling their own wealth, without the guiding influence of men. The independent woman is at best a man, at worst a freak. Riddell's own experiences epitomise the contradictions inherent in mid-Victorian women's lives. Following her improvident husband's bankruptcy, Riddell felt obliged to repay all his creditors, amounting to the enormous sum of £10,000 ("The Court of Bankruptcy", 1871: 9). Although one of the most successful authors of her day, Riddell was reduced to subsistence on a small pension from the Society of Authors. She was not compelled to make good her husband's losses, but essentially believed her money to be his, and opted to sacrifice her income. Furthermore, Riddell was unperturbed in 1871 when her stolen purse was described in court as the property of her husband (*Old Bailey Proceedings Online*). This was because she too was his property, a position in which she felt comfortable. In her life Riddell's response was one of mute acquiescence; in her writing she made a fervid plea to uphold the status quo.

"That blessed Property Act": Marryat's Political Fiction

Rather than presenting these laws as an opportunity for women to abandon domesticity, Marryat demonstrated in her fiction how they could be employed to negotiate an identity as equal marriage partner. *Her World Against a Lie* (1878) was published between the Married Women's Property Acts, praising and explaining the progress already made, but also demanding more. Heroine Hephzibah Horton is described as "the spirit of a man cased in a woman's body" (Marryat, 1879: 1:4) and is a thinly-disguised portrait of her creator – almost an avatar. And she is someone who reads the papers and keeps abreast of current affairs:

> "A fine speech!" she thinks as she finishes a long discourse on the injustice of taxing landowners who are ineligible for representation in Parliament. "I wonder what the Ministry will say to it! Ah! if the time had only come for them to give us a voice in such matters, I would move heaven and earth until I had seen some of these radical wrongs set right. But what's the use of talking when the greatest wrong of which they are guilty – the position of our unfortunate sex – is right under their noses, and they will not even notice it. For eighteen centuries they have cramped our minds as the Chinese have cramped their women's feet, and for the same reason – the fear that we should prove as strong a body as themselves – and it will be a hard fight to get the swathing-bands off now. But I see it coming in the distance – the hour when we shall assert our right to stand side by side with the other half of creation, and be heard in our own cause. Heaven grant I may live to see it come!" (1:2)

Like Margaret Oliphant, Marryat is sensitive to the fact that non-existence in law does not exempt her from taxation.

Hephzibah uses her legal knowledge to help Delia Moray, a young woman married to a violent alcoholic.[15] Before the main action has even begun, Marryat makes an impassioned political speech through her avatar, supporting the idea of female suffrage. Sensing that another leap forward is required before equality is achieved, Marryat explains this will be facilitated only when women have a direct political voice: "if women had but ventilated their wrongs from the commencement, instead of hiding them in their own breasts, they would have been emancipated before now! ... We have suffered in silence too long not to be afraid of our own voices" (1:30). There is acknowledgement that the first Act made a difference to the legal position of wives. Hephzibah praises it to Delia, effectively assuming the position of the author addressing the reader:

> "Not that I'm an advocate for marriage, as you well know; though, since that blessed Property Act has passed, it's not half the slavery it used to be ... We haven't been standing still for the last fourteen years. If I warned you not to place your foot upon the rotten plank, because it would give way and precipitate you into the stream, that's proper caution. But when this same rotten plank has been propped up by a stout support from beneath, I should say you might cross with safety". (2:35)

Hephzibah goes on to explain the Act's provisions, ostensibly to Delia, but actually to the reader:

> "the 'Married Woman's Property Act' is more comprehensive than any bill that has been passed for the protection of women before. It embraces a wide area of possibilities, and it provides that the earnings of any married woman, however obtained, and all investments of such earning, shall be held as her separate property, and settled to her separate use ... No

more use for drunken or dissolute husbands, whose wives can earn a little money, to try and make their homes miserable as yours was made. The women can spend their earnings as they will, and snap their fingers in the men's faces". (2:41–2)

Hephzibah herself eventually marries, retaining her own name and choosing for her husband a tiny man she can patronise without fear of him asserting his superior strength. Marriage provides Hephzibah with a room of her own and leisure to write what she pleases, while her attentive husband assumes the household cares. For Marryat this was probably wish-fulfilment realised in fiction. Marryat's polemic is woven into a sensational, compelling and labyrinthine plot, mitigating the didacticism suggested by the above quotations. However, repeated references to women's property legislation, along with many examples to illustrate their application, demonstrate that Marryat's aim was to inform as well as to entertain. The figure of Hephzibah – a strong woman who is not subjugated by marriage – offers a role model to her readers. Although it is impossible to gauge the impact of such novels, an opinion piece in a Welsh newspaper from 1880 certainly suggests that fiction played a role in enlightening women:

> Until we attended the [women's rights] meeting last Thursday week I was (and I believe many others were) ignorant of certain technicalities of the law which seem to be especially oppressive to women, and I have lately read a book, written by the well-known novelist, Florence Marryat, "Her World Against a Lie", and one of her characters, dubbed "Mrs. Hephzebah [sic] Horton", in one of her many diatribes against it, painfully enlightened me on certain points of the statute dealing with a subject about which all women feel strongly. (A. Lady, 1880: 3)

When Marryat adapted the novel for the stage in 1880, she took for herself the role of Hephzibah, thereby reinforcing her link with the character and her opinions, and also reaching a wider audience. Unfortunately, most of the script has been lost,[16] so it is difficult to know the extent to which the radical elements of the novel were recreated on stage. However, a detailed review of the London première suggests that the plot was left untouched, with Hephzibah retaining her stridency: "Miss Florence Marryat made a hit as Mrs Horton. The strong-minded asserter of woman's rights was hit off to the life" ("The London Theatres", 1881: 6). This adaptation – and Marryat's direct involvement with it – exemplifies the lack of distinction between her life, opinions, and work. As with *Miss Chester* (see Chapter 1), the author publicly associated herself with the drama. Had she restricted herself to just fiction, Marryat would have limited her audience; by also writing and performing plays, giving lectures, and delivering one-woman shows, her message reached a much broader range of people.

Of Marryat's later novel *Miss Harrington's Husband* (1886), a reviewer for *The Graphic* remarked: "Internal evidence would lead anybody to imagine it to be inspired by personal rancour" ("New Novels", 1886: 582). They were absolutely right. The novel, also published as *The Spiders of Society*, was based mainly on Marryat's marriage to Francis Lean. Actress Georgie Harrington has been married for three years to Gerard Legh, a military man discharged for dishonourable conduct and disowned by his family. Their first twelve months together were tolerably happy, but then Georgie was forced to return to the stage due to Gerard's extravagance. Since then he has been violent and abusive and refuses to work. Although he makes no financial contribution to the household, he still considers himself its head. Furthermore, he disparages his wife's profession, even though they are entirely dependent on her considerable earnings. When confronted, he declares that he intends to do exactly what he pleases. This includes having an affair and hitting his wife and young sister-in-law.

At the end of her tether, Georgie consults a lawyer, who assures her: "Your money is your own, and the entire disposition of it lies in your hands. You may bank it, or invest it, or spend it as you choose, and Captain Legh has no more right to touch it, or to order how it shall be expended, than I have. The Married Woman's Property Act leaves you completely free" (Marryat, 1886a [1891]: 38–9). To which the delighted wife responds: "Free! ... Is it possible? ... But my husband told me yesterday that a man is always master in his own house" (39).

As in *Her World Against a Lie*, Marryat uses her novel as a platform from which to educate women on their rights. Like Marryat herself, Georgie escapes her husband by taking to the stage and negotiates a US tour. A reviewer in *The Academy* commented that the novel is basically the same as Marryat's theatrical memoir, *Tom Tiddler's Ground*, written just after the final breakdown of her marriage to Lean (Noble, 1886: 305). This willingness to blur fact and fiction and to share the most harrowing episodes of her life reveal Marryat as a highly political writer. Indeed, a great deal of nineteenth-century fiction is autobiographical in nature, but Marryat is unusual, I argue, in making little (and often no) attempt to pretend that it is anything other than a true story. She served as an example herself, and also created fictional prototypes to dispense sound advice on how to deal with intractable husbands.

"I don't like to see a woman do such unfeminine things": Women in Charge

In *A Harvest of Wild Oats* (1877), Marryat shows that women would not have to accept the sexual double standard if they were allowed to manage their own wealth, as financial dependency forces wives to tolerate husbands' unreasonable behaviour. When her husband Frank starts making nocturnal visits to an old flame, Clare Iredell resolves to separate from him. As an independently wealthy woman with a fortune held in trust, she can act with more autonomy than most unhappy wives. The worldly but odious Addy Seymour advises: "a married woman cannot be too independent. The fact serves to keep her husband in order" (Marryat, 1878 [nd]: 222), also providing Clare with anecdotes of other women disposing of mendicant husbands. When Frank demands that Clare move with him to an unattractive garrison town, she responds: "Well, it seems very hard that with twelve thousand a year of one's own, one should not be allowed to choose one's residence." Frank is "thunderstruck" and "her words go through him like a sudden stab" (335). He realises that a wife who controls the purse strings is no mere chattel to be moved around at whim. When the couple finally resolve their differences, they embark upon a marriage of two equals. Addy Seymour's advice was not altruistic – she hoped to divide the couple, believing that no man would want an independent wife. Marryat is keen to prove that strength is both attractive and necessary in a woman. Clare's femininity is stressed throughout the narrative – she is a loving, forgiving, *and* emancipated wife.

Elsa Carden in *Gentleman and Courtier* (1888) suddenly finds herself the owner of the imposing Newton Hall in Yorkshire, along with an income, like Clare Iredell's, of £12,000 per year. She soon attracts the attention of a much younger man, Jocelyn Yorke, who is drawn more to her wisdom and maturity than he is to her fortune. In a reversal of the traditional May-December courtship plot, Yorke begs Elsa to advise and guide him, impressed by her financial acumen. In this novel Marryat again shows that a financially independent woman does not equal disaster, instead such women can make excellent wives. Similarly, in *How Like a Woman!* (1892), Rachel Saltoun is sufficiently wealthy to become a patron of the arts and to choose a lover outside of her immediate circle. The *Athenaeum* found Rachel unacceptable, identifying her faults as "chiefly those of early independence, wealth, and want of discipline" ("Novels of the Week", 1892: 660). A likeable character and a responsible employer, her "fault" is to challenge a prescriptive model of femininity.

Of *Mount Eden* (1889), the *Athenaeum* reviewer complained

that heroine Evelyn Rayne "is not so pretty as the heroines of fiction are expected to be" ("Novels of the Week", 1890: 382). Growing up, she is expected to marry – a role in which looks are certainly more prized than brains. Her cousin Will is set to inherit the family fortune and he tells her that keeping house "is the best thing a woman can do" (15). After he commits a crime and is obliged to abscond, Evelyn inherits the family's vast estate: Mount Eden. A visiting misogynist is prompted to remark, "And it all belongs to a bit of a girl! How absurd" (107). He does not like to "see a woman do such unfeminine things" (120). Yet Evelyn proves an effective landlord and an admirable leader of her exclusively male staff. Captain Philip, the bailiff, is content to serve a female boss who "wields her sceptre over Mount Eden royally" (107). A neighbouring landowner comments: "It was an immense responsibility to lay upon the shoulders of so young a woman, but Evelyn has proved herself to be quite equal to it. ... What do you say to the Women's Rights Bill after that?" (167) Evelyn is a compellingly drawn character who deftly rebuffs her critics. She does not simply marry a man who bestows his worldly goods upon her. In Mount Eden it is the man who sins and causes his downfall; the woman protects the land and secures it for future generations.

Rachel, Elsa, and Evelyn are shown to be responsible and pleasant, in contrast with the grotesque monsters created by Riddell and the demure creatures imagined by Trollope. For Marryat's heroines, their money permits them the freedom to live like gentlemen, controlling their own space without the obligation to fulfil a feminine ideal. They assume a self-created identity, rather than the 'feminine' one imposed upon them by patriarchal discourses. Their identity emerges from a role they have defined for themselves, not from one assumed upon marriage.

As shown above, most women writers were reticent on the issue of property, or vehemently opposed to increasing the rights of wives. Other than Marryat, only Dinah Craik used her platform to argue for change, albeit in an overwhelmingly sentimental fashion that privileged motherhood over womanhood. Marryat alone made a heartfelt and unqualified plea for wives to be given the right to be treated as individuals, and not as the slave of their husband. And, increasingly, she would suggest that women did not need a husband at all.

"The Majesty of Work"

In March 1882, the Church and State Guild bravely invited Marryat to speak on a topic of her own choosing. The Guild was a society whose purpose was "to assert and vindicate the right of religious people to take part in theatrical amusements whether as performers or spectators" (Orens, 2003: 38). Its founder was Stewart Headlam, a Christian Socialist who opposed land ownership, supported Oscar Wilde, and accidentally married a lesbian (37). Not without good reason was he described as "the most bohemian priest in the history of the Church of England" (1), and it is no surprise that Marryat associated with him. Marryat addressed the audience on "The Majesty of Work". Beginning with a quote from Thomas Carlyle – "What a man can do is his greatest ornament, and he always consults his dignity in doing it" (Marryat, 1882b: 1) – she called for a widening of the employment opportunities open to women so they might also consult *their* dignity. Arguing against the idea that it is the "province of men to support women," Marryat claims men are unwilling or unable to do so any longer, so women must be granted the means to earn their own living (3). Here she takes issue with Eliza Lynn Linton's claim that the Girl of the Period married for "his house, his balance at the banker's, his title" (Linton, 1868: 340). If a woman could achieve these aims herself, she would have no need to pursue them vicariously.

The ultimate aim of her lecture, though, was to address the institution of marriage. For Marryat, the real majesty of work was in its ability to give young women more control over their lives: "one of the most beneficial results of bringing girls up to work for themselves, would be the rendering them independent of marriage. To make marriage the end aim of life, to say to a young girl "you must marry", is the most degrading idea you can put into her mind, yet it is the most common" (6). Whereas Trollope thought the best right of a woman was "the right to a husband," Marryat insisted it was instead the right to *autonomy*.

Marryat's lecture was subsequently published by the Women's Printing Society, a workers' co-operative led by Emily Faithfull and staffed by women. The pamphlet was reviewed in *The Women's Union Journal*, a publication likely to be sympathetic to Marryat's position. Yet reviewer John W. Overton failed to see the need for the changes she demanded. Believing England a Christian and civilised country, he "look[ed] forward in faith to a day when work for women outside the house will be unnecessary" (1882: 51). Given the Journal and the Press were essentially run by the same people (most of them working women), it seems curious that the review should be unsympathetic to an argument in favour of increased employment opportunities. Perhaps the Journal hired a conservative reviewer to counteract the radicalism of Marryat's demands. Such vehement criticism of marriage as an institution could have attracted condemnation of both the Journal and the Press, undermining their mission. Marryat's ideas were too strong to disseminate without mediation.

Although in his review Overton chose to focus on the pamphlet's bolder arguments, Marryat does distinguish between "the women who work because they must, and the women who work because they will" (Marryat, 1882b: 2). But the former was a growing demographic. The number of unmarried women over the age of forty-five doubled in the second half of the nineteenth century, to almost half-a-million (Vicinus, 1980: 27). The issue had been memorably addressed by W. R. Greg in his article "Why Are Women Redundant?" (1862). His ingenious solution was to export the bulk of single ladies to Canada, Australia, and the United States (where men outnumbered women). Those not suited to colonial life "should make themselves so agreeable that men would prefer marriage to their mistresses and clubs". The "artificial" state of the leftover spinsters could be solved by "coquetry and commonsense" (quoted in Vicinus, 1980: 4). In a spirited response – "What Shall We Do with the Old Maids?" (1862) – Frances Power Cobbe challenged the "old assumption that marriage was the sole destiny of woman, and that it was the business of her husband to afford her support" (Quoted in Cobbe, 1868: 86). For Marryat, the solution was simple: work. With "suitable occupations" available to all, "we shall not only extirpate the race of discontented and hopeless single women, but we shall have happier and healthier-minded wives" (Marryat, 1882b: 7).

The notion of these "suitable occupations" was a sticking point for Overton. Observing that there was already a surfeit of women writers – with the effect of pushing down wages – he concludes that wives should resist the urge to enter a crowded workplace. His fundamental assumption (in which he was not alone) was that writing was the only conscionable profession for a middle-class woman. But Marryat's ambitions for her sex were much broader. Working women abound in her novels: artists, writers, secretaries, doctors, nurses, estate managers, actresses, teachers, and detectives. All are able to "consult their dignity" and enjoy the majesty of work.

Jane Farrell, heroine of *In the Name of Liberty* (1897), is a sterling example. When her husband Maurice deserts her to join the Fenian Brotherhood, she initially supports herself by working in a West End department store. Concerned the job is beneath her, a police inspector friend offers Jane a position in the newly-formed CID. She shows her creator's ability of turning her hand to almost any profession. Naturally, Jane's first assignment is to investigate the activities of her estranged husband and his associates. In the face of opposition from colleagues who insist it is no job for a woman, Jane volunteers to avert a bomb plot at the home of an aristocratic landowner. On reaching the grounds of the house,

Jane spies a shifty-looking man who reminds her of Maurice. She apprehends him in the name of the law and is aghast to discover that he really is Maurice. She pleads with him to abandon his plot, but he refuses, instead lighting the fuse of his bomb. Jane blows her whistle to summon her colleagues and then seizes the dynamite. She flings it into the fish pond, where it explodes, "sending all the little gold fish to kingdom come" (Marryat, 1897b: 185). Jane is hailed for her bravery, having remained calm and professional, even when her personal involvement in the case became apparent. She is not a genteel lady detective, but a professional woman who proves the equal of any man when confronted with danger.

Although Marryat was keen to project exemplary women, she was no supporter of affirmative action, adding in "The Majesty of Work": "I am always glad when I hear that an incompetent woman has been turned out of her situation, it is a lesson for the whole sex, and I am afraid they will need many such before they are able to the offices they most aspire to fill" (1882b: 11). She wants women to achieve equality on their own merits to prove their detractors wrong. This position is illustrated in her short story "The Countess of Sorrento" (1898), in which a woman detective fails to reach the standards of professionalism set by Jane Farnell. Mrs Thompson pursues an investigative career to distract herself from a loveless marriage. She is assigned a brief to incriminate Mrs Percoral, a woman suspected of adultery. Disguised as the Countess of Sorrento, Mrs Thompson contrives a social occasion and plies her target with alcohol to winkle out the truth. Alas, Mrs Percoral proves inscrutable and Mrs Thompson (after many glasses of champagne) starts confiding her own infidelities. Defeated, the 'Countess' returns home to find divorce papers from her husband. He had hired Mrs Percoral to investigate *her*.

Marryat is clear that women must achieve emancipation on their own merits. If they prove themselves competent, no opportunity should be denied them. As her avatar in *Driven to Bay* proclaims: "When women do more work in England, they will have a better claim to be acknowledged on an equality with men" (Marryat, 1887b: 2:202).

Conclusion

For Marryat, the status conferred upon women by the right to control their own earnings and property was a crucial stage in the struggle for their rights. While female suffrage is generally seen as the ultimate prize for the women's rights movement – and support for it the primary criterion for recognising nineteenth-century women as feminists – granting wives their independence was arguably of greater importance. In her autobiographical novel *The Nobler Sex* (1890), Marryat provides a retrospective view of the legal advances she witnessed and from which she benefited:

> The Acts which have been lately passed for the protection of married women and their earnings are the greatest blessings ever bestowed upon the daughters of England, although one half of the sex does not yet know the privileges it has gained. Had these Acts been passed twenty years sooner my life would have altered from beginning to end, and the greatest sins I have committed been avoided. (Marryat, 1890b: 97)

Here Marryat acknowledges that, like her heroines, she was forced to be transgressive to overcome the limitations placed upon her.

The Married Women's Property Acts were the fulcrum on which the women's rights movement turned. The fact that no fewer than twenty related Bills were presented to Parliament during the nineteenth century demonstrates their importance and pervasiveness during this period (Holcombe, 1983: 208). Despite this prominence, few authors were willing to engage with such a contentious issue, one that radically redefined the institution of marriage. Those who portrayed the consequences of women's independence often did so conservatively, keen to avoid disrupting the reassuring ideology of consistent gender boundaries. Marryat, however, sensed the beginning of a new phase: "For woman is just now in a transition stage, she is but half awakened; she is not the chrysalis she was a century ago, when she went to the husband her parents chose for her, obediently, and tendered him the homage due to a superior. Nor is she the full winged butterfly, able to soar by herself and choose the flower upon which she shall light" (Marryat, 1882b: 7).

Having twice experienced the misery of an unequal marriage, Marryat believed the institution should be "a companionship, a mutual help, the bond that links two true friends together for life" (Marryat, 1882b: 7) not "the chains that gall" (Marryat, 1890b: 141). Whereas the ideal of female behaviour was the "submission of self, voluntary labour, and a minimum of mobility outside the family home" (Vicinus, 1980: 4–5), Marryat and her heroines demanded subjectivity, control of property, and the right to enter professions traditionally reserved for men. As I discuss in the next chapter, some of those professions fought vigorously to exclude women.

CHAPTER 4

In Bluebeard's Chamber: The Conflation of Medical and Patriarchal Authority

"you women have unlimited power in your hands, if only you would recognise it"

An Angel of Pity

"Medicine is a science of uncertainty and an art of probability," proclaimed eminent nineteenth-century physician William Osler (R. Taylor, 2010: 227). But many in his profession thought otherwise. As Lynda Nead observes, medical authority "rests on the belief that, unlike law and religion, it has a rational, scientific foundation and that its moral values are ratified by advanced forms of knowledge" (1988: 144). The development of these moral values, as I argue throughout this study, formed part of a wider agenda to control women.

As discussed in Chapter 2, the 1857 Matrimonial Causes Act represented a legal landmark, bringing both marriage and wifely behaviour under unprecedented scrutiny. The following year the Medical Registration Act was passed, professionalising the role of doctor and creating the General Medical Council to regulate standards (Parry and Parry, 1976: 130). Many feminist historians have noted how, from the early 1700s onwards, medical men gradually displaced women who had traditionally assumed responsibility for midwifery and healing in their communities.[17] Consequently, the domestic sphere – the only place where female authority was tolerated – became the domain of male physicians, who enjoyed privileged access and significant power over their patients.

One vivid example of medical power was the Contagious Diseases Acts, a series of legislation passed in the 1860s that gave police the power to arrest women suspected of prostitution. They were subsequently detained and forced to undergo an intimate examination. While proponents such as William Acton claimed that the Acts presented no "practical threat to modest women," he acknowledged that authorities might have trouble distinguishing between sex workers and wives whose behaviour attracted attention (Walkowitz, 1980: 87). The impetus for the programme was ostensibly to control the spread of venereal disease, but no equivalent treatment was meted out to sexually promiscuous men. Like the Matrimonial Causes Act, this legislation succeeded in enshrining the sexual double standard in law. And by largely successful attempts to exclude women from the medical profession, doctors ensured that "the medical encounter between patient and practitioner was ... firmly one between an implicitly masculine subject and feminine object" (Bashford, 1998: xviii).

Doctors thus exerted a regulatory effect upon women, who were perceived as a medical problem in need of solution. By consolidating their power through legislation and the creation of professional bodies, doctors increased their influence and established a scientific foundation for their moral authority. As Jane Ussher proposes, "Nineteenth-century discourse placed women firmly on the side of nature, infirmity and superstition, and men on the side of learning, direction, management and science" (1991: 69). Thus the rational man sought to regulate the irrational woman. The maintenance of this dichotomy was essential to perpetuating the dominant gender ideology.

In this chapter I examine three aspects of how medical authority was used to regulate women, considering the ways in which Marryat represented and opposed this regulation in her fiction. Firstly, I assess the role of the doctor, often presented by Marryat as a malevolent figure more concerned with the exercise of power than with patient care. By focussing on those novels where the doctor marries the heroine, I identify the conflation of medical and patriarchal authority, a situation regarded by Marryat as highly dangerous. Secondly, I explore the practice of mesmerism, a controversial therapy beyond the regulation of the medical profession, yet still practised by doctors. Finally, I discuss the medical profession's determination to exclude women from its ranks, inhibiting a feminine influence deemed essential by Marryat. This evaluation of Marryat's fiction within the context of contemporary debates and the work of comparator authors reveals her challenge to a gender binary that privileged masculine moral authority – an authority she proved to be specious.

"beholden to him for all things": The Doctor in Victorian Fiction

The 1858 Medical Registration Act was a major landmark, signifying the elevation of the tradesman to the position of middle-class professional (Parry and Parry, 1976: 131). By the time the next Medical Act was passed in 1886, this higher status was being questioned. In this year Robert Louis Stevenson's *Strange Case of Dr Jekyll and Mr Hyde* appeared, a disturbing novella that disputed the apparent respectability of the medical profession. Stevenson wrote it while living next door to Charles-Édouard Brown-Séquard, a vivisector whose research into the spinal cord caused controversy. This year also saw the repeal of the Contagious Diseases Acts, legislation that had permitted doctors to forcibly examine women suspected of being prostitutes. In less than thirty years, then, the fictional doctor had gone from being an unquestioned authority to a figure viewed with suspicion and even contempt.

This transformation can be charted in the fiction of the period: the doctor of mid-Victorian fiction is often an affable character, such as the hero of Trollope's *Doctor Thorne* (1858), a pillar of the community whose treatment relies more on sage advice than on medical intervention; and in George Eliot's *Middlemarch* (1870), Tertius Lydgate is an idealistic young physician who wants to "resist the irrational severance between medical and surgical knowledge in the interest of his own scientific pursuits" (1874: 105). In Marryat's *Love's Conflict* (1865), Dr Salisbury is a gentle man who is prepared to take counsel from others. Here, however, the reader can also detect the displacement of feminine influence. When Elfrida Treherne asks for her sister during a difficult labour, her husband insists that no women should be in the room with her, allowing only a male doctor to accompany him. By the end of the nineteenth century, the doctor has become a monstrous figure, such as Dr Raymond in Arthur Machen's *The Great God Pan* (1894), and H. G. Wells's vivisector in *The Island of Dr Moreau* (1896), whose aim is to harm rather than to heal.

Marryat's fiction marks this change, too. The genial family physician of the earlier novels is replaced by the phlegmatic man of science who views his position as unimpeachable. While many of these malevolent doctors are hidden from view, Marryat "brings the threat to women out of the doctor's surgery and into the marital bed" (Depledge, 2013: 220). As I argue, by illustrating the conflation of medical and patriarchal authority, Marryat showed the consequences of unfettered masculine power, also alerting her readers to the ways in which it was exercised.

"it must be difficult to breathe there": *Nelly Brooke*

Marryat's first novel to feature a doctor as protagonist is *Nelly Brooke* (1868), a dark story in which a young woman agrees to marry an unpleasant man who promises to provide medical care for her twin brother, Bertie. Bertie suffers from an unspecified spinal weakness that confines him to the couch for much of the time, a fate usually reserved for Victorian heroines. This is a reversal of the traditional roles, with Nelly undertaking the physical labour and Bertie circumscribed by his physical limitations. He is a demanding and irascible patient, whose emotional blackmail makes a domestic slave of the robust Nelly. When Dr Monkton appears on the scene proposing a cure, Bertie insists that Nelly must marry him, even though she finds him utterly repellent. Monkton's intentions are no more honourable than Bertie's, as he seeks only a domestic servant who is strong in body and not subject to womanly emotions.

Monkton is described as "cold-blooded" (Marryat, 1869b: 2:2) with a passion that only extends as far as his temper; the narrator implies that he is asexual and unlikely to satisfy a healthy woman like Nelly. Indeed, his name suggests celibacy. His marriage proposal is characteristically unromantic, revealing the complicity between would-be husband and brother: "Robert and I have been discussing this subject far more in detail that I have done with yourself ... you should become my wife, and make your brother's interests mine" (1:313). Patriarchal and medical authority unite here to deny female subjectivity and to regulate Nelly's behaviour. Her wishes are immaterial. Nelly rejects his offer, overwhelmed by an instinct that causes her to recoil, subsequently mirrored by a physical flinch when he tries to touch her (1:5). Bertie later rebukes her for having privileged her happiness over his, and the local vicar warns that her failure to marry the doctor might result in her brother's untimely death.

Worn down by this patriarchal conspiracy, Nelly relents and agrees to marry Monkton. Approaching her marital home for the first time, Nelly thinks it looks "like a prison, and that it must be difficult to breathe there" (2:26). It is on a "well-guarded" (3:183) street, adding to the sense that Nelly's behaviour is regulated. This is compounded by the continual attendance of Monkton's sister, Mrs Prowse, whom he expects to behave like a second wife. Inevitably, Monkton's interest in Bertie vanishes once he has attained his goal, and he is keen to establish his supremacy. When Bertie acts the martinet, Monkton informs him: "You talk very glibly, young man, of what you will allow 'your sister' to do, but you seem to forget that your sister is my wife" (2:209).

Monkton later informs Nelly that "[Bertie] has already monopolised the best part of your life, the rest belongs to me" (2:235). She exists purely to serve men and is to have no life of her own. Realising the failure of his plan, Bertie admits to his sister: "I have sold you for very little, indeed. I made a bad bargain of you, Nell" (2:190). Sensing his imminent death, he ponders: "I wish we were both dead ... I often think what a good thing it would be if I just took one of my grandfather's old pistols, or the carving knife, and put a bullet through your head, Nell, or cut your dear little throat, and made away with myself directly afterwards" (2:171). Bertie can conceive of no separate existence for Nelly, and her own identity has been completely effaced. At the beginning of the novel, "[Bertie] was his sister struck down and withered by sickness: [Nelly] was her brother, glowing with health and strength" (1:26), by the end they are equal: Nelly's cheeks have fallen in, and her eyes are lifeless. Monkton has reduced the once blooming Nelly to a husk, and she now resembles her brother, rather than being his antithesis. Denied the medical care he was promised, Bertie soon dies, causing Nelly further distress.

Monkton's response is to medicate her, which serves only to weaken her further. Her lack of energy and interest suggest clinical depression, and her doctor husband treats it with sedatives, ensuring that she does not become emotional. The medication prevents her from reproaching Monkton for Bertie's death and guarantees appropriately feminine docility. A reviewer in *The Spectator* described Nelly as the "most perfect" heroine ("Nelly Brooke", 1868: 1378), a heroine who is depressed and entirely subservient to her sadistic husband. Through this character, Marryat parodies the selflessness expected of literary heroines, and the *Spectator*'s praise exposes critics' unrealistic expectations.

Even Nelly's dog Thug is controlled. When he barks at his hated master, Monkton orders that he be muzzled and then thrashes him, a punishment metaphorically similar to his drugging of Nelly. The usually lamb-like dog later retaliates by sinking his teeth into the doctor's throat, an attack that turns out to be fatal: Thug is rabid. It was believed at the time that hydrophobia was caused by cruelty (Turner, 1980: 135), so this is a fitting fate for a doctor who abuses his power. In fiction of the period, mistreatment of animals is often a signifier that the perpetrator also abuses women, a trope I discuss in the next chapter.

Although the widowed Nelly remarries, this time to a man of her own choosing, "subdued melancholy seemed to pervade every feeling and tone down every pleasure," and she claims there is "no such thing as happiness" (2:334–5). She is ostensibly content in her new life, but the scars persist from the old one. The novel's ironic subtitle, *A Homely Story*, conveys the idea that the domestic space is not safe, especially when it is inhabited by a doctor who is also a husband. Geraldine Jewsbury implored Richard Bentley not to publish the novel, complaining that Nelly was "as merry as a cricket" after the death of her husband (Bentley Archives, Add. MSS 46658).[18] She even included a dreary three-page synopsis to make it sound thoroughly unappealing. As an arbiter of literary morality, Jewsbury was uncomfortable with a story that showed resistance to male medical authority. Nelly certainly was not merry, but she survived both of her oppressors.

"You stand in the position of her father": *Petronel*

In *Petronel* (1870), Dr Ulick Ford seems a less sinister character than Monkton, but nevertheless he commits a significant abuse of his power. Learning that his quondam lover is on her deathbed, he rushes to see her and agrees to adopt her thirteen-year-old daughter, Petronel. Although his actions are portrayed as largely altruistic, he is motivated partly by the girl's extraordinary resemblance to her mother. Even though her behaviour is portrayed as juvenile, even immature, Ford projects sexual maturity upon her, seeing her as: "A tall girl ... who carried her thirteen summers bravely, standing upright as a young poplar, and who, although younger by three years than her mother had been when first he saw her, looked almost as old as she had done" (Marryat, 1870a: 1:111). This is echoed by one of Petronel's uncles, who demands a kiss and a lock of her hair in return for some pocket money, remarking that she is "Doosidly handsome" (1:227). He and other family members make lewd remarks about her body, making her feel "uncomfortable at their scrutiny" and "wondering what right they had to make such observations about [her] personal appearance" (1:227). Although certainly tall, the narrator observes that Petronel grows half an inch over the Christmas holiday (1:293) – a clear signal that she is still going through puberty. This is a girl and not yet a woman. When Petronel sneaks into Ford's consulting room – that she refers to as "Bluebeard's Chamber" – she is intrigued by his medical books. As an ingenue, she has no idea of human anatomy: "I had never seen to strange a book before, nor yet such curious pictures, and I laughed aloud as I turned over the coloured prints which it contained, and puzzled my ignorant little head to find out what they were intended to represent" (1:188–89).

Marryat describes Petronel's awkwardness by misquoting Henry Wadsworth Longfellow's poem "Maidenhood": "Standing with reluctant feet / Where womanhood and childhood meet" (Marryat, 1870: 2:103). Ford's friend Mr Bertram is also drawn to Petronel's pubescent state. He ogles her and makes unnecessary body contact, to the point where she feels "nervous in fact of being left alone in the room with him" (3:107). Rather than protect her, Ford insists that she makes friends with Bertram, even insisting that she go and stay with him. When Bertram makes his intentions plain, Ford asks: "And so you wish to commence courting this child as soon as she returns from school. Perhaps you have already done so!" Bertram responds: "You stand in the position of her father, and we shall have to submit to your tyranny" (3:145). Like

Nelly Brooke, Petronel's own wishes are irrelevant.

At the time *Petronel* was published in 1870, the age of consent was twelve; five years later, the Offence Against the Person Act would raise it to thirteen – hardly a significant increase.[19] And, as Ornella Moscucci explains, the age of consent laws applied only to girls (1990: 120). As with much legislation relating to sexual behaviour, they were concerned mainly with protecting property, in this case a father's right to control his daughter's sexuality. If she was under the age of sixteen, he could sue a seducer for loss of services. Female virginity, then, was a prize to be carefully controlled; here Ford ultimately realises that this prize is one that he wants for himself. As Petronel's male guardian, he is in complete control of the situation. Later in the story, another character poses as Petronel's biological father. He insists that she is his property and that he has the right to carry her away if he so chooses. When Petronel refers to herself as a "silly, stupid, intractable piece of goods" (2:88), she is partly right. Petronel's virginity is a commodity, or piece of goods, that is variously protected and traded to serve family interests and to cement friendships. She is definitely not intractable, though. Her tractability makes her vulnerable to Ford's attentions, as does her complete dependence on the only person who will take any responsibility for her.

The apparent competition for Petronel inspires jealousy in Ford and he allows himself to entertain thoughts of marrying her, despite the twenty-two-year age gap. Even *The Spectator* thought this May-December plot "almost revolting" ("Petronel", 1870: 1328). Petronel herself realises that she is vulnerable to predatory men and welcomes his protection. She also feels "beholden to him for all things" having nobody else to take care of her (3:101), and speaks of her "veneration" for him (1:176). He refers to her as "that soft girlish creature ... whom one could influence with a word, and who succumbed to a kind look" (3:247). As a doctor, he exerts considerable influence over his female patients, some of whom refuse to eat until he revisits them. They become entirely dependent upon his ministrations, with his bedside manner designed to evoke desire. Eventually, he has the same effect on Petronel and she succumbs to his power, finding herself "weak and languid, and lying on the sofa" (2:251). Now assuming the role of her doctor "he proceeded to ask me various questions concerning my health, in a methodical and professional manner, which drove me nearly wild. I longed to throw my arms around his neck, and tell him that I wanted nothing except the assurance of his love for me" (2:168). Petronel has become addicted to Ford's attention. When he decides she is "nervous", he writes a prescription for her (2:169) – just like Dr Monkton in *Nelly Brooke*. Ultimately, though, the only cure is for her to marry him.

Through this course of "treatment", Ford transforms Petronel from daughter to wife. When they agree to a marriage date, Ford cautions her "till that time you must remain my child" (2:318). He should be beyond reproach and maintain his role of guardian before assuming the equally powerful position of husband. The narrator observes: "The very knowledge of his love had changed her from a child into a woman; what might not the experience of it do?" (2:25). The *experience* of it is apparent from the novel's conclusion. The reader is propelled to the future where Petronel is the mother of six children (her fecundity is noted with distaste by the *Spectator* reviewer), thereby suggesting that her excessive sexual appetite has been channelled into normative, reproductive sex. Although she is apparently happy, the implication is that Ford has used his medical knowledge to achieve his aims and Petronel has been at the mercy of her own sexuality. Aged twenty-six, she describes herself as "an old woman now" (3:293), probably due to childbearing and having entered womanhood before she was ready. Her sense of self-worth is derived entirely from serving her husband and children and she fears that "every one makes more of me than I deserve" (3:295). This is not a woman who has realised her biological destiny, but a girl who had no other option but to marry a man upon whom she was utterly dependent. Through his medical knowledge, Ford convinces her that she is genuinely attracted to him.

Whereas the man of science is generally presented as cold and even repugnant, Ulick Ford is a popular and personable character, which is precisely why he has so much trust conferred upon him. Nobody questions his right to enter the homes of vulnerable young women, and thus he represents a more dangerous figure. Indeed, Petronel's family rejoice that she has been rescued by such a respectable man. He is a popular figure in the seaside town of Rockborough, his "serious and dignified comportment inspir[ing] with confidence all those who had anything to do with him" (1:27). But the narrator confides, "his was a strange character to anyone who tried to dip below the surface, and it was difficult to say what he liked or did not like, or believed or did not believe" (1:21). He is not motivated by the Hippocratic Oath, but by a "love of power" (1:23). Even his sister, a "ferret-faced" battleaxe, is "considerably afraid of him" (1:36). Ford's behaviour is controlled by nobody. Marryat undermines the moral authority of doctors, showing it to be based often on self-aggrandisement rather than a duty of care.

While Dr Ford gently insinuates himself into his patients' lives, in *Dr Phillips: A Maida Vale Idyll* (1887) Frank Danby (the pseudonym of Julia Frankau) presents a gross caricature of the apparently omnipotent doctor.[20] Unfortunately, Danby's agenda is anti-semitic as well as iconoclastic, with many faults ascribed to the eponymous doctor's Jewishness. The novel is an uncomfortable read, even by nineteenth-century standards. Like Ulick Ford, Dr Phillips exerts great influence over women: "the magnetic touch of his smooth palmed hands had a remarkable power of nerve soothing; he had the faculty of at once exciting and gratifying the imagination. He was conscious of this gift, and fond of exercising it; to it he owed his successes among women" (Danby, 1887: 46). The narrator implies that his profession allows him to legitimately spend intimate time with women which would otherwise be unacceptable for a married man, and there are hints that he also visits prostitutes. Resolving to marry his gentile mistress, with whom he has a five-year-old child, Phillips deliberately administers a fatal dose of chloroform to his wife during surgery to remove her unused ovaries. Although his lover forsakes him – realising the danger of a husband with such power – he is never found out. Phillips instead simply initiates a sexual relationship with his housekeeper and carries on as before. The narrator admonishes him for his "moral recklessness" and desire to "unsex women," (341) but he is completely unstoppable, with his behaviour condoned and occluded by the medical fraternity. Jane Jordan argues that Dr Phillips was based on Dr Heywood Smith, a prominent gynaecologist who was notorious for his role in the child prostitution case reported by W. T. Stead in his series "The Maiden Tribute of Modern Babylon" (Jordan, 2016: np). Danby's novel is in many ways more forceful than Marryat's, with its damning indictment of masculine privilege. However, Marryat's subtle portrait of Dr Ford, although ambiguous, does offer a more alarming vision: that those who abuse their power are not always as conspicuous as Dr Phillips.

"Poked and prodded, hypnotised, all-but-anatomised": Mesmerism and Sexual Propriety

One of the aims of the Medical Registration Act was to drive out practices such as mesmerism and hypnotism, which the profession rejected as 'quackery'. They persisted, nevertheless, as "there was widespread feeling that many doctors were not necessarily more successful than those they branded 'quacks'." Harriet Martineau was a high-profile adherent of mesmerism, which she believed cured her uterine cancer (Winter, 1995: 598). Her letters to the *Athenaeum* on the subject provoked a furious response from the President of the Royal College of Surgeons, who made a public diagnosis of hysteria to discredit her opinion (610). In this case, alternative medicine actually empowered a woman, enabling her to resist experimental surgical intervention; more popular, though, were stories of how such powers were abused. Elizabeth

Gaskell, for example, was interested in mesmerism, but feared the possibility of sexual dominance that it implied (Waterfield, 2003: 165). As Alison Winter explains:

> The physical positions of mesmerist and patient ... had to be judged carefully. For example, when a man mesmerised another man, they often sat with their knees touching, hands interlaced ... But when a man mesmerised a woman, he stood over her, either as she sat in a chair or, if she were too ill, lay on a bed. This arrangement satisfied the demands of sexual propriety, and expressed the power relations that justified the trajectory of influence between the male mesmerist and the female patient. (1998: 140)

Marryat explored the abuse of such power relations in *Blindfold* (1890) through the practice of mesmerism, a term she uses interchangeably with hypnotism. This indicates that Marryat saw little difference between mesmerism, a practice that had been discredited, and hypnosis, one that enjoyed a surge in popularity during the preceding decade, largely due to the work of French neurologist Jean-Martin Charcot. In *Blindfold*, mesmerist Paul Adrastikoff boasts that he has "acquired complete control" over his sister (Marryat, 1890a: 1:278), Olga:

> [she] was entirely subservient to him. He had magnetised her so often that in his presence she had no will of her own, although her nature often uprose against the bondage, and made her pant to burst the chains that bound her to him against her better judgement. He could sway her actions when in a normal condition by his unspoken wishes, and even when miles of distance stretched between them he could make her do just as he chose. This awful and mysterious power ... is perhaps the most fatal influence which one human creature can exercise over another. (1:280–1)

During a stay in the Swiss Alps, Paul forces Olga to participate in a stage act where he mesmerises her and invites audience members to perform degrading acts on her while she is in a trance. In one performance, Paul lies on her chest and then invites two men to take their turn in doing the same, prompting one audience member to exclaim: "Fancy that brute inviting two great hulking men to sit on that tender creature's body" (1:274). This extraordinary spectacle is reminiscent of Charcot's hypnotic demonstrations, where he was "ruthlessly insensitive to the pain and anguish of his patients," who were brought on stage "to be examined, poked and prodded, hypnotised, all-but-anatomised" (Scull, 2009: 114).

Paul's behaviour suggests sexual assault and there are hints that he can make Olga have sex while in a trance. He effectively uses mesmerism to control his sister in the way that pimps might administer drugs to manage prostitutes. He pockets all the money from ticket sales and sees Olga's role as earning his living, expressing a desire for her to marry a rich man, preferring "to live upon another person than to make money for himself" (1:279–80). Displeased with Olga's choice of future husband, he hypnotises her and renders her complicit in his murder. He then blackmails her into marrying his friend Jack Dorrian so that they might live in a *ménage à trois*. Paul essentially courts Jack on Olga's behalf, controlling her every movement through mesmerism, and she has no will of her own. Near the novel's conclusion it is revealed that Paul is no relation to Olga: sensing she was susceptible to his power, he hypnotised her into believing they were siblings. Marryat shows how controversial medical practices could be used to reinforce patriarchal authority, or indeed to establish it where none existed.

Novelist and travel writer Iza Duffus Hardy also addresses this theme in *A New Othello* (1890), although through different relationships. Dr Gervas Fitzallan is a creepy and sadistic doctor who repeatedly taunts his wife with accusations of frigidity and threatens to strangle her with her own hair – a plot unnervingly similar to Robert Browning's poem "Porphyria's Lover" (1836). Fortunately for his wife, he soon turns his attentions to Eileen Dundas, an impressionable young woman on whom he practises mesmerism. When a man from his past identifies Fitzallan as an escaped murderer with no medical qualifications, he 'programmes' her to poison him. Fitzallan has assumed the identity of a doctor to practise mesmerism, this illusion of medical authority allowing him to act with impunity. His real name turns out to be George Charcott, an unflattering reference to Jean-Martin Charcot.

Both Marryat and Hardy's novels, published in the same year, express the anxieties surrounding mesmerism and hypnotism. Indeed, the following year the British Medical Association appointed a commission to investigate hypnotism, concluding that "under no circumstances should female patients be hypnotised, except in the presence of a relative or a person of their own sex" (Waterfield, 2003: 210). The Medical Registration Act of 1858 had done nothing to suppress unqualified practice, merely defining a "qualified medical practitioner" (Moscucci, 1990: 60). Patients, especially women, were therefore at the mercy of anyone who offered plausible therapies. Supposedly, the Medical Act Amendment Act of 1886 would ensure that doctors were unified and governed by national standards, but its members could not resist the temptation to dabble in unorthodox practices. Attempts to professionalise medicine, then, had done nothing to stop unscrupulous men from exploiting the power it gave them over women. Having established the doctor as the powerful being and the patient as the helpless woman, abuses were predictable – unless, of course, the doctor was a woman.

"A Bad Imitation of a Man": The Danger of Lady Doctors

Although the 1858 Medical Registration Act did not specifically exclude women doctors, this was purely an oversight. As women were not permitted to study for medical degrees in the United Kingdom it was not deemed necessary to formally debar them.

However, the profession had not given any thought to those who had qualified overseas. Elizabeth Blackwell, who was born in the UK and trained in the USA, was able to register and practice in England in 1859. Nothing could be done to stop her, but an amendment was swiftly passed to exclude foreign degree holders. While this event passed almost unnoticed, in 1867 the arrival in London of US Civil War veteran Dr Mary Walker attracted attention. Having served on the frontline with the Federal army medical service, Walker commanded a certain amount of respect when she visited Middlesex Hospital. Nobody dared to question her professional credentials, but her rational dress excited much comment and opprobrium. The *Lancet* was deferential, yet questioned "the advisability of this lady's example being very generally followed by her sex" ("Medical Annotation", 1866: 502). Even Emily Faithfull criticised Walker, describing her as "such an unfortunate contrast to ladies like Miss Blackwell and Miss Garrett, whose scientific knowledge and medical skill are only equalled by their modesty and quietness of demeanour ... a woman may be a doctor, and yet retain this modesty, purity, and grace, which are her special characteristics" (Faithfull, 1867: 232). Feminists like Faithfull were sensitive to the discovery in 1865 that pioneering surgeon Dr James Barry had been born a woman but lived as a man.[21] There was little chance women would be invited to enter the professions if they did so by imitating the superior sex.

In her novel *The Autobiography of Christopher Kirkland* (1885), Eliza Lynn Linton devotes several pages to the evils of women doctors, referring to them as "flirting, touzled, pretty young creatures" unsuited to the dissecting room (1885 [2011]: 121). Walker is singled out as doing "much to retard the woman question all round" with her "Bloomer costume" (259). Linton cautions that the corollary of equal rights will be "men's virile force toned down to harmony with the woman's feminine weakness; the abolition of all moral and social distinctions between the sexes" (258–9). Although Marryat was seldom in agreement with Linton, her response in 1866 to Walker's appearance was similar:

> There is no reason because women work that they should unsex themselves. We might as well assume men's clothing and say we have a right to it, as try to wrest their proper occupations from them … in all such cases … women silently acknowledge they are overstepping the limits to which they should go, by adopting some part or other of masculine costume. Could anything be more absurd than the appearance of Dr Mary Walker, for instance, unless, indeed, it is herself? Such a hybrid only inspires me with the supremest disgust. (Marryat, 1869b: 127)

As demonstrated below, while Marryat remained sensitive to the supposed "hybridity" of the female doctor, she later argued that medicine needed a feminising influence. And in *Her Father's Name* (1876), she embraced the idea of transvestism for women.

The controversy really started in 1869 when Sophia Jex-Blake and four other women enrolled as medical students at the University of Edinburgh – the only institution prepared to accept them. The following year the women were harassed by an angry mob who tried to prevent them from attending an anatomy lecture. They were pelted with mud and rubbish, and even the college's pet sheep was encouraged to attack them (Todd, 1918: 291–2). Undaunted, the tiny cohort graduated, setting a precedent for those who sought to emulate them. The *Saturday Review* thundered: "it is monstrous to allow so small a minority, moved in great measure by the strange teaching of Mr. Stuart Mill, to disturb the whole relations of social life" ("Women and University Degrees", 1874: 77), a conservative position reiterated by some novelists.

In Wilkie Collins's novel *The Legacy of Cain* (1889) Helena confides to her diary: "A female doctor is, under any circumstances, a creature whom I detest. She is, at her very best, a bad imitation of a man" (3:105). As Kristine Swenson explains, sceptics were grappling with "the radical implications of a woman with the medical knowledge and professional legitimacy to control human bodies" (2005: 3). Critics also feared that women doctors would acquire sexual knowledge, rendering them unfit to become wives. In his short story "Fie! Fie! Or the Fair Physician" (1882) Collins portrays Sophia Pillico, an attractive young doctor who apparently finds a seventy-four-year-old patient with angina sexually irresistible. While it was acceptable for men to treat women, reflecting supposedly innate power relations, the reverse was a dangerous aberration that could cause chaos. It was better for woman to remain ignorant, as medical knowledge would "'unsex' her, make her a 'neuter,' biologically incapable of the conventional womanly duties of marriage and motherhood" (7).

It was this "unsex[ing]" that preoccupied some authors, including Charles Reade. His novel *The Woman-Hater* (1877) is ostensibly an argument in favour of women doctors, but this is significantly compromised by its sensationalism (and also by a regressive main plot involving two women fighting over a useless man). The protagonist, Rhoda Gale (a composite of Elizabeth Blackwell and Sophia Jex-Blake), is presented as a man-hating lesbian, albeit one who is far gentler than her rhetoric suggests. Essentially, she is a good character who successfully campaigns for medical and sanitary reform, but she is also a sexless hybrid. As Patricia Murphy concludes, the novel "undermines its feminist pretensions and reifies unsettling perceptions of femininity" (2006: 214). Rather than endorsing the role of women doctors, Reade instead consigns them to a third, indeterminate sex.

Arabella Kenealy adopts a similar approach in *Dr Janet of Harley Street* (1893), labouring her heroine's masculinity throughout: "The forehead was large and massive, the chin broad and resolute. He would be a bold man who opposed the firm and fiery will of this big woman" (87). Even her womanly tears fall on "large hands" and she prides herself on being a "neuter" (340), conforming to neither male nor female stereotypes. While this gives her great latitude, it also means she must remain single. Her young protégé, Phyllis Eve renounces her medical career upon marriage, realising that the two are incompatible; unwilling to become a neuter, she must instead embrace her biological destiny.

Annie S. Swan also portrayed the woman doctor in *Elizabeth Glen MB* (1895), the conclusion of which might be guessed from the title of its sequel: *Mrs Keith Hamilton MB* (1897). The narrator is at pains to emphasise Glen's femininity throughout, almost apologising for her choice of career, and stressing that her domestic skills have been of most benefit to her patients. Glen eventually sacrifices a successful medical career to marry a partially repentant sexist, finding far more fulfilment as Mrs Keith Hamilton than she did as Dr Elizabeth Glen. In the sequel, she acknowledges that "his career is more interesting to me than any case I ever had," a statement accompanied by a "lovely blush" (1897: 8). Although Swan is offering a partial defence of women doctors, showing what their feminine touch can do for patients, her narrator's relief is palpable when the heroine is returned to normative womanhood through marriage. Like Phyllis Eve, Elizabeth Glen cannot be both wife and doctor. Tabitha Sparks writes of the woman doctor: "When she chooses to marry, she ends her career, and when she chooses her career, she renounces marriage" (2009: 152). Although this is broadly true of Victorian fiction, there are exceptions.

Mona Maclean, Medical Student (1893) was written by Margaret Todd (under the pseudonym of Graham Travers), herself a doctor, and also the life partner of Sophia Jex-Blake. Mona is a clever creation who manages to be intelligent, feminine and non-threatening. Although she encounters hostility during her studies, she wins over her enemies with a combination of charm and self-deprecation. She graduates after several attempts and marries a fellow doctor with whom she sets up a practice. This apparently utopian conclusion offers a counterpoint to Reade and Kenealy's novels, showing that women doctors are not necessarily freaks. However, their adjoining consulting rooms represent an important division: Mona treats only the female patients, an arrangement that goes unquestioned by the narrator. As Swenson argues, "The novel's message about medical women, then, is that they should be afforded an equal though distinct place within the profession" (2005: 144). The seemingly radical narrative also conceals a conservative undercurrent. Complicating Swenson's contention that the female doctor was "the exemplar of the New Woman" (93), Mona is pro-vivisection and a sceptic of women's suffrage, a position that would have placed her outside mainstream feminist thinking – but one that makes her more palatable to the conservative reader. In fact, *The Lancet* pronounced it "a capital book" with a "healthy" tone ("Library Table", 1892: 1394).

In making her argument for the radicalism of fictional women doctors, Swenson asserts that "The nurse was merely an independent rather than a 'New' woman," because she endorsed traditional sex, gender and class distinctions, thereby rendering her no threat to society (Swenson, 2005: 90). But Alison Bashford criticises the "common scholarly insistence on separating historical treatment of nurses, midwives and women doctors," stating that the figure of the female medical practitioner was "ambiguously nurse, midwife and doctor" (1998: xviii). Yet many fictional nurses are idealised and saintly creatures, for example Gaskell's Ruth, or fantasy figures, such as the sexually rapacious Edith Archbold in Reade's *Hard Cash* (1863). They invariably conform to the Madonna/Magdalen dichotomy, allowing little room for complexity or individual expression. The medical profession in Victorian fiction is generally inhabited by the all-powerful male doctor and the depraved or saintly nurse.

The title of Marryat's novel *An Angel of Pity* (1898) gives the impression that heroine Rose Gordon will conform to the Madonna model. However, she has taken up nursing after passing a medical degree with high honours at Edinburgh University. She also holds a BA from Girton, boosting her New Woman credentials and establishing her as someone who is not entirely in the thrall of science. Her decision to nurse rather than practice as a doctor implies a desire to conform to notions of femininity, but, as her colleagues discover, Rose does not consider the role of nurse to be subordinate. One of her colleagues warns her: "We nurses cannot afford to fight the medical men. They have it all their own way. Their word is law, and we can do nothing but obey it" (Marryat, 1898a: 49).

Undaunted, Rose immediately starts challenging Dr Lesquard, a pompous misogynist who disregards the opinions of others. During a ward round he deliberately induces a fit in a female patient for the benefit of his audience, smiling at the result. When Rose complains about the indignity he has inflicted she is cautioned by the matron: "the doctors know best ... If they say she is in no pain, she isn't" (14). Thus, the female patient is denied both her dignity and her subjectivity. This scene is perhaps inspired by Frances Power Cobbe's scathing essay on the abuse of medical power, in which she comments: "No doctor can be dull enough to ignore the fact that the feeling of a woman with a crowd of curious young students round her bed of agony must be almost worse than death" (1881: 311).

When Lesquard realises his behaviour is being questioned, he pronounces: "Women have no business in the profession at all! As nurses, they are useful enough – but for nurses we don't require these very highly-educated young ladies. A little knowledge is a dangerous thing ... I cannot say I relish having to excuse or explain my conduct to a woman, who, had she remained in her proper position, would have been satisfied that a man of my experience could do no wrong" (20). Medical men like Lesquard want nurses whose work is merely an extension of their feminine duty to nurture, rather than knowledgeable professionals capable of making decisions. Rose repeatedly undermines Lesquard, defying his orders and exposing him as a prolific vivisector. Eventually they marry, each believing they can change the other. While Rose makes no attempt to conceal her agenda, Lesquard pretends to be supportive of her medical career, quietly resolving that she will resign her position on marriage. Ultimately, Rose's determination and medical knowledge allow her to triumph over Lesquard. At the novel's conclusion the couple are running a private clinic, with the clear understanding that Rose enjoys equal authority with him. In this respect it mirrors the final scene of Mona Maclean, but there is no implication that Rose treats only female patients. Depledge argues that Marryat introduces resolution and compromise to achieve a traditional "happy" ending (2013: 230), but the explanation lies earlier in the novel, when Rose confesses: "I have no money, and no influence. The doctors do not want to let women advance in the profession – they would turn them out altogether if they could – and I am likely, at this rate, to remain a hospital nurse all my life. As Mr Lesquard's wife, I shall at once possess all that I need to help me on, and if the many advantages are clogged by the chain of matrimony, I must try to bear it" (147).

For Rose, marriage to Lesquard is purely expedient, allowing her to circumvent the problems faced by many other women in the medical profession. By making her heroine a nurse, Marryat neatly avoids the hostility that a woman doctor might have provoked. Rose is plainly shown to possess as much knowledge as the male doctors, but there is no suggestion that she is taking their jobs from them. Furthermore, the nurse's uniform renders her appropriately feminine with no hint that she has adopted a masculine or neuter role. Professional women had to distinguish themselves from the likes of the gin-sozzled Sairey Gamp, but, as Bashford observes, "to be too 'scientific' and 'professional' was to be masculine, and to risk accusations of being unsexed and unnatural, accusations regularly directed to Mary Walker" (1998: 85).

Marryat does not explicitly state that Rose assumes the role of a *doctor* in the clinic. By remaining ambiguous, she portrays a medically competent woman while escaping the criticisms levelled at both real and fictional women doctors. Marryat's solution to the controversy is to empower a traditionally female role, rather than to make her heroine masculine, as Reade and Kenealy felt it necessary to do. For them, a woman could not become a competent doctor without also renouncing her femininity. And, unlike Elizabeth Glen, Rose is also allowed to combine her career with marriage. For Rose, marriage presents an opportunity to further her scientific interests, rather than an institution that ensures her conformity to a feminine ideal.

Conclusion

Throughout her fiction, Marryat warns of the dangers posed by a powerful medical profession, and one entirely dominated by men. The enhanced status enjoyed by doctors from the middle of the nineteenth century gave them even more power, especially when bolstered by the law – as in the case of the Contagious Diseases Acts. By providing a scientific rationale for their moral agenda, they significantly widened their sphere of influence. As Sheryl Burt Ruzek argues, they served as "arbiters of morality and agents of social control" (1978: 17). Marryat exposed the superficiality of men's moral authority, challenging this ideology and encouraging women to develop their own agency.

In *An Angel of Pity*, Rose Gordon is told: "you have unlimited power in your hands" (1898a: 59). Combining humanity with intelligence, she possesses precisely the right skills to be a capable doctor. Marryat argues against the dichotomy of the male subject and the female object, instead creating a character who embodies both masculinity and femininity. Unlike Gervase Monkton in *Nelly Brooke* and Ulick Ford in *Petronel*, Rose is motivated by empathy, rather than by a love of power. Marryat argued that without this feminising influence, medicine became just another form of patriarchal control. And, as the misuse of mesmerism showed, increased regulation failed to prevent male doctors from abusing this power – a situation I illustrate with grisly examples in the next chapter. For some medics, women did not have minds – only problematic bodies.

CHAPTER 5

"Are you not a little prejudiced, dear Doctor?": The Pathologisation of Female Sexuality

"doctors deceive one so."

A Rational Marriage

In 1848, pathologist Rudolph Virchow wrote unchivalrously: "Woman is a pair of ovaries with a human being attached; whereas man is a human being furnished with a pair of testes" (quoted in Dally, 1991: 84). As this quotation suggests, nineteenth-century medicine had not progressed far beyond the Hippocratic model. The ancient Greeks believed that the womb wandered about in search of moisture, thereby causing its owner to behave erratically. While physician W. D. Buck thought the uterus a "harmless, unoffensive little organ, stowed away in a quiet place" (1867: 464), some of his colleagues feared that women – and society – were at the mercy of the female reproductive system. It was in the national interest to regulate those troublesome bodies: this would ensure stability, economic growth, and the birth of future generations. As discussed in the previous chapter, doctors like Ulick Ford wielded considerable power over female patients, who had been counselled to believe that they suffered from a serious disease that gripped Victorian society: hysteria.

For a growing nineteenth-century medical profession keen to assert its authority, hysteria – a disease with no distinguishing features – became a useful diagnosis both to contain women and to pathologise their sexuality. It could be conveniently applied to any woman who displayed transgressive behaviour, whether through sexual promiscuity, or by merely expressing a strong opinion. Establishing women's fundamental instability as a scientific fact allowed doctors to devise methods for controlling them. Edward Tilt claimed that gynaecology was the "accurate study of diseases of women" (Tilt, 1882: vii), but some of its practitioners were propelled by an imperfect understanding of women's bodies that was based more on ideology than on scientific progress. William Acton reassured the public that they were not concerned with "soiled doves," rather with "a class of woman we may almost call 'unsexed'" (quoted in Walkowitz, 1980: 87). By "unsexed", Acton meant unfeminine. The problem for him, and some of his colleagues, was that women were having too much sex; worse still, some of them were even enjoying it.

The prescribed model of Victorian female sexuality was a woman who "did not initiate but reacted" (Wood, 2001: 45). While William Acton's belief that "women (happily for them) are not very much troubled with sexual feeling" was shared by many, Lucy Bland usefully explains that there were an equal number of doctors who viewed women as naturally sexual beings (2002: 56). Indeed, there were many who warned of the dangers of women being able to express their sexuality and the implications this might have for future generations, for example widespread sterility and homosexuality. Acton did himself admit that "there are some few women who have sexual desires so strong that they surpass those of men and shock public feeling by their exhibition" (1862: 101). Marryat's novels abound with heroines who take the sexual initiative, and many "shock public feeling", or at least provoke the ire of contemporary critics.

This chapter discusses the various ways in which Marryat portrayed female sexuality and the medical response that sought to control it. Firstly, I consider three of Marryat's most sexually proactive heroines – Henrietta Stuart, Lola Arlington, and Harriet Brandt – through whom their creator makes complex, and often distasteful arguments about the dangers of promoting ideology over reality. I then move on to Marryat's representation of lesbianism and masturbation in her novel *Her Father's Name* (1876). Whereas the medical profession deemed these behaviours deviant and dangerous, Marryat celebrated them as empowering. Finally, I explore the murky world of late-Victorian gynaecology and the controversial practice of clitoridectomy. Close readings of *Petronel* and *The Strange Transfiguration of Hannah Stubbs* show how Marryat exposed these horrifying 'treatments' and the ideological agenda that inspired them.

A "gorgeous throbbing style": *For Ever and Ever*

Jennifer Carnell believes that, in her novel *For Ever and Ever* (1866), Marryat "probably went further than any other novelist, male or female, of the period" (2000: 170). Henrietta Stuart is a pert young woman who resists marriage to the "pale sickly-looking man" (Marryat, 1866: 1:82) favoured by her parents. Her father, the local vicar, despairs that reading *Guy Livingstone* has given her an unrealistic idea of masculine perfection. When she spies a specimen that meets her standard, Henrietta's response is enthusiastic: "She had hungered and thirsted too long, she had been nearly starved to death for lack of nourishment, and love's feast was spread before her. With a passion almost akin to his own, her pomegranate mouth rested upon his, while the fragrance of her breath came and went upon his face, and made his senses reel beneath its influence" (3:185). Most significantly, she makes the first move on her lover, with Marryat's graphic description ensuring the reader is in no doubt as to the nature of their encounter. One reviewer commented: "We are not quite sure that we know what a pomegranate mouth is, but at all events it sounds very luscious" ("For Ever and Ever", 1866a: 432).

This passionate kiss is heartily defended by the narrator, but the *Saturday Review*'s critic found themselves conflicted. Complaining that Marryat had deteriorated to the level of a penny novelist, they added that "there is an additional piquancy in making the young lady, and not the gentleman, take the initiative in this ardent caress" (433). The reviewer admonishes the novelist's "gorgeous throbbing style", yet provides page references for all the offending passages, presumably so the impatient reader can skip straight to the naughty bits. One of the sauciest passages is quoted in full:

> Miss Marryat … tells us that "the flaming colour mounted higher and higher into the youthful cheeks and brow of the lady, while her lips and nostrils quivered with suppressed emotion, and into the liquid eyes, swimming in tears, there rushed an eloquent light, which without effort on the gentleman's part was quickly answered from his own," the joint result being "an electric light such as only passes between man and woman when they love." (432)

Henrietta's worldliness is contrasted with Winifred Balchin, a shy young girl who is seduced, impregnated, and abandoned by the local roué. She has no idea what has happened to her until the baby arrives; then she is swiftly rejected by her family.

The Athenaeum denounced *For Ever and Ever* as a "feverishly exciting book … that will not be particularly beneficial to its readers" (Doran, 1866: 427), while *The Spectator* charged Marryat with "vulgarity". Their reviewer did offer some modest praise for creating characters who "really move and live," but thought Marryat had a duty to present paragons, asking: "Is a toad worth painting?" ("For Ever and Ever", 1866b: 1171) Monica Fryckstedt distinguishes Henrietta Stuart as the most sexually proactive heroine of the period and a "subversive element in the fiction intended for a middle-class audience and a challenge to its code of morality" (Fryckstedt, 1989: 110). The reviewers' comments exemplify the extent to which women novelists were expected to conform to this code of morality, in both tone and style. Towards the end of her career, an exasperated reviewer commented: "It is a pity that Miss Marryat will not take advice … her faults seem to be inveterate" ("New Novels", 1896b: 752), Ignoring their advice, Marryat presents what she deems 'real' women and resists the ideological impulse. One of the reasons why Marryat was so keen to subvert this 'code' was her belief that the sexually passive woman favoured by (respectable) popular culture was leaving English men and women at risk from a dangerous invader.

"she is not a woman calculated to make a man happy": The Threat of the Racial 'Other'

Marryat's agenda in arguing for more realistic portrayals of female sexuality was partly motivated by racial anxiety. While racism was prevalent in the nineteenth century, Marryat's prejudice was particularly vehement and stemmed from an episode in her family's history. Her grandfather Joseph Marryat was best-known as an MP, but he was also a wealthy slaveowner. In *There is No Death* (1891), Florence claimed he was an abolitionist, but he spoke in Parliament on the benefits of the slave trade and published a pamphlet defending his business interests. The Marryats quickly shifted their position once public opinion had turned against slavery. Apart from the considerable wealth the Marryats had amassed from forced labour, they were left with another, more tangible, legacy: Ann Marryat. As research by Catherine Hall shows, Ann was the illegitimate daughter of Joseph and one of his slaves on a West Indian plantation ("Displaced Memories of Slaves", 2017: online). Although he did not recognise her formally, Joseph manumitted Ann, her brother, and her mother before returning to England. Astonishingly, Ann later held an investment in her own slaves, for whom she was compensated a total of £567/4/6d after the abolition of the trade (C. Hall, 2018: 33). Ann Marryat possibly provided an uncomfortable reminder of the family's shameful past. She remained in her native Grenada but is likely to have been a source of family gossip, and anxiety.

Florence Marryat's fiction and non-fiction is marred by racist rhetoric and an intense fear of hereditary taint. The growth of the British Empire and the social mobility enjoyed by mixed-race women like Ann Marryat suggested that the Englishwoman was facing some unwelcome competition. These fears are first addressed in *A Daughter of the Tropics* (1887), a lively but disturbing novel. When Colonel Escott returns from service in India, he is transfixed by the sight of his friend's Creole housekeeper:

> What a handsome creature she was! What rich outlines! what brilliant colouring! Her lips were scarlet, and there was a glow on her face like the heart of the damask rose. And what an exuberance of vitality seemed to pervade every glance and feature! The worn-out man from India looked at her as he might have looked at a goddess of Health and Beauty. The mere sight seemed to infuse new life into his veins! (Marryat, 1887a 1:19)

Although Lola Arlington oversees Mark Kerrison's household affairs, she also manages his money and writes half the plays that have made him a wealthy man. He is utterly dependent on her and she considers herself his wife in all but name. When Escott suggests their marriage must be imminent, Kerrison exclaims: "she has black blood in her veins!" Escott enquires whether that is "such an insuperable objection to matrimony," to which his friend responds: "To *me* it would be, Jem! I have such a horror of it that I would rather marry a woman 'with a history!' It is never purged from the system! The taint remains for ever!" (1:57). He adds that she "turns green under emotion" (1:57) and that her grandmother once roasted and devoured a love rival. Marryat's racial 'othering' lacks subtlety, but not incident.

Lola's passion and exoticism are contrasted with her rival for Kerrison's affections: Miss Lily Power. As her name suggests: "Her complexion was of a pearly white, without any variation of colour; and her hair, which was of a pale gold, made her look still more bloodless" (1:111). Unlike, Lola, Lily is "unpolluted" (1:249). The respective chapters in which they are introduced are entitled "She has black blood in her!" and "The White Woman". These crude stereotypes are juxtaposed to emphasise their difference. Suddenly, Colonel Escott is revolted by Lola's flashing eyes, dark hair, and crimson lips "because his fancy at that moment was riveted on a slight, fragile form, and pensive eyes that shone through tears like wood-violets bathed in dew". A "white face ... had taken possession of his heart ... all riper charms looked coarse and uninviting beside the image enshrined there" (1:179). Once contrasted with an image of the English ideal, Lola's exotic charms appear specious and her race is all he can see. Escott grasps that Lily is more socially acceptable as a wife, and his exile in India has desensitised him to the need for conformity. His friend's horrified response to the idea of a mixed-race marriage serves as a jolting corrective.

Escott is initially attracted by Lola's overt sexuality, her passion, and her low-cut dresses, but ultimately understands that traditionally feminine – that is, sexless – women are preferable. Now he realises that "she is exactly opposite to my ideal of the sex. Too pushing, and forward, and domineering; what I should call an oppressive woman, especially to live with" (3:27). Whereas Marryat portrays Henrietta Stuart's passion as attractive, in Lola it alerts the reader to her 'otherness'. The suggestion is that she would be acceptable and desirable as a lover, but not appropriate wife material. As the narrator observes, "She had received so many declarations of love – so few offers of marriage" (3:127). She might not be able to compete in the marriage market, but her appeal to men remains palpable. The Colonel's interest is still piqued by Lola, but he decides to marry a middle-aged widow with children – a woman who is strikingly like Marryat herself. The English rose triumphs over the "octoroon", who resembles a "wild beast" when thwarted (3:119); but the triumphant widow is sexually experienced, rather than an ingenue like Lily. A wife should be sexual *and* white.

At least only English *men* are susceptible to Lola's sensuality; in *The Blood of the Vampire* (1897), Marryat introduces a heroine who appeals to both sexes. Harriet Brandt is sexually omnivorous, exerting a powerful influence over nearly everyone she meets. She is a 'psychic vampire' who feeds off her victims' lifeforce, rather than blood. Men and women alike experience a strange and inexplicable attraction to her. Margaret Pullen, a respectable married Englishwoman, describes herself as "scooped hollow" after spending time in Harriet's company:

> [she], glancing up once, was struck by the look with which Harriet Brandt was regarding her – it was so full of yearning affection – almost of longing to approach her nearer, to hear her speak, to touch her hand! It amused her to observe it! She had heard of cases in which young unsophisticated girls had taken unaccountable affections for members of their own sex and trusted she was not going to form the subject for one such experience on Miss Brandt's part. (Marryat, 1897a [2010]: 23)

Despite her apparent respectability, Margaret recognises Harriet's motivation and is determined to resist it. But she finds herself helpless:

> She had become fainter and fainter as the girl leaned against her with her hand upon her breast. Some sensation which she could not define, nor account for – some feeling which she had never experienced before – had come over her and

made her head reel. She felt as if something or someone were drawing all her life away. She tried to disengage herself from the girl's clasp but Harriet Brandt seemed to come after her, like a coiling snake, till she could stand it no longer. (18)

The animal imagery continues: Harriet's "hungry, yearning look was more accentuated than before – it seemed as though she was on the alert, watching for something, like a panther awaiting the advent of its prey," (37) and she is reminiscent of the hideous panther-like figure in Wells's *The Island of Dr Moreau* (1896), that symbol of dangerous female sexuality. Like Lola Arlington, her passion is described as bestial. She "eat[s] like a cormorant" (6) and gorges on bonbons.[22] Among the vapid community of expatriates, Harriet is vivid and alluring.

Octavia Davis writes that Harriet's behaviour "illustrates what contemporary science termed 'primitive bisexuality'" (2007: 45), with Darwinian theory used to argue that certain racial types were regressing to their origins. While this is a convincing reading of Harriet, I argue that Marryat is looking forward as well as back: Harriet represents the modern and sexually liberated woman. She is one of the novel's few likeable characters and is compared favourably with the Englishwomen, who are described as passionless and frigid. Ralph Pullen, who is obsessed with Harriet, describes his English fiancée as "prim and old-maidish" (61) and "enough to freeze the sun himself" (130). The sexuality that Harriet represents may be dangerous, but it is also very appealing when contrasted with the sexual reticence expected of white women. She represents the unregulated woman: unstable, but inherently attractive. Even Marryat's racism is complicated and often contradictory: she is both fascinated and repelled by otherness.

Aware of the power Harriet exerts, local physician Dr Phillips warns Ralph that "she is a woman whom you must never introduce to your wife, and … it is your bounden duty to separate her, as soon as possible, from your fiancée and your sister-in-law" (77).

Harriet is a vector of lesbian contagion. When Harriet consults Dr Phillips as a patient, he urges her not to breed. Astonished, she asks: "And that is the truth, medically and scientifically – that I must not marry?" He explains: "You will always exert a weakening and debilitating effect upon [people] so that after a while, having sapped their brains and lowered the tone of their bodies, you will find their affection, or friendship for you visibly decrease. You will have, in fact, sucked them dry" (162). Susan Zieger makes the important point that "although this novel is about vampirism, it is not a supernatural novel: Harriet's 'proclivity' is rigorously elucidated in medical science" (2008: 266). And, as Ross Forman observes, the doctor's 'diagnosis' uses "very much the terms of late nineteenth-century medical discourse about homosexuality" (2011: 426). Lesbianism was seldom mentioned by doctors until the emergence of sexology in the 1880s (Bland, 2002: 54), when Richard von Krafft-Ebing warned that the behaviour of the sexual invert was contagious (Hurley, 1990: 200). Women like Harriet were capable of seducing and corrupting 'normal,' sexually healthy individuals. In the interests of society, these women needed to be quarantined, and physicians were keen to regulate what they saw as the primary cause of lesbianism: masturbation.

"absurd fancies": The Masturbating Hysteric

"ALAS, that such a term is possible! O, that it were as infrequent as it is monstrous" (Cooke, 1890: 100), cried Nicholas Cooke in *Satan in Society*, in a chapter devoted to the evils of female masturbation. William Acton also warned of the dangers in *The Functions and Disorders of the Reproductive Orders* (1862). Masturbation was one of the obvious manifestations of an unhealthily strong sex drive and became a source of cultural anxiety. Many members of the medical profession feared the consequences of women indulging in an expression of sexuality that was autonomous and divorced from reproduction. Masturbation was also thought to impair a woman's ability to bear children, potentially leading to a loss of desire for "normal" sexual intercourse and an epidemic of lesbianism (Mason, 2008: 32, 34). Luxuriating in many detailed examples, Cooke continues: "Beyond all dispute the crime exists, and incontestably the female boarding-school is the arena where it is most widely acquired and practised" (106)

In *The Blood of the Vampire*, Harriet Brandt describes her time at boarding school: "It's the very last place where they will let you make a friend – they're afraid lest you should tell each other too much! ... us girls, we were never left alone for a single minute! There was always a sister with us, even at night, walking up and down between the row of beds" (16). This passage clearly evokes masturbatory fears, and is also indicative of how girls' behaviour was policed to protect them from their own (and each other's) sexuality. Later Harriet reveals: "If ever I took a liking to a girl, we were placed in separate rooms!" (34). Lesbianism and masturbation excluded men and was purely recreational; it also provided a tantalising alternative to traditional marriage. Bram Dijkstra observes:

> the nineteenth-century middle-class male's *rediscovery* of feminine sexuality, as well as his discovery of the apparently fearful fact that women could actually 'awaken' sexual feelings in each other, was, to a large extent, a metaphoric expression of the late nineteenth-century male's unstated awareness that only by dividing women, by keeping them from working together, they could be kept in a state of economic and social submission. (1986: 68, emphasis added)

Dijkstra's use of the word *re*discovery is significant, suggesting that feminine sexuality was already well understood, and feared. The recognition that its expression posed a profound threat to society provoked a conscious agenda to contain women's sexual agency.

As discussed above, the mutable nature of hysteria meant it "could be modified in order to diagnose all the behaviours which did not fit the prescribed model of Victorian womanhood" (Wood, 2001: 10), that is, behaviours that acted against the perceived interests of the family institution. This agenda is represented unambiguously in *Her Father's Name* (1876). Through the character of Lucilla Evans, Marryat's novel exposes how hysteria was clearly linked with masturbation and lesbianism to pathologize sexual 'deviance' in women. As I explain, Marryat uses the character of the family doctor to uncover the ways in which the medical profession operated to restore female patients to supposedly 'normative' sexuality. Marryat uses these 'deviant' behaviours to assert women's power and to challenge the idea that their role was purely reproductive and subordinate.

After her dead father is wrongly accused of murder, Leona Lacoste dresses as a man and embarks upon an international quest to clear his name. On arrival in London, Leona sneaks into her uncle's house, posing as a merchant by the name of Don Valera. His adopted daughter Lucilla, an hysteric who on medical advice has been confined to her couch since the onset of puberty, is overcome with lust. She is transfixed by Leona and ignores the handsome doctor her parents want her to marry. Lucilla's ailment is non-specific: "She had no organic disease, but she had suffered from a weak spine for many years past, and it prevented her taking an active part in life. And the restraint made her fractious" (Marryat, 1876b [2009]: 131). At first glance, Lucilla is a conventional Victorian invalid, but in the context of contemporary medical debates she becomes more problematic. Isaac Baker Brown in his famous work *On the Curability of Certain Forms of Insanity, Epilepsy, Catalepsy, and Hysteria in Females* (1866) claims that patients like Lucilla display classic signs of hysteria and masturbation: "The patient becomes restless and excited, or melancholy and retiring, listless, and indifferent to the social influences of domestic life" (Brown, 1866: 14). By which he means, of course, indifferent to the social influences of *men*. And his supposedly 'distinguishing' symptoms would apply to all women at least some of the time.

The cause was specifically sexual in nature, Brown believing that "peripheral excitement of the branches of the pudic nerve" – or masturbation – caused a disease with eight stages, progressing from hysteria, through to mania, and ultimately death (vi).

Lucilla's parents are eager for her to marry Dr Hastings – a "bluff, manly fellow" (284) – believing only he can manage her delicate health. For them, his behaviour is endearingly solicitous; for Lucilla, it is overbearing. She is repulsed by him, resisting his repeated attempts to control her:

> It was strange ... that [she] should have taken a distaste (it was scarcely to be called a dislike) to the man who had really benefited her health, and was so constantly attentive to her – strange, that is to say, to anyone who did not know the secret of her heart and his. For the cause lay in the fact that Dr. Hastings was too attentive, and that his attentions bore a deeper meaning than mere interest in her as a patient. He was fond of [her], and she felt the influence without acknowledging it; and not being prepared to return his affection, it worried instead of pleasing her. (137–8)

The narrator explains that Lucilla's aversion is not specific to him: "she would be as happy in the future with [him] as she would have been with anybody else" (323). The reason for her antipathy is revealed when the disguised Leona makes her entrance: "Lucilla Evans raised her eyes to the stranger's countenance and withdrew them instantly, blushing deeply. There was something in the face of the newcomer that attracted her at once" (142). Under the influence of this newcomer, the invalid becomes animated and mobile. When Leona kisses another woman during an amateur theatrical performance, Lucilla is overcome by jealousy and must be carried shrieking to bed. Her reaction is indicative of the fits Brown associated with the masturbating hysteric.[23]

The disruption caused by the disguised Leona has not gone

unnoticed by Dr Hastings, who makes frequent disparaging comments about 'his' appearance, such as "He looks more like a woman stuck into boy's clothes to me. I should like to try my biceps against his, though I believe he's taller than I am, and broader into the bargain" (145). Hastings is apparently threatened by this person who exerts such a powerful influence over women, and especially over the woman he wants for his wife. His repeated references to Leona's womanly shape make it apparent that he sees through her disguise. Realising what is happening, he admonishes his patient: "Now, Lucilla," he said, sternly, "I cannot have any more of this nonsense, or I shall speak to your father about it … I know far more than you have any idea of. But I have been watching you closely for some time past, and the absurd fancies you have got into your head are no secret to me" (183–4). Here the man of science asserts himself as a moral arbiter, regulating gender and exposing deviant behaviour. These "absurd fancies" are abnormal desires and must be denounced. Like Isaac Baker Brown's hypothetical patient, Lucilla has become "indifferent to the social influences of domestic life" and must be carefully managed.

Everyone apart from Lucilla comments on Leona's womanliness, yet all – except Dr Hastings – are prepared to collude in her artifice. They accept both her transvestism and her often mutual attraction to women. When Dr Hastings asks Lucilla's father to send her to the country, beyond harm's reach, he refuses. Acknowledging that only the disguised Leona makes his daughter happy and calm, he encourages them to spend time together, even telling Leona that a marriage proposal would be welcome. There is no suggestion that Lucilla's parents are convinced by the unfeasibly handsome youth who suddenly appears in their lives, yet they are prepared for him to 'marry' their daughter. The narrator says of Lucilla: "[she], who in her weakness and timidity shrunk from the generality of the sterner sex, as something too rough and loud-spoken to give her any pleasure, considered Leona Lacoste, in her male attire, to be the very perfection of all she had ever dreamed of as amiable, and gentle, and winning in a man" (189).

The perfect man turns out to be a woman. When Lucilla tells a servant about Leona's "pretty little hands and feet," she responds: "Dear me, miss! that seems more like the description of a young lady than a gentleman to me" (269). Perhaps Lucilla, at least unconsciously, perceives that Leona is really a woman. Either way, her classically hysterical behaviour is explicitly linked with lesbian desire, or what Dr Hastings diagnoses as "absurd fancies". The implication is that Leona makes an utterly unconvincing, if extremely attractive, man. Here, hysteria is not a disease but an expression of unacknowledged sexual impulses. Furthermore, Marryat's 'cure' for Lucilla's hysteria is the realisation of her deviant sexual desires; Isaac Baker Brown's solution was more extreme, and it involved scissors.

"Are you going to cut me up?" The Rise of Gynaecology

In *Practical Gynaecology* (1877), Dr Heywood Smith noted that the prognosis for hysteria was "Unfavourable as a rule" (1900: 175). This did not prevent him from recommending invasive 'cures' including the application of leeches to the uterus ("hold to … cervix until it has bitten") and "removal of nymphae or clitoris, or both" (176). Smith explained that it was important to "Distinguish between hysteria and local mischief [i.e. masturbation]" (143), but his treatments were similar for all gynaecological complaints. While dubious in medical terms, they were no doubt remarkably effective in curing excessive sexual appetite. In the 1860s obstetrician Isaac Baker Brown established The London Surgical Home in which he performed clitoridectomies on women and girls as young as ten, later publishing accounts of the operations that had made him a wealthy man. In at least five of his cases, the 'illness' he was treating was "a desire to obtain a divorce under the new divorce act of 1857" (Dally, 1991: 167).

Although Brown was eventually expelled from the Obstetrical

Society, this was for the method he used (scissors), rather than for the procedure of clitoridectomy itself (Easlea, 1981: 134), which was often seen as a lamentable necessity. Even the *Church Times* defended practitioners, describing it a suitable "remedy for some of the most distressing cases of illness which [the clergy] discover among their parishioners" (quoted in Moscucci, 1996: 67). The *British Medical Journal* reprinted this article, with its claim that "The clergy will be doing a service, especially to their poorer parishioners, by bringing [the operation] under the notice of medical men" (67). The procedure was deemed successful by some, as patients usually (and unsurprisingly) became docile afterwards, yet were still capable of fulfilling their reproductive duties with no troublesome expectations of sexual pleasure. As Dally observes: "The clitoris symbolised the aspect of women that men could arouse but not control" (1991: 163). By making it the source of unacceptable female behaviours, doctors were justified in removing it, and by barbaric means: "the clitoris is freely excised by scissors or knife — I always prefer the scissors" (Brown, 1866: 117).

Some historians, such as Dally and Wood, have cautioned against ascribing sinister and misogynistic motives to surgeons, but there are no recorded instances of surgical interventions to cure men of sexual misbehaviour. Furthermore, Brown's claim that "Clitoridectomy is nothing more or less than circumcision" is demonstrative of the lack of medical knowledge behind the procedure (Jalland and Hooper, 1986: 263). Other doctors were perfectly aware that the clitoris played an important role in sexual enjoyment. In *On Single and Married Life* (1847), Dr R. J. Culverwell – a member of the Royal College of Surgeons – wrote: "It is exquisitely sensitive, and believed to be the seat of pleasure in the sexual embrace" (Nead, 1988: 19). Perhaps unlike Brown, he had bothered to ask his wife. Ovariotomy was also a popular procedure for 'curing' a range of female ailments, and it is estimated that between 1870 and 1900 around 150,000 women had their ovaries removed (Easlea, 1981: 135). Brown thoughtfully performed the procedure on his own sister, even though his three previous patients had died on the operating table. So, surgical intervention was the regulatory solution to a variety of undesirable behaviours, and exclusively for women. Despite the opposition of such authorities as *The Lancet*, who denounced ovariotomy as "spaying" (quoted in Bland, 2002: 166) and insisted "we have scarcely more right to remove a woman's clitoris than we have to deprive a man of his penis" (Moore, 1866: 699), these practices persisted. One of the reasons for this persistence was that women were not educated about their own bodies and lacked the vocabulary to described what was happening to them. Doctors could offer "a harmless operative procedure" without the need to explain precisely what was involved (Sheehan, 1981: 43). Naturally, the topic was also far too indelicate for discussion beyond the medical press but Florence Marryat portrayed these practices obliquely in her fiction, while exposing the underlying ideology more forcefully.

Petronel

In *Petronel* (see previous chapter), Dr Ulick Ford's mere presence has a powerful effect upon his hysterical patients. But his ulterior methods are also hinted at darkly. When the teenaged Petronel tries to explore his consulting room, she is sternly admonished: "This is not the place for little girls" (Marryat, 1870a: 1:196). When caught in the act, she has been examining some of Ford's instruments: "I had never met with such a collection before. There were long thin scissors, which looked as though they had been nearly starved to death, and short fat scissors, that seemed as though they had been cut in two, and scissors that shrugged their shoulders; and others again, all curly-wurly, which reminded me of nothing but a corkscrew" (1:190). Given the emergence of gynaecology and the controversy it caused, this description is unsettling. Ford is concerned not with hygiene or safety, rather that his methods should not be uncovered. His older sister, who acts as his housekeeper, is also barred from entering his professional space. The novel appeared after the repeal of the Contagious Diseases Acts, so to the enlightened reader Ford's instruments would have had a political connotation, as well as suggesting his use of the speculum to examine his patients – an instrument that was also known as the "steel penis" (Walkowitz, 1980: 146). As Louise Foxcroft notes, the abuse of the speculum was widely discussed in the medical press during the 1850s and 60s, with men such as William Acton concerned that it was being used in cases where patients were not suffering from a gynaecological complaint (2009: 150). In 1853 the physician, Robert Brudenell Carter, wrote:

> I have, more than once, seen young unmarried women, of the middle-classes of society, reduced, by constant use of the speculum to the mental and moral condition of prostitutes; seeking to give themselves the same indulgence by the practice of solitary vice; and asking every medical practitioner, under whose care they fell, to institute an examination of the sexual organs. (69)

This offers an explanation as to why Dr Ford's patients become so dependent on him. The father of one patient tells him: "She seemed so well when you were here last ... but since then she has had fits of hysterics every day, generally an hour or two after the time that your visits are usually paid; and neither yesterday nor to-day have we been able to induce her to touch any solid food; and she has scarcely done anything but weep" (1:48). Like Lucilla Evans, this patient is a textbook hysteric, and in the advanced stages of the condition. Ford "had guessed the nature of that disease," and "Were he correct, it could be nothing but a sick girl's fancy, the consequence of seeing no one but himself, and to be easily eradicated by the *proper means*, the means he should put at once in motion" (189, emphasis added). Eradication by the proper means is not made explicit, but possibly relates to the instruments Petronel discovers in Ford's consulting room.

The Strange Transfiguration of Hannah Stubbs

In *The Strange Transfiguration of Hannah Stubbs* (1896), Marryat makes oblique references to such surgical interventions. Hannah Stubbs is a young servant who has been disowned by her family, as her mediumistic powers are disrupting the household by causing furniture to jump around. Her employer, Mrs Battleby, is also displeased by these events, repeatedly threatening to dismiss Hannah. The strange goings-on attract the attention of lodger Professor Ricardo and his friend, Dr Steinberg. While Ricardo is interested in Hannah's mediumistic powers, hoping that she can contact his dead wife, Steinberg seems more concerned with her potential for experimentation. He is the archetypal callous scientist, who acknowledges: "As a rule, I have not cared for women. I look upon the sex as a necessary evil – something without which population cannot go on" (Marryat, 1896b: 12). Their furtive behaviour does not go unnoticed by the landlady, whose friend muses: "Suppose he should be Jack the Ripper, and congeals the corpusses in your third room" (7). The behaviour of these men is thus explicitly linked with the perpetrator of the Whitechapel murders, whose mutilation of his victims led some to believe he was a gynaecologist (Moscucci, 1990: 159).

Hannah becomes alarmed when her powers cause the table to leap across the kitchen. Ricardo comforts her: "trust yourself to the Doctor and me and we'll cure you of this nonsense" (47). He tells the landlady: "she is a victim to what we call hysteria – and … if she will allow me to treat her for the complaint, I will undertake to cure her" (49). He goes on to explain that it "will be more convenient for me to operate on her here, than at the hospital" (53), and he requires a separate private room for the purpose. As with the vivisectors discussed above, he wants to practice beyond the gaze of society. The suspicious landlady asks: "'O! Lor, Sir, you're never a' going to cut up the pore gal, surely!'" (53) To which he responds, "'No! no! Indeed! ... I intend to treat her by an entirely new process which, if I am not mistaken, will have an almost immediate effect in preventing those nervous tremors which seem to assail her'" (53), adding sinisterly, "'she must be a little worse before she's better'" (53–4).

When Ricardo and Steinberg take Hannah to their room, she reacts badly: "'In there?' she screamed, 'but what for? I've never been in such a dark 'ole in all my life! And what do you want to do with me there? Are you going to cut me up?'" (55–6). They reassure her, then administer a sedative drug. When she regains consciousness, Hannah complains "'but I do feel so queer-like, as if my legs were all bruised'" (61). The doctor later explains that the drugs ensure the patient is unable to recall what has passed. Meanwhile, Mrs Battleby and her friend are speculating as to what might be happening behind the locked door: "'Keep a gal in the dark, indeed, and give 'er summat to make 'er go to sleep – I've 'eard summit like that afore, Mrs. Blarney, and no good came of it'" (89). Mrs. Blarney suggests: "'Why! 'oo knows? that Doctor might be Jack the Ripper – which many said 'e was a doctor – and going to cut Hannah into bits'" (88). When Mrs Battleby complains about the "diabolical practices" (100) going on under her roof, Ricardo and Steinberg decide to take a cottage in Hampstead where they can live together with Hannah. This curious *ménage à trois* becomes even curiouser when Hannah marries the two men in turn, and also reveals later on that she had sex with Steinberg while married to Ricardo (273).

Although Marryat is understandably not explicitly describing genital mutilation, to the educated reader these scenes are suggestive of such practices, Hannah's fear indicating that they were well known. What *The Academy* referred to as a "bewildering narrative" ("New Novels", 1896a: 383) was actually Marryat's way of obfuscating a dark and menacing subplot. Hannah's mediumistic powers that disrupt her environment are used as a metaphor for unacceptable female behaviour, an idea I explore in Chapter 7. As a woman, and especially as one from the lower classes, she should be quiet and demure. The ominous 'cures' proposed by Ricardo and Steinberg suggest the severity of the punishment meted out to women who refuse to submit to more subtle forms of regulation. By the time the novel was published in 1896, Isaac Baker Brown had long since been discredited. He was expelled from the Obstetrical Society in 1867 and died six years later. The controversial procedure that had made him notorious was supposed to have disappeared, too, yet it persisted into the twentieth century. In the second edition of *Practical Gynaecology* from 1900, Dr Heywood Smith was still prescribing clitoridectomies and leeches; Dr Lawson Tait admitted to performing a clitoridectomy in 1886 for "reasons altogether too disgusting for publication" (Tait, 1889: 63). This moral squeamishness absolved Tait from justifying his actions and the reasons are left to the reader's imagination.

It is no wonder that some women's rights campaigners saw little difference between gynaecological procedures and the widespread use of vivisection. The equipment used by gynaecologists for invasive and often painful examinations was not unlike the paraphernalia used in the laboratory, placing the subject in a similar state of helplessness and discomfort. Marryat makes this comparison in *An Angel of Pity* (see previous chapter), where heroine Rose Gordon alerts the vivisector to the misery he is causing to both patients and quadrupeds.[24] As Moscucci observes, "women and animals shared the same fate as the victims of materialist medical men" (1990: 122).

Conclusion

Elaine Showalter concludes that the routine "mutilation, sedation, and psychological intimidation" of women was "an efficient, if brutal, form of reprogramming" (1987: 66). As I have shown above and in the previous chapter, Marryat exposed these practices, depicting the various ways in which the medical profession attempted to regulate women by defining and punishing their sexual behaviour. Her willingness to engage with key scientific debates confirms that her work went beyond mere sensationalism, instead embodying a serious attempt to question the limits of masculine power and moral authority. As Moscucci argues, whereas the medical profession believed they were pushing the boundaries of gynaecology, "The historian will be more inclined to view this development as the expression of an enduring ideology" (1990: 206). It was this *ideology* that Marryat sought to expose and undermine.

Throughout her novels, Marryat uses behaviours deemed 'deviant' to assert women's power and to challenge the idea that their role was purely subordinate. Henrietta Stuart takes control of her own sexuality, while Harriet Brandt has no hesitation in expressing hers. Crucially, although problematically, Marryat also argues that this expression of female sexuality is essential for society if it is to resist the threat of the black woman. In Leona Lacoste and Lucilla Evans, Marryat presents heroines who comprehensively challenge dominant notions of Victorian women's sexuality. Through them Marryat both exposes the regulatory agenda of the medical profession and also confronts the idea that a woman's role was purely reproductive. What society denounces as deviant and hysterical, Marryat celebrates as transcendent femininity, creating heroines who retain their womanliness yet embody powers beyond those generally ascribed to the female sex.

By allowing her heroines a greater range of sexual experience, Marryat resisted Virchow's idea that their role was merely reproductive. A woman was, after all, more than just a pair of ovaries. And, like George Drysdale, she believed that "the control of fertility was an essential element in the general emancipation of ... women" (Nead, 1988: 20). As we shall see in the next chapter, on this issue Marryat found herself a powerful ally who outranked even the medical profession: the Virgin Mary.

CHAPTER 6

Our Mother Who Art in Heaven: The Virgin Mary and Sacred Maternity

"For religion does require a lot of what children call 'making believe' to render it satisfactory."

Parson Jones

At the first Lambeth Conference in 1867, Anglican bishops denounced the exaltation of the Virgin Mary. Fearing that some people were praying to her directly, they insisted that a spiritual relationship with God should be mediated through an appropriate male authority figure (Adams, 2001: 15–6). Essentially, the cult of Mariolatry had created a female figurehead that disrupted the patriarchal authority of the church. This appropriation of the Virgin Mary as an icon of female power provided women like Marryat with an inspirational role model, offering an image of the mother as strong and independent, rather than a submissive creature limited by her biological function. Tensions between the Anglican and Roman Catholic churches were further exacerbated in 1870 by Pope Pius' declaration of Papal Infallibility, reinforcing his authority after the earlier proclamation of the Immaculate Conception. This defined Mary as the only human spared the taint of original sin.

As discussed in the previous chapter, the late nineteenth century saw an attempt to establish a scientific basis for woman's supposed physical inferiority. By claiming that biological difference rendered women hopelessly weak and emotional creatures, men could contain them within the limited domestic sphere and prescribe 'treatments' for their problematic bodies. Now there was a potent image of womanly perfection – one who combined flawlessness with agency. This impetus for Mariolatry was prompted in part by shifting attitudes towards established religion; with the Bible's authority under attack by historicist critiques, the scriptural foundation for women's subordinate position was also called into question. Ben Griffin argues convincingly that "without these new religious ideas, a popular women's movement could not have developed to challenge successfully the nostrums of Victorian domestic ideology" (2012: 112).

Throughout the Victorian period, the Virgin Mary remained a pervasive, yet controversial figure. For Catholics she was the embodiment of womanly perfection, while for some Protestants she symbolised the worst excesses of Roman idolatry. An almost fantastical figure, people could project upon her their own image of woman. Even Protestants, particularly women, appropriated her as their spiritual figurehead, a "feminised version of Christ" (Melnyk, 2003: 135). Kimberly Van Esveld Adams's study on the work of Anna Jameson, Margaret Fuller and George Eliot shows how these Protestant women used images of the Virgin Mary to empower women, and she became "their Lady of Victorian Feminism" (Adams, 2001: 226). Marina Warner asserts that the Virgin Mary was an "instrument of ascetism and female subjection" (2013: 50), a man-made image accepted unquestioningly by women. But, as I show, by conflating Spiritualism with Marian imagery, Marryat created an influential symbol of women's spiritual power.

In this chapter I discuss how these new religious ideas are evident in Marryat's fiction, arguing that her radical interpretation of Roman and Anglo-Catholicism allowed her to explore important ideas surrounding women's identity and status. Firstly, I offer an account of Marryat's evolving faith, setting it within the context of Victorian religious upheavals. Secondly, I consider how she used the figure of the Virgin Mary to elevate the role of the mother. Through a close reading of *My Own Child* (1876), I show how Marryat epitomised the "paradigm of sacred maternity" that Alex Owen proposes as central to late nineteenth-century feminist thought (Owen, 2004: 34). By comparing Marryat's work with that of contemporary novelists, I argue that she used religious ideas to empower women, rather than to contain them. Finally, I examine the novella *The Dead Man's Message* (1894) and Marryat's bold vision of female spiritual authority. As I show, Marryat believed masculinity should be regulated by powerful women, rather than the other way around.

"he shall rule over thee": The Biblical basis for male authority

The Bible is liberally scattered with references to male authority. In Genesis, wives are told "thy desire shall be to thy husband, and he shall rule over thee" (Genesis: 3:16); the Epistle to the Ephesians explains "the husband is the head of the wife, even as Christ is the head of the church" (Ephesians: 5:23). St Paul's writings had been hugely influential on domestic ideology, and women's ability to withstand their subjection was equated with Christ-like suffering. As Melnyk observes, "the model of the suffering Saviour was an effective tool for controlling women and encouraging their self-sacrifice in the service of patriarchy" (2003: 131–2). The Church of England, as the established church, sought to use this doctrine to regulate women's behaviour. However, this became increasingly difficult in the early nineteenth century, as the population started moving away from Anglicanism. Already in competition with the Roman Catholic and Presbyterian Churches, "the most serious threat came from the splintering of religious views within the Church of England" (Melnyk, 2008: 19). The three main factions that emerged during the 1840s – the Evangelicals, or Low Church; the Tractarians, or High Church (later the Anglo-Catholics); and the Broad Church – had to negotiate difficult territory, demarcating their many differences without compromising the Church's overall authority.

This process of redefinition, while presenting challenges, also allowed sects to evolve that could accommodate a social diversity that Anglicanism refused to acknowledge. For example, by the 1830s radical Unitarians had already attempted to promote marriage as a "triumph of dual responsibility and commitment, rather than the domination of one sex over the other" (Gleadle, 1995: 113), with the wife maintaining a direct relationship with God, rather than one mediated through either her husband or male clergy. Other dissenting sects, such as the Methodists, also permitted women a more active involvement in the church, as George Eliot showed with her preacher Dinah Morris in *Adam Bede* (1859). However, as Julie Melnyk points out, the novel is deliberately set in 1799 as women preachers were suppressed after 1804, their appointment to positions of spiritual authority becoming "rare and marginal" in most denominations (2008: 128). Logie Barrow's (1986) important research shows that dissenting religion was a clear antecedent for Spiritualism, a movement Owen describes as "capable of containing the full spectrum of beliefs" (2004: 22), absorbing even secularists and free-thinkers. As I discuss in the next chapter, this plasticity allowed women to develop further a faith that could be reconciled with feminist beliefs, granting them latitude far beyond that offered by the established Church.

While the activities of the non-conformists had little impact on wider society, it was the historicist approach to biblical criticism during mid-century that seriously undermined Anglicanism. Already weakened by developments in geological and evolutionary science, the exposure of textual errors showed the Bible to be disappointingly fallible (Griffin, 2012: 114, 115). Furthermore, by studying the Bible in its historical context, its more controversial tenets could be dismissed as anachronisms, rather than accepted as axioms (115). In *The Spirit World* (1894), Marryat questions the sacredness of the Bible, referring to it as:

> a very jumbled history of the times, written long after the events spoken of took place, and in the fantastical and allegorical language of the East, so that is difficult to known what the writers of it did, or did not, mean. The interpretation of it has been made ... by men, who felt compelled to explain it in some way or other, and so made it fit in, with their own doctrines. (Marryat, 1894c: 54–5)

Her complaints are legion, but fundamentally she condemns a church "which solemnizes marriages that are nothing less than prostitution" (37). For Marryat and other iconoclasts, the Bible – and St Paul in particular – were ripe for dismissal. Women's subordination could no longer be dictated by scripture.

After decades of tension, in 1874 Parliament passed the Public Worship Regulation Act, legislation drafted by the Archbishop of Canterbury, who sought to limit the rise of Anglo-Catholicism, or Ritualism, as it was then known. This controversial Act established a court with powers to prosecute those who indulged in Ritualist practices, leading to many high-profile trials and convictions (Yates, 1999: 333, 245). Nigel Yates argues that the Act was prompted by panic, and resulted in more panic when people realised that their private worship could be subject to state intervention (276). The ruling judge was Lord Penzance, who had previously reigned over the Divorce Court, and now achieved increased authority to regulate many areas of people's lives. This dual role epitomises the law's imbrication with the Church, consolidating male power and excluding feminine influence.

This desire to defeat the "hybrid" of Ritualism can be seen as a move designed to establish Roman Catholicism as a distinct "other". As Maureen Moran argues, "it serves as a 'heretical' foil against which orthodox middle-class beliefs and structures can be reaffirmed" (2007: 4). For this model to succeed, the two faiths must remain polarised. It was during this foment that Marryat converted to Roman Catholicism, a profoundly rebellious act in which she adopted a faith that was deemed by some to be "sexually perverse and theologically alien" (O'Malley, 2006: 24). Her daughter Ethel later commented that "The emotional character of that faith was particularly adapted to a temperament like hers" (E. Church, 1899: 588). It was this religious conversion in 1870 that caused the irretrievable breakdown of Marryat's marriage to Thomas Ross Church. While she initially heeded her husband's demand that she return to Anglicanism, a subsequent relapse landed her in the Court of Chancery, where Church sought custody of their children so he could protect them from their mother's Papist tendencies (Bill of Complaint). Marryat remained a Roman Catholic after winning her case, but her faith developed a protean quality, continually adapting to accommodate the vicissitudes of her unconventional life.

Marryat's novel *The Hampstead Mystery* (1894) set in 1875, at the time of her second conversion, is partly a vehicle for her criticisms of the Roman Catholic Church. Despite having "no religion at all" hero Frederick Walcheren becomes a priest (Marryat, 1894b: 1:71), mainly to prevent himself from getting into any more disastrous relationships with women. A widower since his wife was murdered by a jealous admirer, Walcheren also has at least one love child with a woman he seduced. Partly, too, this self-imposed reclusion allows Walcheren to contemplate the spirit of his dead wife, who becomes an object of worship and a symbol of goodness: "she was an angel in heaven, and he might dream of her just as soon as of the Virgin Mary, or any other saint" (3:99). Although he considers himself an independent thinker, Walcheren declines to heed the warnings of a clairvoyant, who prophesies that entering the priesthood would be a grave mistake. Choosing instead to take counsel from his devout cousin, Walcheren is subsequently forced to listen impotently to the confession of his wife's murderer. By submitting himself to the rules of the Church, he must respect confidentiality and allow a killer to go unpunished. Had Walcheren instead yielded to the feminine influence of the clairvoyant, he would have been spared considerable emotional turmoil. This novel embraces many of the themes explored in greater detail in Marryat's other fiction – the challenge to biblical authority, the supremacy of women's spirituality, and the limitations of established religion – all of which I discuss below and in the next chapter.

The "Divine Mother" in *My Own Child*

When Marryat visited Canada in 1885, she was greeted by a deputation of mothers who wanted to thank her for writing *My Own Child* (1876) (Black, 2011: 99). This novel celebrates motherhood and exemplifies Marryat's appropriation of Mariolatry. Within a mawkish plot lies a complex exploration of Marryat's faith and her vision for a new form of gynocentric religion. Here she explores the intersection between Roman Catholicism and Spiritualism, with many of the ideas informing her non-fiction writing. Marryat uses the Virgin Mary as a symbol of feminine power to express radical ideas about marriage, reproduction, and gender roles. The fact that Marryat was greeted so enthusiastically by her Canadian (and probably socially conservative) fans, shows how the novel works on several levels. They were thrilled with her depiction of motherly love and probably oblivious to the author's subversion.

Anxious to escape her disciplinarian aunt, fifteen-year-old Katherine Arundel elopes with handsome neighbour, Hugh Power. During their honeymoon in Paris, Hugh falls ill with cholera, dying intestate after only four weeks of marriage. Distraught, Katherine returns to her hated childhood home, reverting to the status of an unwanted ward. Discovering to her joy that she is pregnant, Katherine visits Ireland shortly after the birth to meet her parents-in-law, a powerful and aloof Catholic family. They object to the agnostic Katherine's nominal Protestantism, and seek custody of their grandchild, along with the right to choose her name. Defiantly, Katherine has her daughter covertly baptised with the unusual name of Hugh Mary (shortened to May) in honour of her father and "the Divine Mother" (Marryat, 1876c: 75).

Although she now finds prayer a comfort, Katherine is uncomfortable with the Powers' insistence on ritual. Her unconsciously deliberate breaking of a holy water stoup symbolises her rejection of such practices (116–7). When she is told that May was to be anointed with holy water every morning and evening, Katherine retorts: "I'm very glad the stupid thing is broken. I never heard such rubbish in my life" (117). Continually excluded by the family, Katherine tries to convert to Roman Catholicism so that their religious differences might be overcome. The priest refuses to admit her into the church unless she agrees that Jesus is more important than her daughter (124). Unwilling to do so, it is only some years later, when they are living on the Continent, that Katherine's conversion is complete. Now sharing the faith of her late husband and her daughter, she professes herself much happier than before (138), drawing strength from her faith and the women around her in the homosocial environment of a convent. This exemplifies Susan Mumm's argument that religious sisterhoods "embody a powerful example of feminist practice" (1999: 210), offering an alternative to marriage. Marryat herself spent a year in a Belgian convent with her daughter Ethel, to whom the novel is dedicated (E. Church, 1899: 588). According to Ethel, this was the point at which her mother converted to Roman Catholicism, and it was also during the time when Thomas Ross Church sought sole custody of the children after their marriage broke down. For Marryat, the convent became a refuge from male authority.

When Katherine receives a marriage proposal from her husband's schoolfriend Eustace Annerley, she travels to Paris and stays in the hotel room where she spent her honeymoon. Hugh appears to her as a powerful vision, convincing her to stay true to his memory. The spurned Annerley is outraged, wreaking his revenge by tricking May into a loveless marriage. He flaunts his adulterous liaisons and is physically violent towards her. Desperate to escape, a half-dressed May runs away on a cold, wet night, collapsing and dying in her mother's arms. Although bereaved once more, Katherine is relieved that May is safely with her father, and, most importantly, beyond the reach of Annerley. The dramatic final scene resembles a pietà, with Katherine as the Virgin Mary and May a Christ-like figure in her arms. This idea is prefigured earlier in the novel when Katherine is told she is pregnant with May. Such is her ignorance of sexual matters, the idea had never occurred to her, and the doctor's portentous words and her disbelief recall the Annunciation. The doctor describes himself as "a messenger to assure you of God's care for and interest in you" (66). Even at her most sensational, Marryat would not allow for actual parthenogenesis.

Ruth Vanita contends that the literary model of the Marian ideal "eroticises the mother-daughter relationship and gives rise to triangles in which the primary energy is between two women" (1996: 2). This idea is particularly apposite in the case of *My Own Child*, with the intense bond between Katherine and May, and the sublimation of Hugh, the father. Carol Dever concludes that, "To write a life, in the Victorian period, is to write the story of the loss of the mother," but this novel subverts the usual trope in Victorian fiction where the mother dies, often in childbirth, becoming an idealised figure who can do no harm. Dever observes, "Mothers were often a source of transgression rather than a passive ideal"; in their absence, however, they can be "constructed retrospectively as virtuous" (2006: 1, 130). Here, this is exactly what happens to the father. Marryat's radical implication is that the family is better off once Hugh is in Heaven. He is freed from concupiscence and any sins he might have committed cannot be visited upon his wife and daughter. When he appears to Katherine, Hugh reveals: "Had I been left longer in this world, I should have ruined not only my own life, but yours. It was necessary for the salvation of both of us that I should be removed" (194). He has been "purged of the grossness of [his] mortal nature" (194). An absent father becomes the ideal – he has performed his biological duty, and now his work is done. Instead Marryat presents a divine motherhood, an all-powerful love that transcends everything else: Katherine's love for May is such that she needs no father, beyond a disembodied and distant figure. Marryat surpasses contemporary Marian worship, relegating the figure of God the Father to a subordinate role.

Hugh has assumed a saint-like status, protecting them from above and interceding with God on their behalf. When he appears to Katherine in the hotel room, he has "waving hair and beard" and his eyes "beamed like fire", his countenance so dazzling that she is almost unable to look at him (194). He inspires awe in Katherine, revealing that he is always with her, like a guardian angel. As Nina Auerbach observes, angels had been traditionally androgynous, but the Victorians saw them as female (1990: 64). Here Marryat returns them to the Miltonian or Blakean model, embodying strength and vitality. Whereas angels are often "soggy dilutions of human complexity," (64) Hugh embodies wisdom, compassion, gentleness and strength – a perfect blend of male and female characteristics. Marryat recreates the angel in the house as an idealised man in Heaven.

In a scene strongly suggestive of masturbation, Hugh appears before Katherine as she lies restless in bed, and the ecstasy he provokes is both religious and sexual: "'Kiss me – kiss me!' I urged, passionately, in my unchastened, earthly desire" (194). It is after this vision that Katherine rejects Eustace Annerley and, indeed, the idea of a relationship with any other man. A superficial reading might suggest an appropriately wifely desire to remain true to her husband's memory, but I propose a more radical interpretation: this spiritual marriage fulfils her, at the same time releasing her from the cycle of womanhood, or what Vanita called the "tying-in of childbirth with heterosexual marriage" (Vanita, 1996: 7). Aged only twenty-eight, a second marriage would likely mean more children for Katherine. By rejecting a marriage proposal from an eligible man, she is denying the teachings of St. Paul, who decreed: "Let not a widow be taken into the number under threescore years old, having been the wife of one man". She must instead "marry, bear children, guide the house, [and] give none occasion to the adversary to speak reproachfully" (1 Timothy, 5:9–14).

As she did elsewhere in her fiction, (see Chapter 2) Marryat is championing elective single motherhood, elevating the status of women who reject the idea of a husband, and establishing a matrilineal heritage. By styling herself in the image of the Virgin Mary, Katherine invokes a figure who is "undomesticated and remarkably mobile" (Adams, 2001: 30), the antithesis of the womanly ideal who is confined within the home. Katherine instead appoints May as her own personal saviour and worships her accordingly. Naming her 'Hugh Mary', she summons the masculine strength of her late husband and the feminine spirit of the Virgin Mary, creating an androgynous ideal, but one that is manifestly 'woman'. As I outlined in the introduction, the growth in nineteenth-century feminism was stimulated by such questioning of the Bible's wisdom and authority; here Katherine rejects the orthodox faith of parents-in-law, instead establishing a heterodox faith that permits her the freedom she craves.

Katherine is anxious that May should remain a virgin, actively discouraging her from marriage. The reference to May having grown during her honeymoon indicates that she is still going through puberty. Like Petronel in the previous chapter, the wife is just a girl, yet is unprotected by the law. The marital violence May subsequently endures vindicates Katherine's anxieties. Virginity and women-only spaces such as convents offer a means of protecting women from abuse. By rejecting remarriage, Katherine also rejects the need for a human father for her child, and the masturbation scene expresses the ultimate in sexual self-sufficiency. As I discussed in the previous chapter, there was a cultural anxiety surrounding an expression of sexuality that was autonomous and divorced from reproduction, and masturbation was also thought to impair a woman's ability to bear children (Mason, 2008: 32). Marryat's choice of 'Katherine' as her heroine's name is significant, as St. Katherine was the patron saint of virginity. Katherine's name also perhaps acknowledges St. Catherine of Alexandria and St. Catherine of Siena, both of whom were reputed to have contracted a mystic marriage with Christ. The former also appeared to Joan of Arc, a feminist icon Marryat invoked in several novels and on her *carte de visite*.

Early in the novel, Katherine's attitude to marriage is equivocal, and she admits that sometimes she would "rather go round the world and seek adventures" (10). Her acceptance of Hugh's proposal is largely an expedient that allows her to leave her unhappy home. She seems smitten by the idea of the name she will assume when Hugh's father dies – Lady Power – a hint of the personal faith she later develops. She repeats the name to herself (14, 17), as if summoning a vision of her future self and invoking the "Divine Mother". This novel prefigures some of the arguments that Marryat later made in her lecture, "The Mistakes of Marriage" (see Chapter 2), where she urged alternatives to matrimony and advocated contraception to limit the number of pregnancies women would have to endure.

Even after the loss of her husband and daughter, Katherine lives a long and fulfilled life. Although she draws strength from her spiritual family, she is not defined by them. She evokes art historian Anna Jameson's insistence that the Virgin Mary should be shown as "a majestic woman of mature age" (Adams, 2001: 67), rather than as an impossibly youthful feminine ideal. An ingénue at the beginning of the novel with "no religion in [her] heart" (122), by its conclusion she has effectively constructed her own religion, appropriating and modifying elements of Roman

Catholicism. Katherine draws strength from the Roman Catholic Virgin Mary, but rejects those elements she deems patriarchal, such as confession. For Katherine, the confession box gives power to a man, investing him with the power to judge her, and providing him with a "long list of frailties" (51). She fears having to "render up an account of every idle word I said" (51). As Susan David Bernstein argues, "confession is largely a site of coercion," a dyadic structure "between the confessing subject compelled to narrate a story of transgression and the authorised audience of this tale who determines its meaning and the speaker's absolution, treatment or punishment" (Bernstein, 1997: 1, 3). In Marryat's *The Hampstead Mystery* (1894), newly-qualified priest Frederick Walcheren, although a "man of the world" (3:100), is shocked by the questions he is required to ask young girls. He feels as though he will be "blushing all over, just as if he were in a drawing-room instead of a confessional" (3:100). Rather than submit to this regulation and penetrative questioning, Katherine simply defines her own codes of behaviour.

This complex novel goes some way to explaining Marryat's own faith, the disparate blend of Roman Catholicism and Spiritualism that she practised. Like Margaret Fuller, Anna Jameson and George Eliot, Marryat found Catholicism "a useful corrective to the exclusions of Protestantism" (Adams, 2001: 226) and the protean nature of the Virgin Mary allowed her to redefine the popular image of womanhood. As Adams argues, the Virgin Mary "acts as a model and justification for unconventional behaviour by both women and men, [and] provides a convention for alternative ways of life" (26). Through the character of Katherine Power, Marryat rejects both the ideal of Victorian womanhood and the patriarchal image of the Virgin Mary as a passive and impotent figure. She also challenges the ways in which women of faith are typically represented by contemporary authors.

"The Protestant Mary was isolated and uncertain, unlike the joyful Catholic Mary," writes Carol Marie Engelhardt (2004: 301).

This dichotomy can be seen by comparing Katherine's strength and agency with the passive heroine of Margaret Oliphant's novel *Madonna Mary* (1867). The goodness suggested by the eponymous heroine's nickname is called into question when it is discovered that she is not actually married to the father of her children. Although it is her 'husband's' fault that their marriage service was 'irregular' and unverifiable, she is described as a fallen woman and becomes the subject of gossip – her legendary piety revealed as entirely specious. Her life as a single mother following her husband's death is further marred by reproach from her sons for the invidious position in which they have been placed. For Mary, maternity becomes a shameful condition, rather than the expression of strength it represents in Katherine Power. Lacking any agency, her life is nearly ruined by her husband's action and is made unpleasant because she has no authority over her sons. She conforms to St. Paul's teaching that widowed women over thirty are "Widows Indeed" whose lives should be dedicated to caring for others. As Carol Herringer concludes, "Far from incorporating a strong and admirable Madonna figure into English discourse, this novel dismissed the viability of the Virgin Mary as a role model for women" (2008: 96–7).

While *Madonna Mary* merely exemplifies the Victorian feminine ideal of passivity and impotence, other novelists ridiculed the idea that women might define and control their own sexuality and faith. It was the very notion of female empowerment that agitated Charles Kingsley. The man who came to symbolise 'muscular Christianity', a movement that saw "an association between physical strength, religious certainty and the ability to shape the world around oneself" (quoted in Paxton, 2013: 215). Kingsley's image of 'masculinity' relied on an oppositional 'femininity': the woman was weak and receptive where the man was strong and authoritative – rather like the relationship between the male doctor and the female patient than was extensively criticised by Marryat (see Chapter 4). As Andrew Bradstock et al. argues,

Kingsley's particular gripe was with elective virginity and the suggestion that the female body should be used for anything other than reproduction. For him it went against his belief that "virility was proof of masculinity" (2000: 48), which could be expressed only through sexual conquest and procreation. In his memoirs he expresses his horror at overhearing a woman advised to "Go to the Blessed Virgin ... She, you know, is a woman, and can understand all a woman's feelings" (Kingsley, 1894: 211). As far as Kingsley was concerned, a woman should go to her husband. Above all, women's spirituality needed to be "channelled and disciplined" through heteronormative marriage (Paxton, 2013: 214).

In his novel *Yeast: A Problem* (1851), Kingsley argues that real Englishmen are both Protestant and manly, contrasting them with Luke, an effeminate and droopy Tractarian priest. His lack of interest in the opposite sex is mirrored by Argemone Lavington, who is "trying in vain to fill her heart with the friendship of her own sex," choosing Sappho as her heroine (31). Her lamentable lesbianism is overcome when she encounters a muscular Christian man whose virility defeats her:

> She was matched, for the first time, with a man who was her own equal in intellect and knowledge; and she felt how real was that sexual difference which she had been accustomed to consider as an insolent calumny against woman. Proudly and indignantly she struggled against the conviction, but in vain. Again and again she argued with him, and was vanquished. (167)

Argemone experiences a "new sensation" of normative sexuality, realising "the delight of dependence – the holy charm of weakness" (126). Her self-defined version of femininity is powerless: "What was her womanhood, that it could stand against the energy of his manly will? The almost coarse simplicity of his words silenced her with a delicious violence" (193). The female intellect cannot defy the essentialism that defines her position purely in relation to man, the "delicious violence" of his words conveying his physical superiority and her inexorable weakness. As Kingsley decrees in his memoirs, a woman should go "not to the indulgent virgin, but to the strong man" (1894: 211). Unlike Katherine Power, she must submit to the traditional Protestant idea of feminine weakness, and, in the absence of a strong image of womanhood, Argemone can be defined only by her difference from a man.

Eliza Lynn Linton's *Under Which Lord?* (1879), published shortly after *My Own Child*, offers an interesting counterpoint to Marryat's family triangle: here the removal of the father causes its collapse. Hermione Fullerton, a wealthy heiress, has ceded all her money to her husband, Richard:

> She was a woman without much reasoning faculty and with no sense of property; but with an overwhelming power of obedience and self-abnegation which made her the docile creature of the man whom she loved. And this sacrifice of her fortune, this transfer of her rights to the husband from whom they had been so jealously guarded, pleased her more than power would have done. (1879: 1:7)

This sacrifice is rewarded by a loving husband and, in a particularly emetic passage, the narrator explains with satisfaction that her life is now "like one long poem" (1:8). However, the marriage is threatened by the arrival of Launcelot Lascelles, an Anglo-Catholic priest who seeks funding for a new church. Richard, a rational man of science and an atheist, refuses to donate any money to what he views as "superstition" (1:14). Lascelles instead preys on the innate suggestibility of Hermione, perverting her with ideas that the money belongs to her.[25] Under his influence, Hermione becomes a Ritualist and her daughter Virginia converts to Roman Catholicism. They are swayed by evil nun Sister Agnes, who refers to herself as Virginia's "spiritual mother" (1:97) and assumes a role that should be reserved for men. The ease with which Hermione's position is usurped suggests the essential fungibility of the mother figure, whereas the marginalisation of Richard is portrayed as disastrous.

The homosocial environment of the convent indoctrinates Virginia against her biological destiny and she resists the robust wooings of a hero with the unlikely name of Ringrove Hardisty. A symbol of male normativity, Hardisty is described as "The Samson of Erastianism" (3:251), conveying his strength and the message that his faith is cultural, rather than spiritual.[26] He valiantly attempts to rescue Virginia from her "lost life" (3:3), exclaiming "A woman can do better for herself and the world than by incarcerating herself and renouncing all practical usefulness. A mother is of more value than a nun" (3:19). For Marryat, celibacy represents the ultimate in female liberation, but for Linton it is self-indulgence that should be challenged. Like Argemone in *Yeast*, Virginia is denied the right to self-determination; her destiny is a matter of public interest and too important to be left in her own hands. The family ultimately disintegrates, the novel concluding with Hermione alone and lamenting the untimely death of her husband. Whereas in *My Own Child* the removal of the father strengthens the family, Linton implies that the strong spiritual bond between mother and daughter is damaging, and that the husband's authority and rationality are necessary to their survival. The malignity of the mother's influence is compounded by that of the nun and the effete priest who espouse feminist principles. Spiritual authority should be masculine. The narrator asks, breathlessly: "And now the final struggle had come. Love or religion – her husband's control or her Director's authority – the obligations of marriage or the ordinances of the Church – which would win? Under which Lord would she finally elect to serve?" (3:139).

Throughout the narrative, Hermione vacillates endlessly between the two: there is never a suggestion of "Under Neither

Lord". For the wife it is a simple choice between two male authority figures, the husband and the priest, and the implication is that masculinity trumps spirituality. Even the *Saturday Review*, the former vehicle of Linton's famously reactionary Girl of the Period articles, thought the novel a product of a "diseased imagination" ("Under Which Lord?", 1879: 668). The tone and rhetoric look back to *Yeast*, written almost thirty years earlier; it is a retrogressive tale that seeks to deny the reality of women's changing lives and faith. Meanwhile, in *My Own Child*, Marryat anticipates the New Woman novel by portraying an autonomous heroine who controls her own spiritual growth, challenging the Church's desire to enforce subordinate female behaviour.

"A Bitter Penance": Neglected Spirituality in *The Dead Man's Message*

Marryat also explores the idea of heavenly parenting in *The Dead Man's Message* (1894). This novella is more closely related to her Spiritualist beliefs but is still expressed within the ideological framework of Roman Catholicism. Although this time the mother is absent, she enjoys considerable spiritual agency, rather than being just a salutary presence to those left behind. Again, a guardian angel acts as a link between the spiritual and the temporal. When Professor Aldwyn dies, he finds a "majestic figure" by his side, who, while in "the prime of manhood" has a "mild, calm" expression (Marryat, 1894a [2009]: 38). Like the apparition of Hugh Power in *My Own Child*, this figure combines masculine strength with feminine qualities, such as compassion and solicitousness. He tells Aldwyn "The spirituality in you has been neglected" (38), as he has been obsessed with rationalism and male supremacy. The authorial voice explains "if he had yielded to the gentle counsel and entreaties of a woman who loved him, he might have turned out a very different man" (45). Instead, his reductive view of a wife is that she could be nothing beyond a housekeeper and mother.

Upon arrival in the Spiritual World, Aldwyn is taken to the "Sphere of Meeting",[27] one of the lowest spheres where the recently deceased are greeted by those who knew them during life (45). He is initially excited, believing his first wife, Susan, will be there to welcome him: "He had always expected, in a vague way, that, when he met his first wife again, all the differences of their married life would be dissolved, in some miraculous manner, and they would be lovers again for eternity" (52). Although he remarried after Susan's premature death, Aldwyn expects her to have remained true to him. She soon appears, but it is not the emotional reunion for which he had hoped. Instead she chides him for having abused her during life and predicts a "bitter penance" for him (51). She has made a much happier spiritual marriage and has been reunited with her two stillborn children.

When Aldwyn claims his paternal rights to the children, Susan impugns his parental abilities, declaring "happily for them, [they] never lived to know you" (52), expressing her reluctance for their purity to be defiled by his grossness (53). As in *My Own Child*, Marryat marginalises the father figure, instead making a bold statement of the supremacy and divinity of both motherhood and femininity. Although she never becomes angry, Susan is far from meek and mild. She refuses to forgive Aldwyn's sins against her. The onus is on him to repent, rather than on her to provide absolution. She reiterates that he is solely responsible for his own actions and the repercussions when he declares:

"This is hell, indeed."

"It is," replied Susan, gently; "the hell you have made for yourself. There is no heaven and no hell in reality, Henry – not such as we are wrongly taught from infancy to believe in. We make our heaven, or we make our hell. What greater hell could there be than for a man to find ... that no one wants him here, and no one wants him there?" (54)

When the Guide takes Aldwyn back to earth, he is surprised to see Susan once more. Questioning her presence, he is told:

> She has never ceased to visit her children, since she was called away from them. But what eyes had you to see her? What ears to hear her gentle counsels? Every good influence which has been brought to bear upon you – every whisper from your better self – every doubt whether, after all, you were quite just and right – has been prompted by the invisible presence of Susan. She has watched like a sister over your second wife; without her aid and solace, Ethel would hardly have been able to bear the trials you put upon her. (67)

Here Marryat firmly establishes Susan as a Marian figure, a powerful maternal divinity, watching over her children and exerting a benign influence on them. Crucially, she also acts as a brake on Aldwyn's patriarchal authority by supporting his long-suffering second wife in a spiritual sorority that he finds disturbing. Susan is a kindly friend to the weak and powerless, but a stern critic of those who abuse them. The description of Susan recalls a Leonardo Virgin Mary, and is also reminiscent of Rossetti's painting *The Blessed Damozel* (1878), a sumptuously dressed spirit who leans over the bar of Heaven: "Her fair hair hung down her neck in waving ringlets; her large blue eyes were soft and ambient; her graceful figure was draped with consummate taste, and her head and waist were wreathed with flowers" (50). Many of the Spiritualist tracts popular at this time portray dead mothers as benevolent maternal spirits, continuing to care for their families from the other side of the veil. Such depictions provided comfort to the bereaved:

> My dear mother was surrounded by little children and young people, who looked to her for knowledge and instruction, and hung on to her words and treasured them up in their minds as jewels of priceless value. I thought her beautiful

upon earth, but here she is exquisitely lovely, youthful, and graceful; her long golden hair floats around her, forming clouds of loveliness and glory, her robes are of spotless white, and all around seems pure and spotless, and unsullied by evil. (A. H. M. W., 1871: 43)

Marryat's "dear mother" is similarly graceful and irreproachable, but she is also a model of female agency, not merely a heavenly vision. Susan provides practical support to her children. When the Aldwyns' daughter Maddy has a photograph taken in a studio, she is mystified by the appearance in the negative of a "tall, slight woman, with long, loose-flowing hair" (72). She eventually realises it is her mother and visits a medium to discover the reason for her manifestation. Susan speaks to her, explaining that she has been looking after her from the "other world" and warning that the man she wants to marry will be unkind to her (90–91). She chose the photograph because "I knew the sight of my features would make you pause and think" (92). This image is like a Marian apparition, imbuing its witness with a sense of the feminine divine.

Disconcerted by Susan's omnipresence, Aldwyn is told by the Guide that Susan has been commissioned to remain by his side, supervising his spiritual growth: "you will see her and feel her presence wherever you go – her influence will lead you aright" (128). Whereas the popular perception is that the naïve wife must be educated by a superior husband, here the roles are transposed. Without this feminine guidance, Aldwyn can never achieve salvation. At the novella's conclusion, he is described as a "repentant child" (122), relegated to the lowest position in the family unit, far from his self-image of unassailable patriarch. Christine Ferguson argues that Susan "is delivered to him in terms that might please even the staunchest defender of traditional gender roles with marriage: silent, dutiful and capable of exerting power only through gentle moral influence," adding that Marryat's afterlife is "deeply patriarchal ... restoring rather than transforming earthly conjugal bonds" (Ferguson, 2012: 110). This analysis overlooks the fact that this arrangement is temporary, designed to last only until Aldwyn progresses to the next sphere. Also, Ferguson does not allow Susan to derive any satisfaction from her position of spiritual superiority, perceiving her only as "dutiful" and "gentle" (110). In fact, Susan is given the opportunity to perform a protracted emasculation of her bullying ex-husband in the afterlife, with the power to decide whether he has atoned for his sins or should endure further "bitter penance". This is immensely satisfying for both her and the reader. There is no suggestion of spiritual bigamy, rather the exaction of an exquisite revenge. While the "earthly conjugal bonds" are in evidence, the dynamics have changed completely.

Just as God's authority and omnipotence were being questioned, so was the position of the father in the microcosm of the family. As Janet Oppenheim writes, "the angry God was another remnant of ancient paganism, to be swept aside by the truly modern religion of progressive spiritualism" (1985: 95). *The Dead Man's Message* represents a challenge to both the omniscient (and male) transcendental deity and his temporal representative in the home. At the same time, Marryat denies the conception of women as weak and passive. Rather than an omnipotent patriarch, many Victorians were craving "humility, tolerance, love, care, and forgiveness – all the virtues which the age prescribed to the feminine sphere, the realm of the mother" (Uglow, 1989: xvii). Susan Aldwyn represents a divine mother who is strong and compassionate, also embodying Adams's idea of the Virgin Mary as "undomesticated and remarkably mobile" (Adams, 2001: 30). She is not confined to the heavenly sphere, and can both intervene and intercede where she sees fit. This is not the feminine ideal – the portrait of male fantasy suggested by Marina Warner (2013) – rather a radical re-envisioning of Victorian woman that builds on the character of Katherine Power from *My Own Child*. Marlene Tromp argues that novels like *The Dead Man's Message* "participated in the evolution of the narrative face of marriage and became a voice in the shifting cultural and material face of marriage as well" (2007: 60). I would go further and suggest that Marryat is not only redefining women's place within marriage, but also allowing them to define their own sexuality and identity.

For Marryat, the afterlife was not a choice between heaven and hell, but a holding to account of one's life and an opportunity for redemption. In *The Dead Man's Message*, death becomes a celestial courtroom where men are on trial for crimes of masculinity. A later edition of the novel was entitled *A Soul on Fire*, conveying a sense of the post-mortem purgatorial journey and linking the ideas more explicitly with traditional Roman Catholic ideology. Although her vision is one of universal salvation, Marryat depicts an extremely uncomfortable teleological experience for those who neglected their spirituality and the feminine divine. Marryat later decreed: "The more spirituality we acquire below, the better fitted shall we be to enjoy a spiritual life above ... and I have been taught that every man remains as he passes away until he aspires to become better. But that may incur a bitter penance first" (Marryat, 1894c: 15). Geoffrey Rowell writes that this "indeterminate state ... fitted better with a dynamic, evolutionary picture of the universe, than the conception of fixed and unalterable state into which men entered at death" (Rowell, 1974; 216). By exploring the idea of alterable states, Marryat was helping to reshape this dominant ideology and imagining a new vital role for women's spirituality.

Conclusion

In her final decade, Marryat noted with satisfaction that "the old, cold faiths have melted away" (Marryat, 1891b: 60). The reconstruction of the Virgin Mary as a feminist icon had provided women with an inspirational role model, offering an image of the mother as independent and powerful, rather than a submissive creature limited by her biological function. The gentle and merciful image was more appealing to some than the vengeful Jehovah who emanated from the Protestant pulpit. This idea that religion should provide spiritual comfort and redemption (at least for women), rather than dispense judgement and punishment, is a key theme in Marryat's fiction. She boldly created her own vision of sacred maternity and female spiritual authority, disrupting the subordinate role prescribed in scripture. Rather than just challenging the Anglican Bishops who denounced the Virgin Mary, she declared them irrelevant.

As Herringer observes, "The Marian controversies became most heated during the decades in which the feminine ideal was dominant" (Herringer, 2008: 25). Marryat rejects the conservative and man-made ideal of the established church. By taking control of her own spiritual identity, she could reconcile her faith with her feminism. Even as a divorcée, adulterer, and author of risqué novels, she believed in her right to redemption. Ben Griffin proposes that the "religious justification for the subjection of women was arguably the single most important component of nineteenth-century 'anti-feminist' thinking" (Griffin, 2012: 52). By unweaving this "complex web of male beliefs" (6), I argue, Marryat articulated radical ideas through fiction that imagined a different spiritual and earthly life for women. Later in her career, she would become more famous as a Spiritualist, joining a formidable movement that supported her vision of a gynocentric faith.

CHAPTER 7

"Courageous Assertions": Spiritualism and Power

"a place where every man may hold his opinion, and no one is permitted to dispute it."
There is No Death

When activists gathered for the first Women's Rights Convention at Seneca Falls in 1848, it was only four months after the Fox sisters famously heard spirit rappings in their home (Braude, 1985: 419). These young girls suddenly found themselves celebrated and wealthy. Unlike controversial medical practices such as mesmerism, which usually facilitated male control, mediumship actually empowered women. The "occult mysteries of the female body" became a strength (Barsham, 1992: viii), rather than a weakness to be managed and medicated. Hysteria was no longer a dangerous illness, but the manifestation of spiritual power. Ann Braude sees the growth of Spiritualism as part of the "rebellion against authority," associating its adherents with some of the most radical reform movements (Braude, 1996: 2, 3). As discussed in the previous chapter, there was already rebellion within the established church, with some women like Marryat converting to Roman-Catholicism and worshipping the Virgin Mary. Spiritualism allowed an even more direct relationship with spiritual authority and women were able to "determine their own 'truth'" (B. Taylor, 1983: 561).

In this chapter, I consider the ways in which Marryat determined her own 'truth' through her life and work, arguing that her spiritualist beliefs allowed her to create a uniquely liberating and utopian vision of a gynocentric faith. Firstly, I provide the context for Marryat's conversion to Spiritualism and the impact it had upon her career. I then discuss her experiences of the séance room, a space she used to pursue progressive ideas around power, gender, and sexuality. Moving on to her fiction, I return to Marryat's novel *The Strange Transfiguration of Hannah Stubbs* (1896), in which she illustrates how mediumistic powers could transform a humble woman. Finally, my analysis of *Open! Sesame!* (1874–5), shows Marryat believed firmly that authority in the spiritual realm should be exclusively female.

"Miss Marryat's Bogus Bogey"?

In 1873 Marryat was encouraged by a fellow journalist to attend a séance at the home of Mrs Holmes, a celebrated American medium. She was accompanied by the novelist Annie Thomas, the two women "having first removed [their] wedding rings … to look as virginal as possible" (Marryat, 1891c: 18). They were determined that the medium would be unable to make educated guesses from their outward appearance. The spirit of an unknown girl appeared before them, and it was only afterwards that Marryat came to believe that she was her daughter, Florence, who had died at just ten days old. The child manifested once more, this time during a séance at the home of novelist and mystic Mabel Collins. Baby Florence had continued to develop in the spirit world and Marryat was able to speak to her; their emotional reunion confirmed her belief in Spiritualism and provided, for her, incontrovertible evidence of its truth (22). Although convinced that her hosts knew nothing of Baby Florence's history, Collins's biographer suggests they had previously obtained details of the child's distinctive deformities through mutual friends to make the medium's performance more plausible (Farnell, 2005: 43). They were keen to recruit a high-profile supporter to their cause, and their efforts were entirely successful.

Marryat became evangelical about Spiritualism, and through her popular novels and non-fiction she convinced many others. She also joined the council of the newly-formed British National Association of Spiritualists, which held séances and gave public lectures (Oppenheim, 1985: 54). In *Notable Women Authors of the Day*, Helen C. Black comments: "Florence Marryat numbers her converts by the hundred and they are all gathered from educated people; men of letters and of science have written to her from every part of the world and many clergymen have succumbed to her courageous assertions" (2011: 100–1). Although this claim is difficult to verify, *There is No Death*, in which Marryat recounts her early experiences, has remained in print since its first publication in 1891. Her reunion with baby Florence, in particular, offered great comfort to bereaved parents. Even if they were unable to summon the spirit of a dead child, they were consoled by the idea of a son or daughter enjoying a second, and healthier, life. There was practical advice, too. Marryat explains how she employed a clairvoyant to help her track down her lost dog, Clytie, who was discovered sniffing hopefully outside a fish and chip shop (Marryat, 1891c: 30).

Marryat invited as many detractors as she did fans and was widely ridiculed in her lifetime; she is regularly held up by more recent commentators as a risible example of late-Victorian credulousness (T. Hall, 1962: 39; Owen, 2004: 227; Oppenheim, 1985: 39). Owen describes Marryat as "an ardent and susceptible believer" (1989 [2004]: 227), and her selection of sensational séance scenes in *The Darkened Room* led an excited tabloid reviewer to label Marryat "a slightly histrionic contemporary novelist" (Hennessey, 1989: 31). Trevor Hall, in his thorough debunking of the famous mediums, wrote that Marryat "could be relied upon to write columns of eulogistic and inaccurate rubbish about spiritualism"

(1962: 60). In *The Diary of a Nobody* (1892), Marryat's quondam professional partner George Grossmith parodied both her and her beliefs, depicting Mrs Pooter reading *There is no Birth* by Florence Singleyet. When his wife holds a séance in their parlour, Mr Pooter mischievously taps on the ceiling with a hammer from above (Grossmith, 1888 [2008]: 123, 124). This was Grossmith's revenge after Marryat became furious with him for his lack of respect during a table-rapping session (Grossmith, 1888: 85–6). The *Athenaeum*, meanwhile, cheekily included *There is No Death* among its "Novels of the Week" (1891: 349) and the newspaper *Truth* titled one of her spiritual encounters "Miss Marryat's Bogus Bogey" (Marryat, 1894c: 20). Her own family were no more supportive, referring to her recollections as "Another of Flo's optical illusions" (Marryat, 1891c: 12). Marryat insisted on styling her beliefs "the science of Spiritualism" (83), an approach deemed "aggressive" by one male journalist (Dolman, 1891: 2). But for her, and others, it perhaps seemed no less fantastical than the invention of the telephone or the phonograph – technologies that allowed the projection of disembodied voices.

It is easy to become distracted by the question of scientific basis for Marryat's claims, and some academics are inclined to place any Spiritualist claims in quotation marks. I do not see any reason to make retrospective judgements, nor to deny Marryat her subjectivity. Furthermore, Marryat was not trying to challenge the laws of physics, rather to reshape a prevailing ideology that had no more basis in fact than did Spiritualism. For Marryat, I propose, the appeal of the séance was twofold: firstly, this contact with the dead provided comfort lacking in established religion, allowing the bereaved to commune with departed souls. The dead were behind a thin veil, rather than separated by a final curtain. Secondly, through Spiritualism the influence of the feminine sphere could be extended in an age where many religious denominations still denied women a voice. I argue that Marryat's enthusiasm for Spiritualism was mainly about pursuing a feminist agenda and challenging the boundaries of established religion.

Marryat did not embrace Spiritualism unquestioningly, even though she found séances a great comfort. As Georgina O'Brien Hill detects, Marryat's editorials in *London Society* chart a transition from dismissal, through open-mindedness, then finally credence (2008: 333). While the Church denounced Spiritualism from the pulpit, Marryat received special dispensation from Father Dalgairn of the Brompton Oratory, who allowed her to pursue this "research" (Marryat, 1891c: 20). Marryat was able, therefore, to reconcile her Roman Catholic faith with her Spiritualist beliefs, an often difficult position she was frequently obliged to defend. In *The Spirit World*, described as her "spiritualistic manifesto" (Dickerson, 1996: 145), Marryat enumerates the failures of established religion and ridicules aspects of Catholic doctrine. She also rejects the authority of the Church to which she belongs, declaring "if to be a Catholic is to be blind, deaf and dumb, I give up all claim to that title" (Marryat, 1894c: 12). Marryat remained open-minded about Spiritualism and female sexuality.

"A scene of active frottage": Queerness in the Séance Room

During the early days of Spiritualism in the 1850s, it was easily dismissed as table-rapping. When two trance mediums, Florence Cook and Mary Rosina Showers, claimed to have achieved full-form spirit materialisations, many people, including Marryat herself, were prepared to give the idea more weight. It was the spectacle of materialisation that convinced her. Her sympathy, open-mindedness and fame meant that Marryat was regularly invited to enter the private space of the medium's cabinet, a privileged position affording her rare access to some of the most astonishing scenes in 1870s domestic life. Not everyone shared Marryat's willingness to believe, and the Society for Psychical Research (SPR), founded in 1882, sought to expose what it saw as fraudulent practice. Showers and Cook were crowned the "two princesses of the spiritualist world" (Owen, 2004: 51) and many sceptics were keen to dethrone them. The faith of believers like Marryat was a vital bulwark against the constant interrogation and threat of exposure to which trance mediums were subjected.

Marryat was first convinced of Cook's power when she materialised the spirit of her dead daughter, Florence. To establish her authenticity, Cook would be secured in a cabinet while the spirit wandered freely, interacting with the sitters. The focus of William Crookes's investigation was proving that the medium and the spirit were one and the same person. So, a binary emerged of the rational male and the hysterical female (as discussed in Chapters 4 and 5), with the former determined to assert his mental and physical superiority. As I shall argue below, Marryat's passionate defence of Spiritualism was motivated by a desire to protect this female space, as much as by her faith. Marryat wanted to believe in the integrity of Cook, as she derived great comfort from contact with her dead daughter, but she was also claiming a feminine realm, free from the penetrative gaze of the male. As Owen notes, the séance was a "celebration and exercise of female spiritual authority" (2004: iv) – while men were allowed to participate, it was on the understanding that they respected the woman's spiritual superiority and untouchability.

While the male investigators craved the opportunity to verify their suspicions, it was Marryat who was granted intimate access once "Katie King" [Cook] was "good enough" to give her "still more infallible proof" ("The Farewell Séance", 1874: 259). When sceptic Serjeant Edward Cox wrote to *The Spiritualist* claiming there was no proof that the body in cabinet was that of Cook, Marryat responded with a letter detailing her own version of events. The homoeroticism of the scene is striking: "When she summoned me ... I again saw and touched the warm breathing body of Florence Cook lying on the floor, and then stood upright by the side of Katie, who desired me to place my hands inside the loose single garment which she wore, and feel her nude body. I did so *thoroughly*" (259, emphasis added). This account is toned down very slightly when it is reused in *There is No Death*, but remains surprising: "she called me after her into the back room, and, dropping her white garment, stood perfectly naked before me. "Now," she said "you can see that I am a woman." Which indeed she was, and a most beautifully-made woman too; and *I examined her well*, whilst Miss Cook lay beside us on the floor. She then knelt down and kissed me, and I saw she was still naked" (Marryat, 1891c: 142, emphasis added).

William Crookes, another attendee at the séance, also contradicted Marryat's account, and Trevor Hall dismisses it as a "careless and imaginative narrative" (1962: 66). Careless or not, it is illuminating. These conspicuously sensual scenes recall the homoeroticism of *Her Father's Name* (1876), discussed in Chapter 5, which was written just after the séance took place. Marryat describes her heroine's form in the same admiring tones that she uses to confirm the spirit's womanliness. This feminine realm becomes a safe space in which women can explore their own non-reproductive sexuality, free from patriarchal constructions of their identity and the imperative to fulfil their biological duty.

When Cook retired as a medium, she left a note for Marryat, written as her spirit form, saying: "From Annie Owen de Morgan (alias "Katie") to her friend Florence Marryat Ross-Church. With love. *Pensez à moi*. May 21st, 1874" (Marryat, 1891c: 144).[28] The style is reminiscent of a love letter. The lawlessness of the séance room enabled these two women to behave outside of societal norms. By adopting the position of the "rational male", Marryat was able to engage in a sensual and intimate experience under the guise of empiricism. In *The Blood of the Vampire* (1897), the homosocial environment of the boarding school allows Harriet Brandt to explore her own sexuality, and in *Her Father's Name*, Leona Lacoste's androgynous disguise affords her far more latitude. Marryat's real-world experiences, therefore, inform her fiction, where she continues to explore ideas of gender and sexuality.

Sarah A. Willburn argues that "the context of the séance provides a dynamic space for role-playing and social interaction," where the medium is "observed and touched in a scene of active frottage" (2006: 85, 86). As I argued in my previous chapter, male doctors sought to establish themselves as the experts and controllers of the female body, but in the séance room women are the arbiters of their own and each other's bodies, this space offering "hands-on opportunities for radically reimagined social interaction" (87). In her encounters with Rosina Showers, Marryat's behaviour went far beyond active frottage. In *There is No Death* she describes a sequence of events like a seduction: "In a moment it flashed across me to ask her to return to Bayswater and sleep with me, for I was most desirous of testing her powers when we were alone together. ... I took Miss Showers into the bedroom ... Miss Showers and I then undressed and got into bed" (Marryat, 1891c: 67). Initially, the activity is similar to the séance room, with an outbreak of spirit activity, including a ghostly Pope fiddling with Marryat's ornaments. Then matters become more personal. Showers summons a spirit, Peter, and the women feel "as many as eight and ten hands touching [them] at once" (69). When she feels him touching her, Marryat ties Showers's hands together – to which she "consented willingly" (69) – to be sure she is not responsible. Still, the materialised hand touches her face and hair (68–9). Upon investigation, Marryat discovers that the arm responsible "terminate[s] *in the middle of Miss Showers' back*" (70, original emphasis). The hand continues stroking her hair, and Marryat does nothing to prevent it. Later, Marryat comments that she and Showers could not sit together anywhere without a phantom hand menacing them under the table.(109). To the non-Spiritualist, this speaks more of sexual attraction than spectral activity. Subsequently, in the séance room, Showers asks Marryat "to put [her] hands up her skirts," to check that she has half-dematerialised (111).

Tromp proposes that "The darkened parlour of the séance

invited and embodied the disruption of the ordinary," where the sitters "violated customary barriers of age and gender" (2003: 67). She goes on to discuss only heterosexual relationships, which although illicit, are not quite as disruptive as the preamble promises. Notwithstanding this limitation, Tromp poses an interesting question:

> Which experiences are those of the flesh and which are those of the spirit? In which body does the medium's identity lie? Who is responsible for the reaching arms the shared kiss, the embrace? The boundary between the spiritual and the flesh of the medium became indistinct, and, by virtue of this slippage, one could not demarcate the medium's identity, locate her accountability or intention, or distinguish the Victorian woman from the unfettered spirit. (67)

For Marryat, this lack of accountability and corporeality allows her more liberty than she could expect in the temporal world. That the séance room was an area for experimentation is also demonstrated in an episode from *There is No Death*, in which the spirit of baby Florence (grown to a toddler in the spirit world) gleefully reorganises the accessories of the sitters, so that the women are wearing ties and the men are adorned with earrings (Marryat, 1891c: 81–2). This gender fluidity is indicative of the liberation that Spiritualism affords. Tromp argues that full-form materialisation mediumship participated in "a shift of codes that made increased sexual freedom less a subject of spectacle and more a part of the norm" (2003: 78). Tromp's analysis is of heteronormative transgression, whereas the accounts of Cook, Showers and Marryat suggest a far more radical upheaval in gender roles. While it is important not to read too much into Victorian same-sex friendships, the bed scene especially suggests an unusual level of intimacy.

In maintaining a sustained and passionate defence of

Spiritualism, Marryat was, in fact, protecting a space that allowed freedom of self-expression, where women could reject traditional feminine ideals with impunity. Marryat's remarkable experiences endorse Owen's contention that the séance "effected a truly radical challenge to cultural orthodoxy and the stunning subversion of the nineteenth-century feminine ideal" (2004: 212). Often frustrated by the limitations placed on women in daily life, Marryat imagines a world in which women reign supreme. Men's innate rationality prevents them from colonising this female space: in the séance room the masculine imperial imperative is checked.

Marryat's recollections have been thoroughly debunked by fellow Spiritualists, sceptics, and even her own family. In her memoirs, Marryat's niece, Viva King, described her as "rather dotty on the subject of spiritualism but ... quite terrified when her time came to meet those spirits with whom she had claimed so much familiarity in life" (King, 1976: 4). This recollection suggests that Marryat was not as ardent as many people thought, indicating that her adoption of Spiritualism was motivated by something more than a desire for eternal life. In *Mount Eden* the rational male character proclaims that "all the stories you hear about ghosts and apparitions are nonsensical lies," to which the heroine responds: "I shouldn't like to believe that ... it would rob me of one of my greatest comforts" (Marryat, 1889 [nd]: 38). But for Marryat, Spiritualism was not just about comfort – it was also about female power.

"It isn't all jam to have a medium in the house": The authoritative female voice in *The Strange Transfiguration of Hannah Stubbs*

"[S]triking is the number of middle-class housewives who discovered powers of trance communication, clairvoyance, and furniture re-location during the 1850s, 1860s, and 1870s" (1985: 9), notes Janet Oppenheim. While Oppenheim sees these activities as assuaging boredom and frustration, the possibilities went beyond mere entertainment and diversion. Instead, they afforded women a status above that which their class and gender might dictate. In Marryat's novel, working-class protagonist Hannah has been ejected from the family home because her mediumistic powers are proving disruptive to domestic life. As discussed in Chapter 5, these powers make her the victim of medical experiments by Professor Ricardo and Dr Steinberg. Hannah's unusual powers have made her a far more valuable commodity than just a servant, and, as the narrative progresses, she develops a sense of her own worth. By marrying her, Ricardo believes Hannah's powers will be entirely at his disposal, but it must be pointed out to him: "performing the office of a medium does not come within the legalities of Marriage, and if she will not do it of her own free will you have no means by which you can compel her!" (Marryat, 1896b: 126) Hannah's gift, therefore, allows her to act more independently than the traditional wife. Ultimately, the roles are reversed and Hannah has the upper hand in the relationship: "The woman had magnetised his every sense, and he was a tool in her hands" (223). The newly-empowered Hannah informs him, "It isn't all jam to have a medium in the house, Professor!" (202)

It transpires partway through the novel that Hannah's burgeoning confidence is due partly to her body having been possessed by the spirit of Ricardo's first wife, the Marchesa, whom he murdered in a fit of sexual jealousy. Identifying Hannah as a weak and vulnerable host, the Marchesa controls her speech and actions to make Ricardo's life a misery.[29] Through Hannah, Marryat shows that exploited women are responsive to stronger members of their own sex, and also that revenge is no longer confined to the temporal sphere – a concept she had also explored in *The Dead Man's Message* (1894). The spirit of the Marchesa urges Hannah to murder her husband and marry someone richer and more powerful. Her only motivation is money, mimicking the idea that in marriage women should privilege financial security over emotional fulfilment.

Vanessa Dickerson argues that novels such as *Hannah Stubbs* show that "the angel in the house has become a demon hell-bent on getting money" (1996: 143). While it could be argued that Hannah's transfiguration is a grotesque image of women's desire for freedom and money, it is also a morality tale, showing that abused women might become resurgent in unexpected ways. As I showed in Chapter 5, Hannah had been sexually exploited by Professor Ricardo and Dr Steinberg, so her transformation into a depraved nymphomaniac is condign punishment for their actions. Their attempt to reconstruct her identity to suit their needs yields surprising results, with the usually passive Hannah harnessing the strength of a formidable woman. She becomes the embodiment of what the two men want: Ricardo craves money to restore his social status, while Steinberg wants a highly sexualised woman. Hannah is as much a projection of male fantasy as of woman's desire for agency, and Marryat is showing the dangers of men getting what they want. Ricardo and Steinberg are punished for using Hannah's powers for their own ends, instead of allowing her to provide spiritual comfort to others. Dickerson claims that Hannah's powers are purely "for the benefit of the male" (145), but she does also use them at séances, bringing together the bereaved and their loved ones. She is not a complete "demon," since much of her agenda is dictated by a vengeful revenant. Hannah combines her talent with a sense of her own worth. Although Hannah dies at the end, her transfiguration has given her a sense of fulfilment she would not otherwise have enjoyed. Her death is joyful: "The plain face glowed with delighted anticipation – the swollen hands were stretched out with rapture – the eyes, lovely to the last, beamed upon the apparition that stood before her, and the spirit of Hannah Stubbs, with the most gratifying result of all her mediumship, flew into the arms of her waiting mother, whilst her body fell back lifeless on the pillows" (287).

Through Spiritualism and her strange transfiguration, this "plain and uninteresting" girl has become "beautified and refined and enlightened" (288). Perhaps Marryat's argument would have been more satisfying (and less classist) if it Ricardo and Steinberg had died, rather than Hannah. In her short story "The Ghost of Charlotte Cray" (1883) the heroine exacts her revenge on her cheating lover only after she dies suddenly of peritonitis. Her post-mortem activities are certainly undignified, but she succeeds in scaring out him of his wits. Thoroughly spooked, he gives up his job and settles for an uneventful life in Streatham. Her death means that she can confront him with the consequences of his actions far more effectively than when she was alive. For a Spiritualist like Marryat, death did not mean the end – it meant new possibilities. Diana Barsham writes "Where the stereo-typical image of the male mesmerist and his passive female somnambule re-informed the gendered power structures encoded in English law, Spiritualism reversed them, offering to the female medium ... the active role of penetrating the minds of her audience" (1992: 127). This transformation can be traced in Marryat's fiction, from the supine and assailable form of Olga Adrastikoff in *Blindfold* (discussed in Chapter 4), to Hannah Stubbs, initially a vulnerable victim of human vivisection, who subsequently becomes a feted member of fashionable society and the nemesis of two dishonourable husbands. The spiritual woman, even when dead, is disruptive to male hegemony.

Vested Interests: Hyperfemininity and Homosexuality in *Open! Sesame!*

In typically combative fashion, *Punch* dismissed Spiritualism as a "species of revelation ... derived from the mouths of soothsayers who are generally either nervous or epileptic youths, or females afflicted with hysteria" (quoted in Pearsall, 2003: 28). *The Strange Transfiguration of Hannah Stubbs* exemplifies Owen's argument that "medicine linked spiritualism with hysteria ... alerting the profession to the prospect of femininity gone awry" (2004: 147), with Marryat reconfiguring hysteria as female power. In *Open!*

Sesame! (1874–5), Marryat instead pathologises the behaviour of the male protagonist. Written during the period when she was forming her own opinions on Spiritualism, Marryat uses this colourful novel to explore her nascent ideas and to establish firmly the spiritual sphere as feminine. The novel is also a coded representation of homosexuality, a theme Marryat uses to expose the fragility of masculinity and to argue the ascendance of the feminine, topics that were to dominate the debates of the *fin de siècle*.

Everil West-Norman, a robust and horsey young heiress, is appalled to discover that her father's will stipulates she must marry her cousin, Bernard Valence, if she is to inherit the family wealth. She dismisses him as an "invalid – a bookworm – a lunatic!" (Marryat, 1874–5 [nd]: 25) Bernard is bookish and effeminate, eschewing outdoor pursuits in favour of the Stygian gloom of his castle in Ireland. Whereas Everil is "tall" with "more energy than softness in her expression" (10), Bernard is "about the middle height, extremely fair and delicate in appearance" and his mouth is "too finely cut to betoken energy or much endurance" (29). Bernard immediately declares that he is willing to "fulfil [his] part of the business" even though the "idea of marriage is distasteful to [him]" (32). This resignation is motivated by a persistent belief that he is doomed to an early death. Everil, meanwhile, frantically resists the idea, hoping for a turn of events that will render their union unnecessary, as he's "not my idea of a husband" (18). Like Evelyn Rayne in *Mount Eden* (see Chapter 2), she is repelled by an "effeminate sham" (222).

Bernard's indifference to women is openly discussed by his family, and his widowed sister-in-law Agatha tells Everil: "I don't suppose dear Valence ever paid attention to a woman in his life" (25), also apprising her of his preference for homosocial environments. Everil remarks, "I hate a man who isn't a man" (73). Bernard discusses his likely fate with his best friend Bulwer, explaining that he and Everil would be able to lead separate lives and still fulfil the terms of the will. An incredulous Bulwer asks, "but your wife will surely have your company, Valence?" To which he responds, "No! Bulwer, no! or at best, very little of it … It is the one thing my cousin must not ask of me. She may have everything I possess, except —" (43). The ellipsis and concluding dash connote the unspeakable: Bernard's homosexuality. He is prepared to countenance marriage purely as a financial transaction, but the idea of a sexual relationship with a woman is repugnant.

Realising that an unfulfilling marriage is preferable to destitution, Everil agrees to marry Bernard, adding "I should marry you, under the circumstances, if you were a chimpanzee" (164). Indeed, Everil shows herself no more suited to marriage than her cousin. During an awkward dinner party, Everil asks why women should not enjoy the same freedoms as men. Bernard in a "nervous, half-diffident manner" enquires whether men would then be free from responsibility for women. Sensing his fear and discomfort, Everil gleefully responds: "Leave you free! Why, what should we want with you then? By Jove! … it would be the best day's work we had ever done!" A "dark flush rises to the very roots of Lord Valence's hair" and the other men start examining the pattern on their dinner plates (98).

When Everil discovers that Bernard spends hours alone in a darkened room, pursuing his spiritualist studies, she responds "I have the greatest contempt for anything like belief in the supernatural" (205). Bernard's beliefs become an area of conflict within their marriage, as Everil attempts to make him more rational and, indeed, masculine. His housekeeper is quietly optimistic that Everil will be successful:

> He's very bad in his head, poor gentleman, and has been all along, as every one about him can say; and the dreadful things as go on in this house, sir, words, couldn't tell you of them; and it's a wonder anyone can bear to stay here – and not more they wouldn't if they hadn't loved him, boy and man, as their

own ... it's only the Lord above as knows all. And if I thought the lady as is coming could win him from such dark deeds, why, I'd bless her on my bended knees, that I would. (171)

The "dreadful things" and "dark deeds" are an explicit metaphor for homosexuality, which can be cured only by the presence of a woman. His physician, Dr Newall tells him, "Shake off this slough of superstition and blind bigotry which has *unsexed* you" (280, emphasis added). Bernard's study represents the dark side of his character, and it becomes both a literally and metaphorically contested space, as he endeavours to retain his "harbour of refuge" (166). Bernard reveals to Everil that he spends long nights practising his dark arts and regularly conjures up a spirit control called Isola, who has told him he will die on the stroke of noon on 3rd February. Obsessed with the idea of his own mortality, he waits patiently for her to appear with her "diaphanous drapery – and a veil of flowing golden hair" (252).

Isola is all softness and femininity compared with the tomboyish Everil, her blonde hair and elaborate clothing representing the hyperfemininity of the mid-Victorian womanly ideal. It also suggests the exaggerated appearance of the drag artist. *Open! Sesame!* was written only a couple of years after the infamous 1871 trial of Boulton and Park, also known as Fanny and Stella, two young men who were charged with conspiring to incite others to commit unnatural offences – namely, wearing women's clothing and having sex with other men (McKenna, 2013: 36). To be decadent in an age of utility was unforgivable, and they were ridiculed as the "He-She Ladies". Until they were subjected to the glare of publicity, however, many men were duped by Stella's flaxen curls and elaborate dress – the very epitome of feminine attire. The case was mentioned in *London Society* under Marryat's editorship, so she was undoubtedly aware of it. The details of this sensational story would have been in her readers' minds, too, and the coded references to Bernard's homosexuality and his fascination with an almost grotesque form of 'femininity' were intended to evoke this collective cultural memory. Through this character, Marryat anticipates the homosexual panic and crisis of masculinity of the *fin de siècle*.

When Everil conceals herself in Bernard's study one night, she too sees Isola and becomes jealous, this apparent competition prompting her to desire a more conventional marriage with her husband. The next morning, Everil comes bouncing down the stairs, looking radiantly happy, and then devours an enormous breakfast (Marryat, 1874–5 [nd]; 256) – a clear signal to the reader that the marriage has been finally consummated. As his taste for normative sexuality grows, Bernard starts noticing other women and comparing them unfavourably with his own wife, praising her "fire and energy and action" and musing "I can't understand any man falling in love with any woman whilst Everil is within the range of sight" (282). The feminine strength that initially repelled him has now become overwhelmingly attractive. As discussed in Chapter 5, Marryat believed women should project their sexuality, rather than conform to the sexless Victorian ideal. In *A Daughter of the Tropics* (1887) and *The Blood of the Vampire*, the consequences are the ascendancy of the mixed-race woman; here she warns that a lack of strong women might lead to male homosexuality. It is one of Marryat's many contradictions that she sees lesbianism as empowering, yet portrays homosexual men as weak. Indeed, her view of acceptable masculinity is often no less restrictive than the model of femininity demanded of women.

Notwithstanding his heterosexual epiphany, Bernard remains firmly convinced of his own imminent demise, and Everil is unable to convince him otherwise. Increasingly agitated, she consults Dr Newall, who advises that she must provoke jealous rage in her husband to rouse his manly instincts. Everil reluctantly affects disinterest in Bernard and instead starts responding to the flatteries of an old flame, Maurice Staunton. A disturbed and dejected Bernard starts regressing to his former weakly self.

He seeks consolation in the company of Isola, who reiterates his appointment with death, thereby reassuring him that his agony will soon be over. In the face of Bernard's visible decline, Everil organises a grand ball to take place at the castle, an elaborate subterfuge to facilitate a feigned elopement with the asinine Staunton, who believes himself irresistible. They slip away under cover of darkness, leaving a note for the devastated Bernard. Urged by Bulwer to pursue the 'lovers' and reclaim his wife, Bernard races to the hotel for an angry confrontation. As the doctor predicted, his manly instincts are roused: "His eyes are flaming fury, his hand grasps a pistol. His adversary feels that … he is not a man to be trifled with" (371). Bernard's transformation into a red-blooded heterosexual is complete. When Staunton claims that Everil loves him, Bernard retorts: "Don't presume to mention her name with your dastardly lips, or I will cram this pistol down your throat" (371). This is an image that requires no further commentary. He then strikes Staunton across the mouth and throws him into the passage. Bernard has gone from penetrating Everil to penetrating everything. Marking this transition from deviance to normalcy, Bulwer comments: "You have awakened, Valence, thank God, from the saddest dream your life has ever known" (374). And he has awakened to the importance of female influence.

Bulwer also reveals that Isola is, in fact, Bernard's sister-in-law Agatha, who donned a wig and robes in a ploy to frighten him into an early grave. Eager that her own son should inherit the family fortune, Agatha has a vested interest in convincing Bernard that he is deviant, sterile, and doomed. When her "veil of flowing hair" is shown to be a wig, her hyperfemininity is exposed to be as inauthentic as that of Boulton and Park. In this overwrought denouement, Marryat deploys the *East Lynne* plot, but, unlike Lady Isobel, Everil remains firmly in control throughout. Combining strength and intelligence, she is superior to both the men vying for her attention. At the novel's conclusion, Bernard resolves to retain his spirituality while renouncing his former credulousness. Everil's vigour and rationality have proven a positive influence on him, in a transposition of the traditional gender roles. Such was the fragility of Bernard's masculinity, it could be stabilised only by feminine strength – a strong woman, not one who is traditionally feminine. Agatha represents an atavistic threat to the female sex, an asexual woman who is interested solely in money; her tenacity is employed only in securing an inheritance for her son. Marryat proposes that humankind's only hope of salvation is through allowing women sexual liberation, rather than expecting them to conform to unrealistic ideas of chastity and financial dependence. Here it is the husband, not the wife, who is forced to adapt, and Everil's strong-mindedness is displayed as an asset, rather than as something that should be tamed: *she* is the standard to which *he* should aspire. Whereas women were supposed to be sexually reactive, Everil here is the instigator. Like the New Woman whom she anticipates, she craves financial independence *and* sexual fulfilment.

While Marryat is making a bold claim for women's equality (and, arguably, superiority), she is also establishing their preeminence in spiritual matters. Bernard's deviance and narrowly averted downfall were precipitated by dabbling in what Marryat sees as the feminine domain: Spiritualism. As Barsham observes, trance mediumship was "widely regarded as providing access to the 'female' side of the human psyche" (1992: 7), and Owen explains that it was thought to undermine "the strength of mind (will-power) which differentiated the masculine from the feminine psychological profile" (2004: 10). By pursuing his interests despite the opposition of those around him, Bernard unwittingly becomes effeminate and feminised. There are apparent similarities between Bernard and the celebrity Spiritualist Daniel Dunglas Home, who divided opinion with his flamboyant performances.

Robert Browning thought Home "weak and effeminate," accusing him of "unmanliness" and resenting his wife's endorsement of his mediumistic powers (Lamont, 2006: 50). Home was widely rumoured to have been imprisoned in Paris for "an unnatural offence" and in 1869 Lord Adare disclosed that he had shared a bed with Home, ostensibly to create greater intimacy with the spirits (96, 97). Home was obliged to retire following this scandal, but Marryat's novel would probably have refreshed the memories of those familiar with his disgrace. There is a marked resemblance between Home and the physical description of Bernard Valence. Owen writes that Home's "long hair, sensitive hands, and personal vanity" would have been enough to prompt "persistent rumours" (2004: 10), and Marryat aims to elicit a similar response from her reader. Furthermore, Home was debilitated by chronic illness and suffered an early death – the fate Bernard avoids by renouncing Spiritualism and becoming more masculine. Marryat exposes the destruction that can ensue when men encroach upon Spiritualism and compromise the sanctity of the divine feminine. Bernard redeems himself by admitting the limits of masculine knowledge, concluding: "we can never 'have done' with spiritual companionship. It is beneath us, over us, and round about us; appointed by the wisdom of the Almighty to be our protection and our guide … for the future you and I will be content to feel and know this care without striving to *penetrate* the mysteries that He has hidden from us" (Marryat, 1874–5 [nd]: 374, emphasis added). Bernard continues to derive comfort from an awareness of the spiritual, but he has renounced the need to penetrate or master this realm, instead focusing those energies on a healthy sexual relationship.

In writing a novel in which the medium turns out to be fraudulent, Marryat is demonstrating her willingness to approach Spiritualism objectively, employing 'male' rationality, rather than succumbing to 'female' credulousness. As O'Brien Hill explains, Marryat had an "acute awareness that unquestioning belief and uninformed scepticism could both do damage to the 'cause of spiritualism'" (2008: 334). Marryat was as quick to denounce a fraud (or ineffectual medium) as to embrace one she considered gifted, so long as they were female. Men could be supporters of Spiritualism, but not practitioners; for Marryat, the spiritual realm was one regulated by women. Men might make the laws on earth, but women reigned supreme in the spiritual realm.

Conclusion

Although *The Spirit World* is credited as Marryat's "spiritualistic manifesto" (Dickerson, 1996; 145), as I have shown above, she made equally powerful arguments through her fiction, much of which would have reached a wider and more diverse readership. In the novels discussed here, women appropriate power through mediumship and men are punished for their attempt to interfere in the spiritual realm. While Owen discerns that "women's involvement with spiritualism was at one level all about gender expectations, sexual politics, and the subversion of existing power relations between men and women," she is quick to dismiss Marryat as "an ardent and susceptible believer" (2004: i, 229). An analysis of Marryat's life and work, however, shows that Spiritualism was much more than a faith to her, allowing her to imagine possibilities denied her by conventional religion.

Oppenheim complains that "the vivid detail that enlivens her séance accounts owes something to a novelist's imagination" (1985: 39) but it was precisely this imagination that allowed Marryat to reinvent women's spiritual identity. Furthermore, the "vivid detail" of those séance accounts conveys provocative ideas around sexuality that Marryat would have been unable to express through conventional modes. As Tatiana Kontou observes, her "spiritualist experiences are hybrids between life and death, memory and fantasy, performance and reality" (2012: 226). It is irrelevant and distracting to focus on whether Miss Marryat's spirits were bogus. Even if imaginary, they were irresistible agents of social change. By establishing and affirming the concept of female spiritual authority, Marryat disrupted the basis of the gender binaries mandated by the law, medicine, and the established church. Her "courageous assertions" imagined a radically different world for women.

CHAPTER 8

Woman of the Future: Conclusion

"I have a well-known name and a public reputation, a tolerable brain, and two sharp eyes."

There is No Death

As the lights dimmed on a New York stage, the audience was confronted by an extraordinary spectacle: a tall woman, clad in fiery red robes, with fluffy blonde hair poking out from a mortarboard ("What to do with the Men: Miss Florence Marryat's Glimpse Ahead to the Year 1995", 1885: 4). Electra Thucydides, Senior Wrangler of St Momus, was poised to deliver a lecture entitled "What shall we do with our Men?" The syllabus she intended to cover included:

> Man in the Past and the Present. The qualification of Gorillas and Chimpanzees to sit in Parliament. The Marriage Lease Act. The Separated Wife's Grandmother Bill. The Rearing of Fathers. The Patent Infant Incubator. The Management of Nurserymen. Preparation of Daughters for the Army and Navy. Can men be allowed to appear in public without detriment to their natural modesty? The question solved. (Marryat Family Papers, "Notebook: Love letters/Woman of the Future": np)

The ladies and gentlemen in the plush seats were understandably confused. They had come to see a performance of *My Sweetheart*, a light musical on "the difference between the love of a good, pure girl and the designs of a woman of the world" (Bordman and Norton, 2011: 74). Now they were receiving a lecture on a subject that made no sense. Only after ten minutes did realisation dawn. Electra Thucydides was a visitor from 1995 (110 years hence), and she was played by the best-selling novelist Florence Marryat. Sensing the thrust of her argument, many of the men either left the auditorium or chatted to their male friends at the back. Some initial laughter subsided when the audience realised this was not purely entertainment – it was a manifesto, too.

In a deep voice, and occasionally lurching to emphasise her points, Marryat explained that the United Kingdom had been under "feminine rule" for the last fifty years, and "Man is, today, kept in his proper position".[30] He is restricted to occupations befitting his lowly status, especially those that "demand muscle rather than brain". Men are entitled to seats in Parliament but are confined in the lower house and allowed only to vote on issues that affect their sex. With glee, Marryat added that the women were also obliged to allow gorillas and chimpanzees to sit in the House of Commons, explaining:

> it would have been impractical for us to pass the one bill without the other. It would have been the height of injustice to declare <u>men</u> qualified to vote for the Government & to refuse the same privileges to their prototypes … And to be impartial – the Gorillas & Chimpanzees appear to say quite as much worth remembering as their more advanced brethren. They say it also in fewer words & they certainly look wiser whilst they are saying it.

In much of her later fiction, Marryat repeatedly portrayed wives who were superior to their husbands (see Chapters 2 and 7), but here she makes a much cruder argument: women are a separate species and one that is more evolved. Men are regressing, while women are steadily becoming the master race.

Most of the lecture is similarly rooted in the realms of fantasy, but there are glimpses of practicality. The New Marriage Lease Act, for instance, transforms marriage into a purely civil contract ("it used to be a very <u>uncivil</u> one") that must be renewed after 3, 5, or 7 years. Just in case any of the men in the audience were warming to her ideas, Marryat added that the contract was dissoluble by the female partner only. The sexual double standard remained, but now women had the upper hand. Women are also liberated by technology in the twentieth century. Although men were initially making themselves useful in the nursery, they were eventually met by "the absolute refusal of all females over the age of 3 to submit to their control". Even toddlers were rebelling against patriarchy. The advent of the Patent Infant Incubator rendered "the domestic circle a fiction of the past," as this "marvellous little machine" feeds and entertains small children. Women of the future are still responsible for childbirth, but no longer confined to the home or reliant on a male breadwinner. Marryat imagines that other technological advances will also obviate the need for housework. By making a series of preposterous suggestions, Marryat cleverly rendered some of her moderate ideas more palatable.

Marryat's vision is bold, ambitious, and occasionally deranged. If she had hopped into H. G. Wells's time machine, what would she have thought of the year 1995? Well, Parliament was far from the gynocracy she had imagined. At the 1992 General Election, only sixty female MPs were returned to the House of Commons – 9.2% of the total ("Women MPs and Parliamentary Candidates Since 1945", 2017: online). And marital rape – which Marryat had described painfully in her fiction – only became illegal in 1991. She would no doubt have been pleased that more than 70% of women had entered the workplace ("Report Summary", 2017: online), but less impressed that they were still shouldering most of the responsibility for housework and childcare. The battle for equal pay – which still rumbles on – would have left her utterly perplexed. Back in 1875, her status as family breadwinner allowed Marryat to retain custody of her children. Her ability to command sizeable advances and royalties, along with changes in the property laws, meant that she could enjoy greater independence than many other wives. Marryat was ahead of her time in 1885 and remains radical almost 150 years later. She had witnessed a transformation in the position of women during the second half of the nineteenth century, yet it still was not enough for her.

Far from being the cosy domestic novelist suggested by Helen C. Black in *Notable Women Authors of the Day*, Marryat was at the sharp end of the struggle for women's rights. Her insistence on creating heroines in her own image met with hostility from critics, and Marryat's unconventional personal life ensured her exclusion from polite society. Her characteristics – industriousness, extroversion, and a fondness for sexual adventure – would have been prized in a man. As a woman, though, they rendered her at best eccentric, at worst dangerous. Consequently, her extraordinary character tends to be either suppressed, caricatured, or misinterpreted. Jules Eisenbud, for instance, concludes that "the unconscious standard against which she was always inwardly compelled to measure herself was the unrealistically unachievable one of being a man" (1983: 218). This interpretation ignores Marryat's aim in both her life and her work, which was to imagine radically different possibilities for women. Her controversial lifestyle and polemical novels were motivated not by gender dysphoria, but by frustration with the circumscribed role of the mid-Victorian woman. As Marryat's daughter wrote in her obituary, "femininity was too narrow a platform for her" (E. Church, 1899: 591), so she sought a much broader idea of female identity, both for herself and her heroines.

Instead of responding to criticism and becoming a more conservative writer, Marryat remained a provocative novelist, her sensational plots persisting into the 1890s. With women largely denied an official voice in legal, medical, and religious discourses, she used her literary fame to make herself heard, thereby reaching a wide audience with her radical ideas. Through her novels, Marryat showcased the ways in which women diverged from the Victorian feminine ideal. Rather than spotless, subordinate paragons, her heroines were elective single mothers, businesswomen, lesbians, and spiritual authorities. It must be reiterated that Marryat is not always an exemplary feminist – her attitudes towards class and race often make for uncomfortable reading – but she remains an important and compelling voice. Then, as now, there was no one way of being a feminist.

Inevitably, it has been possible to address only a small proportion of Marryat's fiction here. There are many more novels and themes to explore in detail, and other scholars will bring their own perspective to Marryat's writing. More work is needed, too, on her non-fiction, which constitutes a notable body of work. However, I hope this study offers a starting point both for further research on Marryat and other neglected Victorian women writers. By evaluating the vast literary output of these largely forgotten authors, we can greatly expand our understanding of Victorian women's writing, building on the valuable work already done by Lyn Pykett, Pamela K. Gilbert, Elaine Showalter, and Andrew Maunder. Historicising sensation novels in this way helps us to understand what was important to its practitioners, creating what Beverley Southgate calls "a history that incorporates some aspects of experience that have hitherto been relegated to the domain of fiction" (2009: 200). More specifically, I argue that sustained critical attention to marginalised 'sub-literary' fiction like Marryat's offers us an account of the individual struggles that together formed the nineteenth-century women's rights movement – a movement that succeeded in transforming wives from chattels to individuals in their own right. As Janice Radway concludes, "Interstices ... exist within the social fabric where opposition is carried on by people who are not satisfied by their place within it," adding that we should "not overlook this minimal but nonetheless legitimate form of protest" (1984: 222). If Marryat's fiction now seems ephemeral, it is partly because many of the issues she addresses have been resolved, thanks to oppositional voices such as her own.

Thanks to various digitisation projects, we have now unprecedented access to thousands of Victorian novels, including many that probably have remained unread for over a century. This presents a wonderful opportunity to increase the range of women's writing that we can study, teach, and enjoy. To paraphrase Carol Poster, writers become important because they are written about, and scholars continue writing about them *because* they have become important (1996: 293). We must establish and maintain some momentum, as critical attention tends to coalesce around recently recovered authors and specific texts. It is undoubtedly a mark of progress that *The Blood of the Vampire* regularly appears in conference papers and reading lists, but there is much more to discover in Marryat's work. And there are other authors just like her, waiting to be rediscovered. Seen in her historical context, Marryat emerges as a woman who dared to be different in fact and fiction. A similar analysis of other neglected writers may reveal a diverse, rewarding, and often challenging map of nineteenth-century literature.

Notes

Introduction
1. For example, Everil West-Norman in *Open! Sesame!* (1875) (see Chapter 6) and Joan Trevor in *A Rational Marriage* (1899) (see Chapter 2).

Chapter 1
2. There is some confusion over Marryat's birthdate and it is normally given as 9 July 1837. This date appears in the latest printed edition of the *Oxford Dictionary of National Biography* and has been consequently perpetuated through secondary materials. Marryat mischievously lied about her age in interviews and deducted six years on her second marriage certificate. Although no birth certificate exists (such records were not yet mandatory), her christening record, first marriage certificate, divorce records, and death certificate all cite her birthdate as 9 July 1833. This has been amended in the online version of the ODNB.
3. Marryat demanded intelligence in domestic staff, but was concerned that they might be educated beyond their station. She remained an opponent of the Board School system ("The Real Florence Marryat": 591).
4. Either Marryat was mistaken in her claim, or the details were so heavily disguised as to render the article's retrieval impossible.
5. For analysis of Jewbury's influence on Marryat's novel, see Catherine Pope, 2014.
6. Charles Dickens to Florence Marryat, 6 August 1867.
7. Letter: Florence Marryat Lean to George Eliot, 8 February 1879 (The George Eliot and George Henry Lewes Collection).
8. Last Will and Testament of Florence Marryat. Of course, nowadays, a portfolio comprising four London properties would make Marryat a multi-millionaire.
9. Last Will and Testament of Thomas Ross Church.
10. Accounts of Marryat's output vary: I have identified 68. Some novels were published under multiple titles, and some of her sisters' work was also mistakenly attributed to her.

Chapter 2
11. Geraldine Jewsbury to Richard Bentley, 19 June 1861.

12. Reviewers often referred to Marryat by her married name, even though she seldom used it professionally.
13. The husband made several further appearances in front of the magistrate, mainly for brutal assaults on his wife.
14. Mr Gaskell's wish was granted in 1893, with the passing of a Third Married Women's Property Act.
15. For a discussion of marital violence in Marryat's fiction, see Catherine Pope, 2017.
16. The MS included in the Lord Chamberlain's Plays collection at the British Library comprises only a few soot-blackened pages.

Chapter 4

17. For example, Ornella Moscucci, 1990; Sheryl Burt Ruzek, 1978; India Nead, 1988; Ann Dally, 1991.
18. Geraldine Jewsbury to Richard Bentley; 29 February 1868.
19. It was raised to sixteen by the 1885 Criminal Law Amendment Act.
20. For more information on Frankau and her novel, see Tabitha Sparks, 2009.
21. For more information on Barry, see Rachel Holmes, 2002.

Chapter 5

22. For a detailed consideration of Harriet's appetite, see Mariaconcetta Constantini, 2013.
23. For a more detailed exploration of the lesbian theme in *Her Father's Name*, see Catherine Pope, forthcoming.
24. For a detailed consideration of this novel and vivisection, see Greta Depledge, 2013.

Chapter 6

25. Technically, it does, as her father placed her inheritance in trust, thus circumventing the limited married women's property laws at the time.
26. The doctrine of Erastianism holds that the state is superior to the Church in ecclesiastical matters.
27. Predominant views of the spirit world involved a series of concentric spheres, arranged hierarchically, through which the soul would progress.

Chapter 7

28. Upon retirement, Cook adopted the less poetic name of Mrs Elgie Corner.
29. Hannah, a Yorkshirewoman, goes from speaking like a Cockney to adopting an Italian accent not heard beyond the music hall. Marryat was terrible at writing convincing dialogue.

Conclusion

30. All subsequent quotations are from this unpublished manuscript and so have no page numbers.

Bibliography

Archival Material

3 Hansard 134 (13 June 1854), 7. n.d.
Bentley Archives, British Library, London
British Library, 1885. Florence Marryat, "The School of Literary Art: Conducted by Florence Marryat", MSS.C/194.a.117.
General Register Office, Marylebone: Death Certificate for Florence Lean, 28 October 1899, File no. 313938. Certified copy in possession of author.
General Register Office, Pancras: Death Certificate for Eva Florence Stevens, 20 July 1887, File no. 597549. Certified copy in possession of the author.
General Register Office, Winchester: Death Certificate for Florence Church, 10 February 1861. File no. 676262. Certified copy in possession of the author.
The George Eliot and George Henry Lewes Collection, 1834–1981, Beinecke Rare Book and Manuscript Library, Yale University.
Marryat Family Papers, Uncat MSS. 104, Beinecke Rare Book and Manuscript Library, Yale University.
Mayes Family Papers, Harry Ransom Archive, University of Texas.
Public Record Office: Bill of Complaint Filed 10 June 1875. C16/997
Public Record Office: Divorce Court Proceedings, 1877. J77/186/4810.
Public Record Office: Divorce Court Proceedings, 1878. J77/209/5660.
Public Record Office: Marriage Certificate of Florence Marryat and Thomas Ross Church.
Public Record Office: Military Records, Madras Army.

Primary and Secondary Sources

A. H. M. W., 1871. *Glimpses of a Brighter Land*. London: Balliere, Tindall, and Cox.
A. Lady, 1880. "Feminine Foibles, Fancies, and Fashions". *Weekly Mail*, (15 May), p. 3.
Acton, William, 1862. *The Functions and Disorders of the Reproductive Organs in Childhood, Youth, Adult Age, and Advanced Life Considered in Their Physiological, Social, and Moral Relations*. London: John Churchill.
Adams, Kimberly Van Esveld, 2001. *Our Lady of Victorian Feminism: The Madonna in the Work of Anna Jameson, Margaret Fuller, and George Eliot*. Ohio University Press.

Anderson, Nancy Fix, 2002. "The Rebel of the Family: The Life of Eliza Lynn Linton". In *The Rebel of the Family*, edited by Deborah T. Meem, 428–40. Ontario: Broadview Press.

Auerbach, Nina, 1990. *Woman and the Demon: The Life of a Victorian Myth*. Cambridge, Mass.: Harvard University Press.

Austin, Alfred, 1870. "Our Novels". *Temple Bar* 29 (June), pp. 410–24.

Barker, Pat, 2018. "For Women, European Literature Begins with Silence", *The Guardian* (1 September), sec. Online Review.

Barrow, Logie, 1986. *Independent Spirits: Spiritualism and English Plebeians, 1850–1910*. London; New York: Routledge & Kegan Paul.

Barsham, Diana, 1992. *The Trial of Woman: Feminism and the Occult Sciences in Victorian Literature and Society*. Basingstoke: Macmillan.

Bashford, Alison, 1998. *Purity and Pollution: Gender, Embodiment and Victorian Medicine*. Basingstoke, Hampshire: Macmillan Press.

Bassett, Troy J., 2010. "Living on the Margin: George Bentley and the Economics of the Three-Volume Novel, 1865–70". *Book History* 13 (January), pp. 58–79.

"Belles Lettres", 1882. *Westminster Review* (October), pp. 574–89.

"Belles Lettres", 1892. *Westminster Review* 138 (July), pp. 687–92.

Beresford Hope, A. J. B., 1880. *Strictly Tied Up*. 3 vols. London: Hurst & Blackett.

Bernstein, Susan David, 1997. *Confessional Subjects: Revelations of Gender and Power in Victorian Literature and Culture*. University of North Carolina Press.

Bittner, Donald F., 2013. "Florence Marryat and Lieutenant Colonel Francis Lean, RMLI", (5 July), email.

Black, Helen C., 1893 [2011]. *Notable Women Authors of the Day*. Edited by Catherine Pope and Troy Bassett. Brighton: Victorian Secrets.

Blackstone, Sir William, and William Draper Lewis, 1922. *Commentaries on the Laws of England: In Four Books*. 4 vols. Philadelphia: George T. Bisel.

Bland, Lucy, 2002. *Banishing the Beast*. New York: Tauris Parke.

Bodenheimer, Rosemarie, 1988. *The Politics of Story in Victorian Social Fiction*. Ithaca: Cornell University Press.

Bonhams, 2017. "Dickens (Charles) Autograph Letter Signed ('Charles Dickens'), to 'Dear Miss Marryat', Concerning a Story That He Refuses to Publish, Tavistock House, 13 February 1860". n.d. [Accessed 30 October]. https://www.bonhams.com/auctions/23459/lot/169/.

Bordman, Gerald and Richard Norton, 2011. *American Musical Theatre: A Chronicle*. New York: Oxford University Press.

Bradstock, Andrew, Sean Gill, Anne Hogan, and Sue Morgan, eds. 2000. *Masculinity and Spirituality in Victorian Culture*. Basingstoke: Palgrave Macmillan.

Braude, Ann, 1985. "Spirits Defend the Rights of Women: Spiritualism and Changing Sex Roles in Nineteenth-Century America". In *Women, Religion and Social Change*, edited by Yvonne Yazbeck Haddad and Ellison Banks Findly, Albany: State University of New York Press, pp. 419–32.

———. 1996. *Radical Spirits: Spiritualism and Women's Rights in Nineteenth-Century America*. Boston, Mass: Beacon Press.

Brown, Isaac Baker, 1866. *On the Curability of Certain Forms of Insanity, Epilepsy, Catalepsy and Hysteria in Females*. London: Robert Hardwicke.

Browning, Robert. 2009. 'Porphyria's Lover'. In *The Major Works*, edited by Adam Roberts, 122–24. Oxford World's Classics. Oxford: Oxford University Press.

Buchanan, Robert, 1862. "Society's Looking-Glass". *Temple Bar* (August), pp. 129–37.

Buck, W. D., 1867. "A Raid on the Uterus". *New York Medical Journal* 5 (August), pp. 464–65.

Caine, Barbara, 1993. *Victorian Feminists*. Oxford: Oxford University Press.

Carnell, Jennifer, 2000. *The Literary Lives of M. E. Braddon*. Hastings: The Sensation Press.

Carter, Robert Brudenell, 1853. *On the Pathology and Treatment of Hysteria*. London: John Churchill.

"Charles Dickens Sent This Sassy Reply to Writer Florence Marryat | Metro News". n.d. [Accessed 30 October 2017]. http://metro.co.uk/2016/03/06/charles-dickens-sent-this-sassy-reply-to-a-wannabe-writer-5736987/.

Chase, Karen, and Michael Levenson, 2000. *The Spectacle of Intimacy: A Public Life for the Victorian Family*. Princeton, New Jersey: Princeton University Press.

Church, Ethel, 1899. "The Real Florence Marryat. By Her Daughter". *St Paul's: An Illustrated Journal of the Day* (December), pp. 588–89.

Church, Eva Ross, 1888. *An Actress's Love Story*. London: F. V. White & Co.

Cobbe, Frances Power, 1868. "'Criminals, Idiots, Women, and Minors'". *Fraser's Magazine* 78, 468, pp. 777–94.

———. 1881. "The Medical Profession and Its Morality". *Modern Review* II (April), pp. 296–328.

Colley, Linda, 1996. *Britons: Forging the Nation 1707–1837*. London: Vintage.

Collins, Wilkie, 1889. *The Legacy of Cain*. 3 vols. London: Chatto & Windus.

———, 1886 [1994]. *The Evil Genius*. Edited by Graham Law. Ontario: Broadview Press.

Cooke, Nicholas Francis, 1890. *Satan in Society*. Chicago: C. F. Vent.

Constantini, Mariaconcetta, 2013. "Abnormal Female Appetites in Wilkie Collins and Florence Marryat", *Il Confronto Letterario*, 59, 1, pp. 81–96.

"The Court of Bankruptcy", 1871. *The Times* (28 September), p. 9.

Craik, Dinah, 1858 [nd]. *A Woman's Thoughts About Women*. London: Hurst & Blackett.

———. 1870. *A Brave Lady*. London: Hurst & Blackett.

Cvetkovich, Ann. 1992. *Mixed Feelings: Feminism, Mass Culture, and Victorian Sensationalism*. New Brunswick: Rutgers University Press.

Dally, Ann, 1991. *Women Under the Knife: A History of Surgery*. London: Hutchinson Radius.

Danby, Frank, 1887. *Dr Phillips: A Maida Vale Idyll*. London: Vizetelly & Co.

Davidoff, Leonore, and Catherine Hall. 2002. *Family Fortunes: Men and Women of the English Middle Class 1780–1850*. Abingdon, Oxon: Routledge.

Davis, Octavia, 2007. "Morbid Mothers: Gothic Heredity in Florence Marryat's *The Blood of the Vampire*". In *Horrifying Sex: Essays on Sexual Difference in Gothic Literature*, edited by Ruth Bienstock Anolik. Jefferson; North Carolina; London: McFarland & Company, pp. 40–54.

Depledge, Greta, 2011. "Ideologically Challenging: Florence Marryat and Sensation Fiction". In *A Companion to Sensation Fiction*, edited by Pamela K. Gilbert. Chichester, West Sussex: Blackwell, pp. 306–18.

———, 2013. "Experimental Medicine, Marital Harmony and Florence Marryat's *An Angel of Pity* (1898)". *Women's Writing* 20, 2, pp. 219–34.

Dever, Carolyn, 2006. *Death and the Mother from Dickens to Freud: Victorian Fiction and the Anxiety of Origins*. Cambridge; New York: Cambridge University Press.

Dickens, Charles. 2011. *Bleak House*. Edited by Patricia Ingham. Peterborough, Ont.: Broadview Press.

'Displaced Memories of Slavery and Slave-Ownership | Legacies of British Slave-Ownership'. n.d. Accessed 7 November 2017. https://lbsatucl.wordpress.com/2013/05/09/displaced-memories-of-slavery-and-slave-ownership-2/.

Dickerson, Vanessa, 1996. *Victorian Ghosts in the Noontide: Women Writers and the Supernatural*. Columbia: University of Missouri Press.

Dijkstra, Bram, 1986. *Idols of Perversity: Fantasies of Feminine Evil in Fin-De-Siècle Culture*. New York: Oxford University Press.

Dolin, Tim, 1997. *Mistress of the House: Women of Property in the Victorian Novel*. Aldershot: Ashgate.

Dolman, Frank, 1891. "Miss Florence Marryat at Home". *Myra's Journal: The Lady's Monthly Magazine* XVII, 5, pp. 1–2.

Doran, John, 1866. "For Ever and Ever". *The Athenaeum* (6 October), pp. 427–8.

Downey, Edmund, 1905. *Twenty Years Ago: A Book of Anecdotes Illustrating Literary Life in London*. London: Hurst & Blackett.

"The Dream That Stayed", 1896. *The Academy* (12 December), p. 528.

Easlea, Brian, 1981. *Science and Sexual Oppression: Patriarchy's Confrontation with Woman and Nature*. London: Weidenfeld and Nicolson.

Eisenbud, Jule, 1983. "The Case of Florence Marryat". In *Parapsychology and the Unconscious*. Berkeley: North Atlantic Books, pp. 209–26.

Eliot, George. 2005. *Adam Bede*. Edited by Mary Waldron. Peterborough, Ont.: Broadview Press.

Eliot, George, 1874. *Middlemarch: A Study of Provincial Life*. Edinburgh and London: William Blackwood & Sons.

Engelhardt, Carol Marie, 2004. "Mother Mary and the Victorian Protestants". In *The Church and Mary*, edited by R. N. Swanson. Rochester, NY: Ecclesiastical History Society/Boydell Press, pp. 298–307.

"Exeter Guildhall – Wednesday", 1858. *Trewman's Exeter Flying Post* (4 February), p. 5.

"The Fair-Haired Alda", 1880a. *The Athenaeum* (19 June), p. 788.
"The Fair-Haired Alda", 1880b. *The Spectator* (14 August), p. 1044.
Faithfull, Emily, 1867. "Dr Mary Walker and Dr Elizabeth Blackwell and Miss Garett". *Victoria Magazine* 8, pp. 232–3.
"The Farewell Séance of Katie King, The Spirit", 1874. *The Spiritualist* (29 May), pp. 258–9.
Farnell, Kim, 2005. *Mystical Vampire: The Life and Works of Mabel Collins*. Oxford: Mandrake.
Ferguson, Christine, 2012. *Determined Spirits: Heredity and Racial Regeneration in Anglo-American Spiritualist Writing, 1848–1930*. Edinburgh: Edinburgh University Press.
"Florence Marryat on Marriage", 1898. *Sacramento Daily Record-Union* (3 March), p. 6.
"For Ever and Ever", 1866a. *Saturday Review* (6 October), pp. 432–3.
"For Ever and Ever", 1866b. *The Spectator* (20 October), pp. 1171–2.
Forman, Ross G, 2011. "Queer Sensation". In *A Companion to Sensation Fiction*, edited by Pamela K. Gilbert. Chichester, West Sussex: Blackwell, pp. 414–29.
Forster, John, 1873. *The Life of Charles Dickens*. 3 vols. Philadelphia: Lippincott & Co.
Foxcroft, Louise, 2009. *Hot Flushes, Cold Science: The History of the Modern Menopause*. London: Granta.
Fryckstedt, Monica Correa, 1989. *On the Brink: English Novels of 1866*. Uppsala: University of Uppsala.
Furniss, Harry, 1923. *Some Victorian Women, Good, Bad, and Indifferent*. London: J. Lane the Bodley Head.
Gaskell, Elizabeth Cleghorn. 2008. *Ruth*. Edited by Alan Shelston. Oxford: Oxford University Press. Gibbons, Stella, 1998. *Cold Comfort Farm*. London: Penguin.
Gilbert, Pamela K., 1997. *Disease, Desire, and the Body in Victorian Women's Popular Novels*. Cambridge: Cambridge University Press.
Gill, Joanne, 2004. "The Imperial Anxieties of a Nineteenth-Century Bigamy Case". *History Workshop Journal* 57, pp. 58–78.
Gissing, George, 1904. *The Private Papers of Henry Ryecroft*. London: Archibald Constable.
Gleadle, Kathryn, 1995. *The Early Feminists*. Basingstoke: Macmillan Press.
Glendinning, Victoria, 1993. *Trollope*. London: Pimlico.
Gribble, Francis, 1929. *Seen in Passing: A Volume of Personal Reminiscences*. London: Ernest Benn.
Griffin, Ben, 2012. *The Politics of Gender in Victorian Britain: Masculinity, Political Culture and the Struggle for Women's Rights*. Cambridge University Press.
Grossmith, George, 1888 [2008]. *A Society Clown: Reminiscences by George Grossmith*. Bristol: J. W. Arrowsmith.
———, 1892 [2008]. *The Diary of a Nobody*. Oxford: Oxford University Press.
Hall, Catherine, 2018. "Gendering Property, Racing Capital". In *History After*

Hobsbawm: *Writing the Past for the Twenty-First Century*, edited by John H. Arnold, Matthew Hilton, and Jan Ruger. Oxford: Oxford University Press, pp. 17–34.

Hall, Trevor, 1962. *The Spiritualists: The Story of Florence Cook and William Crookes*. London: Gerald Duckworth & Co.

Hamilton, C. J., 1900. "Florence Marryat". *Womanhood* 3, pp. 2–5.

Hammerton, A. James, 1992. *Cruelty and Companionship: Conflict in Nineteenth-Century Married Life*. London: Routledge.

Hardy, Iza Duffus. 1890. *A New Othello*. London: F V White & Co.

Hennessey, Val, 1989. "The Darkened Room". *Daily Mail* (18 May), p. 31.

Herringer, Carol Engelhardt, 2008. *Victorians and the Virgin Mary: Religion and Gender in England, 1830–1885*. Manchester: Manchester University Press.

"Holborn Theatre", 1872. *The Athenaeum* (12 October), p. 72.

Holcombe, Lee, 1983. *Wives and Property: Reform of the Married Women's Property Law in Nineteenth-Century England*. Oxford: Martin Robertson.

Holmes, Rachel, 2002. *Scanty Particulars: The Life of Dr James Barry*. London: Viking.

Horstman, Allen, 1985. *Victorian Divorce*. London: Palgrave.

"How They Loved Him", 1882. *The Spectator* (23 September), p. 1234.

Hughes, Winifred, 1980. *The Maniac in the Cellar*. Princeton: Princeton University Press.

Hull, Simone, 2010. "Florence Marryat", 14 April. Email.

Humpherys, Anne, 1999. "Breaking Apart: The Early Victorian Divorce Novel". In *Victorian Women Writers and the Woman Question*, edited by Nicola Thompson. Cambridge: Cambridge University Press, pp. 42–59.

Hurley, Kelly, 1990. "Hereditary Taint and Cultural Contagion: The Social Etiology of *Fin-de-Siècle* Degeneration Theory". *Nineteenth-Century Contexts* 14, 2, pp. 193–214.

"The Idlers Club", 1893. *The Idler* (July), pp. 229–41.

Jalland, Patricia, and John Hooper, 1986. *Women from Birth to Death: The Female Life Cycle in Britain 1830–1914*. Brighton: Harvester.

Jewsbury, Geraldine, 1866. "New Novels". *The Athenaeum* (17 February), p. 233.

Jordan, Jane, 2011a. "Ouida". In *A Return to the Common Reader: Print Culture and the Novel, 1850–1900*, edited by Beth Palmer and Adelene Buckland. Farnham, Surrey: Ashgate, pp. 37–54.

———, 2011b. "The Law and Sensation". In *A Companion to Sensation Fiction*, edited by Pamela K. Gilbert. Chichester, West Sussex: Blackwell, pp. 507–15.

———, 2016. "Julia Frankau's *A Babe in Bohemia* (1889) and the Rehabilitation of Dr Heywood Smith" (presented at "Victorian Popular Genres", Victorian Popular Fiction Association Annual Conference, London).

Joseph, Tony, 1982. *George Grossmith: Biography of a Savoyard*. Bristol: Tony Joseph.

Kenealy, Arabella, 1893. *Dr Janet of Harley Street*. London: Digby, Long & Co.

King, Viva.,1976. *The Weeping and the Laughter*. London: Macdonald and Jane's.

BIBLIOGRAPHY

Kingsley, Charles, 1851. *Yeast: A Problem*. London: John W Parker.

———, 1894. *Charles Kingsley: His Letters and Memories of His Life*. 2 vols. London: Macmillan.

Kontou, Tatiana, 2012. "The Case of Florence Marryat". In *The Ashgate Research Companion to Nineteenth-Century Spiritualism and the Occult*, edited by Tatiana Kontou and Sarah Willburn. Farnham: Ashgate, pp. 221–29.

Lamont, Peter, 2006. *The First Psychic: The Peculiar Mystery of a Notorious Victorian Wizard*. London: Abacus.

Landow, George P., 1979. *Approaches to Victorian Autobiography*. Athens, Ohio: Ohio University Press.

"The Late Miss Florence Marryat", *The Era*, 4 November 1899, p. 13.

Law, Graham, 2000. *Serializing Fiction in the Victorian Press*. Basingstoke: Palgrave.

Leckie, Barbara, 1999. *Culture and Adultery: The Novel, the Newspaper, and the Law, 1857–1914*. Philadelphia: University of Pennsylvania Press.

Levine, Philippa, 1987. *Victorian Feminism, 1850–1900*. London: Hutchinson Education.

"Library Table", 1892. *The Lancet* (17 December), p. 1394.

Linton, Eliza Lynn, 1868. "The Girl of the Period". *Saturday Review* (14 March), p. 340.

———, 1879. *Under Which Lord?* 3 vols. London: Chatto & Windus.

———, 1885 [2011]. *The Autobiography of Christopher Kirkland*. Edited by Deborah T. Meem and Kate Holterhoff. Brighton: Victorian Secrets.

"The London Theatres", 1881. *The Era* (19 February), p. 6.

Lush, Montague, 1901. "Changes in the Law Affecting the Rights, Status, and Liabilities of Married Women". In *Twelve Lectures on the Changes in the Law of England During the Nineteenth Century*. London: Macmillan and Co., pp. 342–378.

Machen, Arthur, and Roger Luckhurst. 2005. "The Great God Pan". In *Late Victorian Gothic Tales*. Oxford: Oxford University Press, pp. 183–233.

Marryat, Florence, 1865a. *Love's Conflict*. 3 vols. London: Richard Bentley & Son.

———, 1865b. *Too Good for Him*. 3 vols. London: Richard Bentley & Son.

———, 1865c. *Woman Against Woman*. 3 vols. London: Richard Bentley.

———, 1866. *For Ever and Ever: A Drama of Life*. 3 vols. London: Richard Bentley.

———, 1867. *The Confessions of Gerald Estcourt*. 3 vols. Leipzig: Bernhard Tauchnitz.

———, 1868a. *Gup: Sketches of Anglo-Indian Life and Character*. London: Richard Bentley.

———, 1868b. "The Box with the Iron Clamps". *London Society* 13, pp. 77–8.

———, 1869a. *The Girls of Feversham*. London: Richard Bentley.

———, 1869b. *Nelly Brooke: A Homely Story*. 2 vols. Leipzig: Bernhard Tauchnitz.

———, 1869c. *Veronique*. Leipzig: Bernhard Tauchnitz.

———, 1870a. *Petronel*. 3 vols. London: Richard Bentley.

———, 1870b. *The Poison of Asps*. Leipzig: Bernhard Tauchnitz.

———, 1870c. *The Prey of the Gods*. Leipzig: Bernhard Tauchnitz.

———, 1872. *Life and Letters of Captain Marryat*. Leipzig: Bernhard Tauchnitz.
———, 1874 [nd]. *Open! Sesame!* London: R E King & Co.
———, 1876a. "A Lucky Disappointment". In *A Lucky Disappointment and Other Stories*. Leipzig: Bernhard Tauchnitz, pp. 7–118.
———, 1876b [2009]. *Her Father's Name*. Edited by Greta Depledge. Brighton: Victorian Secrets.
———, 1876c. *My Own Child*. London: Richard Edward King.
———, 1877 [nd]. *A Harvest of Wild Oats*. London: The Standard Library Company.
———, 1878. *Her World Against a Lie*. 3 vols. London: Samuel Tinsley & Co.
———, 1879. "To Henry Irving", letter 16 March. THM/37/7/30, Henry Irving Foundation Centenary Project http://www.henryirving.co.uk [accessed 12 April 2010].
———, 1880. *The Fair-Haired Alda*. London: Tinsley & Co.
———, 1881. *With Cupid's Eyes*. London: Tinsley & Co.
———, 1882a. *How They Loved Him*. 3 vols. London: F. V. White & Co.
———, 1882b. "The Majesty of Work: A Paper Read by Florence Marryat at a Meeting of the Church and Stage Guild on Thursday, March 2nd, 1882". London: Women's Printing Society.
———, 1883. *The Ghost of Charlotte Cray, and Other Stories*. Leipzig: Tauchnitz.
———, 1885. "The School of Literary Art: Conducted by Florence Marryat". Prospectus. MSS.C/194.a.117. British Library.
———, 1886a [1891]. *Miss Harrington's Husband*. London: Hutchinson & Co.
———, 1886b. "Our Daily Bread". *The Era*. 7 August 1886, p.11.
———, 1886c. *Tom Tiddler's Ground*. London: Sonnenschein & Co.
———, 1887a. *A Daughter of the Tropics*. 2 vols. London: F. V. White & Co.
———, 1887b. *Driven to Bay*. 3 vols. London: F. V. White & Co.
———, 1888. *Gentleman and Courtier*. 3 vols. London: F. V. White & Co.
———, 1889 [nd]. *Mount Eden: A Romance*. London: Hutchinson & Co.
———, 1890a. *Blindfold*. 2 vols. Leipzig: Tauchnitz.
———, 1890b. *The Nobler Sex*. New York and London: Street & Smith.
———, 1891a. *A Fatal Silence*. New York: Hovendon Company.
———, 1891b. "Collaboration". *The Morning Post* (30 December), p. 3.
———, 1891c. *There Is No Death*. New York: National Book Company.
———, 1892. *How Like a Woman*. London: R. E. King & Co.
———, 1894a. [2009]. *The Dead Man's Message*. Edited by Greta Depledge. Brighton: Victorian Secrets.
———, 1894b. *The Hampstead Mystery*. 3 vols. London: F. V. White & Co.
———, 1894c. *The Spirit World*. New York: Charles B. Reed.
———, 1895a. *At Heart a Rake*. London: H. Cox.
———, 1895b. *The Beautiful Soul*. New York: The Cassell Publishing Co.
———, 1896a. *The Dream That Stayed*. London: Hutchinson & Co.
———, 1896b. *The Strange Transfiguration of Hannah Stubbs*. Leipzig: Bernhard Tauchnitz.

———, 1897a [2010]. *The Blood of the Vampire*. Edited by Greta Depledge. Brighton: Victorian Secrets.
———, 1897b. *In the Name of Liberty*. London: Digby & Long.
———, 1898a. *An Angel of Pity*. London: Hutchinson & Co.
———, 1898b. "The Countess of Sorrento". In *The Summer Holiday*. London: Bliss, Sands & Co.
———, 1899. *A Rational Marriage*. New York: F. M. Buckles & Company.
Mason, Diane Elizabeth, 2008. *The Secret Vice: Masturbation in Victorian Fiction and Medical Culture*. Manchester: Manchester University Press.
Maunder, Andrew, 2004. *Varieties of Women's Sensation Fiction, 1855–1890*. 6 vols. London: Pickering & Chatto.
McKenna, Neil, 2013. *Fanny and Stella: The Young Men Who Shocked Victorian England*. London: Faber.
"Medical Annotation". 1866. *The Lancet* 88, 2253, pp. 498–502.
Melnyk, Julie, 2003. "'Mighty Victims': Women Writers and the Feminization of Christ". *Victorian Literature and Culture* 31, 1, pp. 131–57.
———, 2008. *Victorian Religion: Faith and Life in Britain*. Westport, Conn: Praeger.
"A Military Divorce Case", 1878. *Reynold's Newspaper* (10 November), p. 5.
Mill, John Stuart, 1859 [2006]. *On Liberty and The Subjection of Women*. Edited by Alan Ryan. London; New York: Penguin.
"Miss Florence Marryat's New Novel", 1880. *Pall Mall Gazette* (7 August), p. 11.
"Mistakes of Marriage", 1898. *Daily Mail* (26 January), p. 3.
Mitchell, Sally, 1977. "Sentiment and Suffering: Women's Recreational Reading in the 1860s". *Victorian Studies* 21, 1, pp. 29–45.
———, 1981. *The Fallen Angel: Chastity, Class and Women's Reading 1835–1880*. Bowling Green, Ohio: Bowling Green University Popular Press.
Moore, Harry Gage, 1866. "Clitoridectomy". *The Lancet* 87, 2234, p. 699.
Moran, Maureen, 2007. *Catholic Sensationalism and Victorian Literature*. Liverpool: Liverpool University Press.
Moscucci, Ornella, 1990. *The Science of Woman: Gynaecology and Gender in England, 1800–1929*. Cambridge: Cambridge University Press.
———, 1996. "Clitoridectomy, Circumcision, and the Politics of Sexual Pleasure in Mid-Victorian Britain". In *Sexualities in Victorian Britain*, edited by Andrew H. Miller and James Eli Adams. Bloomington and Indianapolis: Indiana University Press, pp. 60–76.
Mumm, Susan, 1999. *Stolen Daughters, Virgin Mothers: Anglican Sisterhoods in Victorian Britain*. London; New York: Leicester University Press.
Murphy, Patricia, 2006. *In Science's Shadow: Literary Constructions of Late Victorian Women*. Columbia: University of Missouri Press.
Nead, Lynda, 1988. *Myths of Sexuality: Representations of Women in Victorian Britain*. Oxford: Basil Blackwell.
"Nelly Brooke", 1868. *The Spectator* (21 November), pp. 1378–9.
"New Novels", 1886. *The Graphic* (27 November), p. 582.

"New Novels", 1896a. *The Academy* (9 May), pp. 382–3.
"New Novels", 1896b. *The Athenaeum* (28 November), p. 752.
Newey, Kate, 2001. "Women's Playwriting and the Popular Theatre in the Late Victorian Era, 1870–1900". In *Feminist Readings of Victorian Popular Texts*. Farnham, Surrey: Ashgate, pp. 147–67.
———, 2005. *Women's Theatre Writing in Victorian Britain*. Basingstoke, Hampshire; New York: Palgrave Macmillan.
Noble, James Ashcroft, 1886. "New Novels". *The Academy* (6 November), pp. 304–5.
"Novels of the Week", 1890. *The Athenaeum* (20 September), p. 381–2.
"Novels of the Week", 1891. *The Athenaeum* (12 September), p. 349.
"Novels of the Week", 1892. *The Athenaeum* (12 November), p. 660.
O'Brien Hill, Georgina, 2008. "'Above the Breath of Suspicion': Florence Marryat and the Shadow of the Fraudulent Trance Medium". *Women's Writing* 15, 3, pp. 333–47.
"Obituary: Florence Marryat", 1899. *The Times* (28 October): 8.
Offen, Karen, 1988. "Defining Feminism: A Comparative Historical Approach". *Signs* 14, 1, pp. 119–57.
Old Bailey Proceedings Online (www.oldbaileyonline.org, version 7.2), May 1871, trial of WILLIAM BRADLEY (20) (t18710501-404) [Accessed 8 November 2017]
Oliphant, Margaret, 1856. "The Laws Concerning Women". *Blackwood's Edinburgh Magazine* 79, pp. 379–87.
———, 1863. "Novels". *Blackwood's Edinburgh Magazine* 94 (August) pp. 168–83.
———, 1867a. *Madonna Mary*. 3 vols. London: Hurst & Blackett.
———, 1867b. "Novels". *Blackwood's Edinburgh Magazine* 102 (September), pp. 257–80.
———, 1880. "The Grievances of Woman". *Fraser's Magazine* 21 (May) pp. 698–710.
O'Malley, Patrick R., 2006. *Catholicism, Sexual Deviation and Victorian Gothic Culture*. Cambridge: Cambridge University Press.
Oppenheim, Janet, 1985. *The Other World: Spiritualism and Psychical Research in England, 1850–1914*. Cambridge: Cambridge University Press.
Orens, John Richard, 2003. *Stewart Headlam's Radical Anglicanism: The Mass, the Masses, and the Music Hall*. Urbana & Chicago: University of Illinois Press.
Ouida, 1880 [2005]. *Moths*. Edited by Natalie Schroeder. Ontario: Broadview Press.
Overton, John W., 1882. "The Majesty of Work". *The Women's Union Journal: The Organ of the Women's Protective and Provident League*, 77, p. 51.
Owen, Alex, 1989 [2004]. *The Darkened Room: Women, Power, and Spiritualism in Late Victorian England*. Chicago: University of Chicago Press.
Palmer, Beth, 2009. "'Chieftaness', 'Great Duchess', 'Editress!' 'Mysterious Being!': Performing Editorial Identities in Florence Marryat's *London Society Magazine*". *Victorian Periodicals Review* 42, 2, pp. 136–54.

Parry, Noel, and José Parry, 1976. *The Rise of the Medical Profession: A Study of Collective Social Mobility*. London: Croom Helm.

Paxton, Amanda, 2013. "Charles Kingsley's Saintly Trials and Husbandly Duties". *Journal of Victorian Culture* 18, 2, pp. 213–29.

Pearsall, Ronald, 2003. *The Worm in the Bud: The World of Victorian Sexuality*. Stroud: Sutton Publishing.

Peterson, Linda H., 2009. *Becoming a Woman of Letters: Myths of Authorship and Facts of the Victorian Market*. Princeton University Press.

"Petronel", 1870. *The Spectator* (5 November), p. 1328.

Pocock, Tom, 2000. *Captain Marryat: Seaman, Writer and Adventurer*. London: Chatham.

Poovey, Mary, 1988. *Uneven Developments: The Ideological Work of Gender in Mid-Victorian England*. Chicago: University of Chicago Press.

Pope, Catherine, 2014. "The Regulation of Female Identity in the Novels of Florence Marryat" (Thesis, University of Sussex).

———, 2017. "'[T]He Chains That Gall Them': Marital Violence in the Novels of Florence Marryat", in *For Better, For Worse: Marriage in Victorian Novels by Women*, ed. by Carolyn Lambert and Marion Shaw. New York: Routledge, pp. 142–55.

———, forthcoming. "'More like a Woman Stuck into Boy's Clothes': Transcendent Femininity in Florence Marryat's *Her Father's Name*", in *British Women's Writing from Brontë to Bloomsbury*, ed. by Carolyn W. de la L. Oulton and Adrienne E. Gavin, 5 vols, London: Palgrave Macmillan, np.

Poster, Carol, 1996. "Oxidization Is a Feminist Issue: Acidity, Canonicity, and Popular Victorian Female Authors". *College English* 58, 3, pp. 287–306.

Powell, Kerry, 1997. *Women and the Victorian Theatre*. Cambridge: Cambridge University Press.

"The Prey of the Gods", 1871. *The Athenaeum* (23 September), pp. 397–8.

"Purely Personal", 1894. *Hampshire Telegraph and Sussex Chronicle* (3 March), p. 9.

Pykett, Lyn, 1992. *The 'Improper' Feminine: The Women's Sensation Novel and the New Woman Writing*. London: Routledge.

Radway, Janice, 1984. *Reading the Romance: Women, Patriarchy, and Popular Literature*. Chapel Hill and London: University of North Carolina Press.

Reade, Charles, 1896. *A Woman-Hater*. London: Chatto & Windus.

"Report Summary: Women in the Labour Market, Two Decades of Change and Continuity | Institute for Employment Studies", 2017. http://www.employment-studies.co.uk/report-summaries/report-summary-women-labour-market-two-decades-change-and-continuity [Accessed 10 November]

Riddell, Charlotte, 1882 [2010]. *Weird Stories*, edited by Emma Liggins. Brighton: Victorian Secrets.

Riley, Denise. 1988. *Am I That Name?: Feminism and the Category of 'Women' in History*. Basingstoke: Macmillan.

Rossetti, Dante Gabrielle, 1878. *The Blessed Damozel*. Painting, housed at Lady Lever Art Gallery, Port Sunlight.

Rowell, Geoffrey, 1974. *Hell and the Victorians; a Study of the Nineteenth-Century Theological Controversies Concerning Eternal Punishment and the Future Life*. Oxford: Clarendon Press.

Rubinstein, David, 1991. *A Different World for Women: The Life of Millicent Garrett Fawcett*. Columbus: Ohio State University Press.

Ruzek, Sheryl Burt, 1978. *The Women's Health Movement: Feminist Alternatives to Medical Control*. New York: Praeger.

"Sad Immorality in High Life", 1878. *Monmouthshire Merlin* (15 November), p.3.

Sadleir, Michael, 1951. *XIX Century Fiction*. Vol. 1. Cambridge: Cambridge University Press.

Scull, Andrew T., 2009. *Hysteria: The Biography*. Oxford; New York: Oxford University Press.

Shanley, Mary Lyndon, 1993. *Feminism, Marriage and the Law in Victorian England*. Princeton, New Jersey: Princeton University Press.

Sheehan, Elizabeth, 1981. "Victorian Clitoridectomy: Isaac Baker Brown and His Harmless Operative Procedure". *Medical Anthropology Newsletter* 12, 4, pp. 9–15.

Showalter, Elaine, 1977 [1982]. *A Literature of Their Own: British Women Novelists from Brontë to Lessing*. London: Virago.

———, 1987. *The Female Malady: Women, Madness and English Culture 1830–1980*. London: Virago.

Smith, Heywood, 1900. *Practical Gynaecology: A Handbook of the Diseases of Women*. 2nd ed. London: Henry J. Glaisher.

"The Society of Authors", 1897. *The Manchester Guardian* (25 May), p. 7.

Southgate, Beverley C., 2009. *History Meets Fiction*. New York: Pearson Longman.

Sparks, Tabitha, 2009. *The Doctor in the Victorian Novel: Family Practices*. Farnham, Surrey: Ashgate.

Steinbach, Susie, 2004. *Women in England 1760–1914*. London: Weidenfeld & Nicolson.

Stevenson, Robert Louis. 2005. *The Strange Case of Dr Jekyll and Mr Hyde*. Edited by Martin A Danhay. Peterborough, Ont.: Broadview Press.

"The Suitors in Our Courts of Law and the Public", 1867. *The Times* (28 May), p.11.

Sutherland, J. A., 2009. *The Longman Companion to Victorian Fiction*. 2nd ed. Harlow, Essex: Longman.

Swan, Annie S. 1895. *Elizabeth Glen, MB: The Experiences of a Lady Doctor*. London: Hutchinson & Co.

———, 1897. *Mrs Keith Hamilton, MB*. London: Hutchinson & Co.

Swenson, Kristine, 2005. *Medical Women and Victorian Fiction*. Columbia: University of Missouri Press.

Tait, Lawson, 1889. *Diseases of Women and Abdominal Surgery*. Philadelphia: Lea Brothers.

Taylor, Barbara, 1983. *Eve and the New Jerusalem: Socialism and Feminism in the*

Nineteenth Century. London: Virago Press.
Taylor, Robert, 2010. *Medical Wisdom and Doctoring: The Art of 21st Century Practice.* New York: Springer.
Thompson, F. M. L., 1988. *The Rise of Respectable Society: A Social History of Victorian Britain 1830–1900.* London: Fontana.
Tilt, Edward John, 1882. *The Change of Life in Health and Disease: A Practical Treatise on the Nervous and Other Affections Incidental to Women at the Decline of Life.* Philadelphia: Lindsay & Blakiston.
———, 1918. *The Life of Sophia Jex-Blake.* London: Macmillan.
Tosh, John, 2007. *A Man's Place: Masculinity and the Middle-Class Home in Victorian England.* New Haven: Yale University Press.
Travers, Graham [Margaret Todd]. 1893. *Mona Maclean, Medical Student.* Edinburgh: William Blackwood & Sons.
Trollope, Anthony. 1884. *An Old Man's Love.* 2 vols. Edinburgh and London: William Blackwood & Sons.
Tromp, Marlene, 2003. "Spirited Sexuality: Sex, Marriage, and Victorian Spiritualism". *Victorian Literature and Culture* 31, 1, pp. 67–81.
———, 2007. *Altered States: Sex, Nation, Drugs, and Self-Transformation in Victorian Spiritualism.* New York: SUNY Press.
Turner, J., 1980. *Reckoning with the Beast: Animals, Pain, and Humanity in the Victorian Mind.* Johns Hopkins University Press.
Uglow, Jenny, 1989. "Introduction". In *Victorian Ghost Stories by Eminent Women Writers,* edited by Richard Dalby. New York: Carroll & Graf, pp. ix-xvii.
"Under Which Lord?", 1879. *Saturday Review* (29 November), p.668.
Ussher, Jane M., 1991. *Women's Madness: Misogyny or Mental Illness?* Hemel Hempstead: Harvester Wheatsheaf.
Vanita, Ruth, 1996. *Sappho and the Virgin Mary: Same-Sex Love and the English Literary Imagination.* New York: Columbia University Press.
Vicinus, Martha, 1980. *Suffer and Be Still: Women in the Victorian Age.* London.
Vickery, Amanda, 1993. "Golden Age to Separate Spheres? A Review of the Categories and Chronology of English Women's History". *The Historical Journal* 36, 2, pp. 383–414.
Walkowitz, Judith, 1980. *Prostitution and Victorian Society: Women, Class, and the State.* Cambridge: Cambridge University Press.
Ward, Ian, 2007. "The Case of Helen Huntingdon". *Criticism* 49, 2, pp. 151–82.
Warner, Marina, 2013. *Alone of All Her Sex: The Myth and Cult of the Virgin Mary.* Oxford: Oxford University Press.
Waterfield, Robin, 2003. *Hidden Depths: The Story of Hypnosis.* New York: Brunner-Routledge.
Wells, H. G. 1896 [2009]. *The Island of Doctor Moreau.* Edited by Mason Harris. Peterborough, Ont.: Broadview Press.
"What to Do with the Men: Miss Florence Marryat's Glimpse Ahead to the Year 1995", 1885. *New York Times* (16 May), p. 4.

Willburn, Sarah A., 2006. *Possessed Victorians: Extra Spheres in Nineteenth-Century Mystical Writings*. Aldershot: Ashgate.

Winter, Alison, 1995. "Harriet Martineau and the Reform of the Invalid in Victorian England". *The Historical Journal* 38, 3, pp. 597–616.

———, 1998. *Mesmerized: Powers of Mind in Victorian Britain*. Chicago: University of Chicago Press.

"Women and University Degrees", 1874. *Saturday Review* (18 July), pp.77–8.

Wood, Jane, 2001. *Passion and Pathology in Victorian Fiction*. Oxford: Oxford University Press.

Wood, Mrs. Henry [Ellen]. 1861 [2000]. *East Lynne*. Edited by Andrew Maunder. Ontario: Broadview Press.

"Women MPs and Parliamentary Candidates since 1945 | UK Political Info" <http://www.ukpolitical.info/FemaleMPs.htm> [accessed 10 November 2017]

Wynne, Deborah, 2011. *Women and Personal Property in the Victorian Novel*. Aldershot, Hants: Ashgate.

Yates, Nigel, 1999. *Anglican Ritualism in Victorian Britain, 1830–1910*. Oxford: Oxford University Press.

Zieger, Susan Marjorie, 2008. *Inventing the Addict: Drugs, Race, and Sexuality in Nineteenth-Century British and American Literature*. Amherst: University of Massachusetts Press.

Zola, Émile, 186 [1998]. *Thérèse Raquin*. Translated by Andrew Rothwell. Oxford; New York: Oxford University Press.

Index

Page references for endnotes are given in the format 179 n.2

abortion, 29
abuse, 50; of animals, 7, 83, 84, 87, 125; in marriage, 19, 84–7, 134, 145–6; sexual, 93–4, 175
acting/actors, 23–4, 26–8, 70–1
Acton, William, 106, 114
adaptations, 26–7
adultery, 19, 38–9, 40–1, 42–3, 46, 48
afterlife, 144–9
agency, 42, 103, 128, 136–40, 147; *see also* power
alimony, 44
All the Year Round (journal), 20
Angel of Pity, An, 100–3, 125
angels, 136, 144
Anglo-Catholicism, 131–2, 142–3
antifeminism, 40–1, 65, 96–7, 98–9, 142–4
At Heart a Rake, 7
Austin, Alfred, 3
authority: medical, 81–2, 86–7, 89–92, 100–3, 125–6; patriarchal, 90, 129–33, 146, 147–8; male, 144; spiritual, 151–2, 155
autobiographical fiction, 13–14
autonomy, 45–7, 51–3, 62–3, 71–2

bankruptcy, 66
Barrow, Logie, 130

Beautiful Soul, The, 31
Bentley, Richard, 20, 87
Beresford Hope, Alexander, *Strictly Tied Up*, 63
Bible scholarship, 130–1
bigamy, 40, 60
birth defects, 18–19, 50
bisexuality, 55, 112–14; *see also* homosexuality
Black, Helen C., 31
Blackwell, Elizabeth, 96
Blindfold, 93–4
Blood of the Vampire, The, 112–14, 115
bodies, of women, 8, 82, 105–6, 141, 158–9
Boulton and Park case, 166–7
"Box with the Iron Clamps", 19
Braddon, Mary, 4
Broughton, Rhoda, 4–5; *Cometh Up as a Flower*, 5
Brown, Isaac Baker, 116–17, 119–21, 125
Brown-Séquard, Charles-Édouard, 83
Buchanan, Robert, 3–4

Caine, Barbara, 6–7
Catholicism *see* Anglo-Catholicism; Roman Catholicism
celibacy, 143

childbirth, 18–19, 50
children: death of, 18–19, 152–3, 159; custody of, 22–3, 41
Church, Edward, 21
Church, Ethel, "The Real Florence Marryat", 13
Church, Eva Ross, *An Actress's Love Story*, 29
Church, Florence Ross, 18–19, 152–3, 159
Church, Thomas Ross, 16–18, 20–1, 22–3, 24–5, 33
Church and State Guild, 74
Church of England, 127, 129–30
clairvoyants, 132–3, 153
clitoridectomy, 119–25
clothing *see* dress
Cobbe, Frances Power, 7, 76, 101
Collins, Wilkie: *The Evil Genius*, 42–3; *The Legacy of Cain*, 97–8
confession, 139
Confessions of Gerald Estcourt, The, 23, 44–6
consent, age of, 89, 180 n.19
Contagious Diseases Acts, 82, 83
convents, 134, 142–3
Cook, Florence, 155–7, 180 n.28
Cooke, Nicholas, 114
copyright, 27, 32, 61–2
"Countess of Sorrento, The", 77
coverture, 36–7, 62–3
Craik, Dinah Mulock, *A Brave Lady*, 64–5
Crookes, William, 156, 157
cross-dressing, 53–4, 116, 117–19, 166–7
Culverwell, Dr R. J., 119–21
Cumming, Lettice Anne, 24, 25
custody of children, 22–3, 41

Danby, Frank (Julia Frankau), *Dr Phillips*, 91–2
Darkened Room, The, 153

Daughter of the Tropics, A, 110–12
daughter-mother relationships, 16, 135, 137–8, 143
Davis, Octavia, 113
Dead Man's Message, The, 144–9
death, 92, 162–3; of children, 18–19, 152–3, 159; murder, 92, 123; afterlife, 144–9; *see also* spiritualism
debt, 66
Depledge, Greta, 5–6, 102
desire, 98
Dickens, Charles, 19–20, 23; *Bleak House*, 47
Dijkstra, Bram, 115
disease *see* illness; medicine
divorce, 22–3, 24–5, 28, 38–44, 119; *see also* marriage; matrimonial causes acts; separation, marital
doctors, 83–92, 94–5, 114, 119–21; as husbands, 84–7, 117, 124; women, 95–103; *see also* medicine
D'Oyly Carte company, 26
Dream that Stayed, The, 31, 48
dress: transvestism, 53–4, 116, 117–19, 166–7; rational, 96–7
Driven to Bay, 56

education of women, 15, 179 n.3
Eliot, George, *Middlemarch*, 84
equality: sexual, 38–9, 45–6, 48, 82, 174; in marriage, 71–2, 130, 148–9; *see also* property

Fair-Haired Alda, The, 43–4
family: critique of, 14–15; mother-daughter relationships, 16, 135, 137–8, 143; diverse forms of, 37–8; fathers/fatherhood, 135–6, 145, 148; *see also* mothers/motherhood
Fatal Silence, The, 19
fathers/fatherhood, 135–6, 145, 148; *see also* patriarchy
femininity, 8, 99–100, 140, 141–2; of

INDEX

men, 52–3, 164–5, 169–70
feminism, 15, 29, 176–7; of Marryat, 4–6, 7–8, 26, 29, 176–7; and sensation fiction, 4–6, 9–10; Victorian, 6–10; gynocracy, 7, 173–5; suffrage, 7, 68, 175; antifeminism, 40–1, 65, 96–7, 98–9, 142–4; and property rights, 78–9; and religion, 129, 130, 137–8, 143, 149–50, 169
Ferguson, Christine, 147–8
fiction: sensation, 2–6, 9–10; autobiographical, 13–14
For Ever and Ever, 107–9
Frankau, Julia (Frank Danby), *Dr Phillips*, 91–2
Fraser, Mrs Alexander, 59–60
Fryckstedt, Monica, 108–9

Gaskell, Elizabeth, 64, 92–3; *Ruth*, 49, 51
gender: construction of, 8–9; roles, 8–9, 49–50, 117–19, 159; disruption, 52–3, 66, 98–9, 117–19, 159, 164–6, 169–70; and dress, 96–7; of angels, 136; and Spiritualism, 163–71; *see also* femininity; masculinity
General Medical Council, 81
Gentleman and Courtier, 30–1, 72, 73
"Ghost of Charlotte Cray, The", 163
Gilbert, Pamela K., 4–5, 177
Gilbert, W. S., *The Palace of Truth*, 27
Girls of Feversham, The, 16
Greg, W. R., 75–6
Griffin, Ben, 128, 150
Grossmith, George, 24, 154
Gup, 17–18
gynaecology, 29, 105–6, 119–25
gynocracy, 7, 173–5

Hall, Trevor, 157
Hampstead Mystery, The, 132–3, 139
Hardy, Iza Duffus, *A New Othello*, 94–5

Harvest of Wild Oats, A, 19, 71–2
Hay, Mary Cecil, *Old Myddleton's Money*, 5
Headlam, Stewart, 74
Her Father's Name, 97, 116–19
Her World Against a Lie, 7, 26, 27, 67–70
heredity, 110–11, 114
Home, Daniel Dunglas, 169–70
homosexuality, 155–60, 164–7, 169–70; *see also* bisexuality; lesbianism
How Like a Woman!, 72, 73
How They Loved Him, 49–51
husbands: abusive, 19, 84–7, 134, 145–6; women's choice of, 43–4, 45–7; doctors as, 84–7, 117, 124
hypnotism, 92–5
hysteria, 106, 115–17, 122–4, 163

illegitimacy, 49–50
illness: of children, 18–19, 50; Contagious Diseases Acts, 82, 83; hysteria, 106, 115–17, 122–4, 163; *see also* medicine
imagery, animal, 113
In the Name of Liberty, 76–7
individuality, 62–3
inequality: separate spheres ideology, 37, 56; sexual, 38–9, 45–6, 48, 82, 174; *see also* marriage; property
inheritance, 17, 24–5, 38, 39, 61, 73
Irving, Henry, 26

Jewsbury, Geraldine, 3, 20, 87
Jex-Blake, Sophia, 97

Kenealy, Arabella, *Dr Janet of Harley Street*, 98–9
King, Viva, 160
Kingsley, Charles, 140–2; *Yeast*, 141–2

Lean, Francis, 24–6, 27, 28, 32, 70–1
legislation: Matrimonial Causes Act

(1857), 36, 38–40, 44, 56, 61;
Matrimonial Causes Act (1878), 44;
Medical Registration Act (1858),
81, 83, 92, 95; Public Worship
Regulation Act (1874), 131; *see also*
married women's property acts
lesbianism, 49, 54–5, 113–19, 141,
156–8, 167; *see also* homosexuality
Levine, Philippa, 7
Life and Letters of Captain Marryat, The,
15–16
Linton, Eliza Lynn: *The Autobiography
of Christopher Kirkland*, 14, 96–7;
Under Which Lord?, 142–4
London Society (journal), 21
Love Letters (show), 27–8
Love's Conflict, 5, 19, 20, 84
"Lucky Disappointment, A", 17
Lush, Montague, 35

Machen, Arthur, *The Great God Pan*, 84
"Majesty of Work, The" (lecture/
pamphlet), 27, 74–6
Mariolatry, 127–9, 133–41
marital violence, 19, 134
marriage, 7, 35–57; abusive, 19, 84–7,
134, 145–6; adultery, 19, 38–9,
40–1, 42–3, 46, 48; separation,
20–1, 28, 38, 44–5, 50, 59–60;
contracts, 22–3, 51–3, 63;
settlements, 22–3, 51–3, 63; and
age gaps, 30–1; coverture, 36–7,
62–3; monogamy, 36; bigamy, 40,
60; women's choices in, 43–4, 45–7;
alternatives to, 49–56, 74–5; female,
49; rational, 51–3; egalitarian,
71–2, 130, 148–9; reform, 71–2,
78; spiritual, 136–7, 138, 145; of
widows, 136–8, 140; women's power
in, 147–8, 161–3, 168–9; civil, 174;
see also divorce; husbands
Married Women's Property Acts, 60–7,
78–9; 1870 Act, 20–1, 59, 61–2,

68–9; 1882 Act, 27, 62–3
Marryat, Ann, 109–10
Marryat, Captain Frederick, 14, 15–16,
38
Marryat, Catherine (Shairp), 14,
15–16, 38
Marryat, Florence, 22–3; reputation,
1–2, 33–4, 176–7; feminism of,
4–6, 7–8, 26, 29, 176–7; biography,
8, 13–34, 109–10, 134, 179 n.2;
Thomas Ross Church, marriage to,
16–18, 20–1, 22–3, 24–5; in India,
17–18; children, 18–19; writing
career, 19–21, 23, 31–2; separation,
20–1, 28; plays, 21–2, 26; religion,
21–2, 31–2, 132, 134, 139, 149–50,
152–60; Catholicism, 21, 132, 134;
editor of *London Society*, 21; court
cases, 22–3; Spiritualism, 22, 31–2,
152–60; acting career, 23–4, 26–8;
earnings, 23, 33; divorce, 24–5;
Francis Lean, marriage to, 24–6, 27,
28, 32, 70–1; in USA, 28; public
speaking, 29; Herbert McPherson,
relationship with, 30, 57; death,
32–3; stage adaptations, 69–70
Marryat, Florence, works: *The Poison
of Asps*, 3; *Woman Against Woman*,
3, 20; *Love's Conflict*, 5, 19, 20,
84; *At Heart a Rake*, 7; *Her World
Against a Lie*, 7, 26, 27, 67–70;
"The Majesty of Work" (lecture/
pamphlet), 7, 74–6; *The Nobler Sex*,
13–14, 25, 31; *The Life and Letters of
Captain Marryat*, 15–16; *The Girls of
Feversham*, 16; *The Spirit World*, 16,
31, 131, 155; *Gup*, 17–18; "A Lucky
Disappointment", 17; "Box with the
Iron Clamps", 19; *The Fatal Silence*,
19; *A Harvest of Wild Oats*, 19,
71–2; *There Is No Death*, 19, 153;
Too Good for Him, 20; *Miss Chester*
(play), 21–2; *The Confessions of*

INDEX

Gerald Estcourt, 23, 44–6; *Veronique*, 23; *With Cupid's Eyes*, 25; *Miss Harrington's Husband (The Spiders of Society)*, 25, 70–1; *The Spiders of Society (Miss Harrington's Husband)*, 25, 70–1; *Love Letters* (show), 27–8; *Gentleman and Courtier*, 30–1, 72, 73; *The Beautiful Soul*, 31; *The Dream that Stayed*, 31, 48; *The Fair-Haired Alda*, 43–4; *The Prey of the Gods*, 46–7; *How They Loved Him*, 49–51; *Mount Eden*, 53–5, 72–3, 160; "The Mistakes of Marriage" (lecture/article), 55–6; *Driven to Bay*, 56; *Tom Tiddler's Ground*, 71; *How Like a Woman!*, 72, 73; *In the Name of Liberty*, 76–7; "The Countess of Sorrento", 77; *Nelly Brooke*, 84–7; *Blindfold*, 93–4; *Her Father's Name*, 97, 116–19; *An Angel of Pity*, 100–3, 125; *For Ever and Ever*, 107–9; *A Daughter of the Tropics*, 110–12; *The Blood of the Vampire*, 112–14, 115; *Petronel*, 121–3; *The Strange Transfiguration of Hannah Stubbs*, 123–5, 160–3; *The Hampstead Mystery*, 132–3, 139; *My Own Child*, 133–9; *The Darkened Room*, 153; *Open! Sesame!*, 163–71; "The Ghost of Charlotte Cray", 163
Marryat, Joseph, 109
Martineau, Harriet, 92
masculinity, 62–3, 140–2, 143, 166–9; of women, 66, 98–9, 166; lack of, 164–5, 169–70
masturbation, 114–19, 136, 138
Matrimonial Causes Acts: 1857 Act, 36, 38–40, 44, 56, 61; 1878 Act, 44
Maunder, Andrew, 4–5, 177
McPherson, Herbert, 30, 57
Medical Registration Act (1858), 81, 83, 92, 95
medication, 86–7

medicine, 81–104; gynaecology, 29, 105–6, 119–25; authority of, 81–2, 86–7, 89–92, 100–3, 125–6; regulation of, 81–2; and power, 82, 84–95; mesmerism, 92–5; quackery, 94–5; nurses, 100–1; and women's bodies, 105–6; and sexuality, 114; clitoridectomy, 119–25; ovariotomy, 120–1; *see also* doctors; illness
mediums, spirit, 123, 124–5, 132–3, 152–3, 155–7, 160–3, 169–70
men: feminine, 52–3, 164–5, 169–70; feminized, 52–4; weak, 52–4; authority of, 129–33; *see also* fathers/fatherhood; husbands
mesmerism, 92–5
Miss Chester (play), 21–2
Miss Harrington's Husband (The Spiders of Society), 25, 70–1
"Mistakes of Marriage, The" (lecture/article), 55–6
money, 44, 66; inheritance, 17, 24–5, 38, 39, 61, 73; marriage settlements, 22–3, 51–3, 63; women's control of, 61, 65–6, 70–3; *see also* property
monogamy, 36
mothers/motherhood, 133, 135–6; and daughters, 16, 135, 137–8, 143; childbirth, 18–19, 50; pregnancy, 18–19, 29, 49–50; single, 50–1, 136–7, 140; spiritual, 142–3, 146–7, 148–9
Mount Eden, 53–5, 72–3, 160
murder, 92, 123
My Lady (anonymous novel), 41
My Own Child, 133–9

Nelly Brooke, 84–7
Nobler Sex, The, 13–14, 25, 31
nuns, 142–3
nurses, 100–1

Offen, Karen, 6

Ogilvie, Charles, *The Lost Diamonds*, 27
Oliphant, Margaret, 3, 62; *Madonna Mary*, 140
Open! Sesame!, 163–71
Oppenheim, Janet, 160–1, 171
Ouida (Maria Louise Ramé), 4–5; *Moths*, 41–2, 49, 51
ovariotomy, 120–1
Overton, John W., 75, 76
Owen, Alex, 171

patriarchy, 90, 129–33, 147–8; and the law, 42; and medicine, 84–95; religious, 127–8, 129–33, 139; *see also* gynocracy
Penzance, Lord, 61, 131–2
Petronel, 87–92, 121–3
Poison of Asps, The, 3
polyamory, 55
power: medical, 81–2, 86–7, 89–92, 100–3, 125–6; and medicine, 82, 84–95; and mesmerism, 93–4; spiritual, 151–2, 155; *see also* patriarchy
power, of women: gynocracy, 7, 173–5; spiritual, 127, 128, 138; in marriage, 147–8, 161–3, 168–9
Powles, John, 18, 19
predation, sexual, 88–90, 91–2
pregnancy, 18–19, 29, 49–50
Prey of the Gods, The, 46–7
priests, 139, 142, 143
property, 59–79; money, 17, 24–5, 38, 39, 61, 73; legislation, 20–1, 27, 59, 60–7, 68–9; of married women, 59–67; women's control of, 61, 65–6, 70–3; and motherhood, 64–5
Public Worship Regulation Act (1874), 131
purgatory, 144–9
Pykett, Lyn, 4, 5, 177

quackery, 94–5

race, 110–14
racism, 109–14
Radway, Janice, 4, 177–8
Ramé, Maria Louise (Ouida), 4–5; *Moths*, 41–2, 49, 51
rape, 175–6
rational dress, 96–7
Rational Marriage, A, 51–3
Reade, Charles, *The Woman-Hater*, 98
religion, 127–50; Mariolatry, 127–9, 133–41; Anglicanism, 127, 129–30; Church of England, 127, 129–30; and feminism, 129, 130, 137–8, 143, 149–50, 169; Bible scholarship, 130–1; dissenting, 130; and women, 130, 142–3, 149–50, 154–5, 160, 170–1; Anglo-Catholicism, 131–2, 142–3; convents, 134, 142–3; ritual, 134; visions, 135, 136; angels, 136, 144; saints, 136, 138; confession, 139; priests, 139, 142, 143; Protestantism, 141–2; nuns, 142–3; afterlife, 144–9; purgatory, 144–9; gynocentric, 154–5, 160, 170–1; *see also* roman catholicism; spiritualism
Riddell, Charlotte, 65–7; "The Old House on Vauxhall Walk", 65–6; *Weird Stories*, 65–6; "Nut Bush Farm", 66
Riley, Denise, 7
Roman Catholicism, 127, 128, 131–4, 142–4; conversions, 21, 22, 132, 142; and Spiritualism, 149, 155
Russell, Dora, *Beneath the Wave*, 5

saints, 136, 138
School of Literary Art, 28–9
séances, 152–3, 155–60
sensation fiction, 2–6, 9–10
separate spheres ideology, 37, 56
separation, marital, 20–1, 28, 39, 44–5, 50, 59–60; *see also* divorce
sex, biological, 97, 98–9

sexology, 114
sexual double standard, 38–9, 45–6, 48, 82, 174
sexual predation, 88–90, 91–2
sexual violence, 93–4, 175
sexuality, 141; and marriage, 49–50; lesbianism, 49, 54–5, 113–19, 141, 156–8, 167; bisexuality, 55, 112–14; consent, age of, 89, 180 n.19; virginity, 89, 137, 141; and mesmerism, 92–4; desire, 98; of women, 106–9, 111, 112–21, 126; and race, 110–14; masturbation, 114–19, 136, 138; celibacy, 143; queer, 155–60; and Spiritualism, 155–60; homosexuality, 164–7, 169–70
Showalter, Elaine, 4, 5, 125, 177
Showers, Mary Rosina, 155–6, 158
single mothers, 50–1, 136–7, 140
Skene, Felicia, *Hidden Depths*, 5
slavery, 109–10
Smith, Dr Heywood, 92, 119, 125
social class, 161–3, 179 n.3
Society for Psychical Research (SPR), 155
Society of Authors, 32
speculum, 122
Spiders of Society, The (*Miss Harrington's Husband*), 25, 70–1
Spirit World, The, 16, 31, 131, 155
Spiritualism, 22, 31–2, 123, 130, 146–7, 151–71; mediums, 123, 124–5, 132–3, 152–3, 155–7, 160–3, 169–70; clairvoyants, 132–3, 153; and Catholicism, 149, 155; séances, 152–3, 155–60; critique of, 153–4; and queer sexuality, 155–60; and gender, 163–71
Stead, W. T., 92
Stevenson, Robert Louis, *Strange Case of Dr Jekyll and Mr Hyde*, 83
Strange Transfiguration of Hannah Stubbs, The, 123–5, 160–3
strength, of women, 52–4
subjectivity: feminine, 56; denial of, 84–7, 89–91, 101
suffrage, 7, 68, 175
Swan, Annie S.: *Elizabeth Glen MB*, 99; *Mrs Keith Hamilton MB*, 99

Tait, Dr Lawson, 125
taxation, 62
There Is No Death, 19, 153
Todd, Margaret (Graham Travers), *Mona Maclean, Medical Student*, 99–100
Tom Tiddler's Ground, 71
Too Good for Him, 20
transvestism, 53–4, 116, 117–19, 166–7
Trollope, Anthony: *An Old Man's Love*, 63–4; *Doctor Thorne*, 84
Tromp, Marlene, 148–9, 158–9

United States of America (USA), 28

vampirism, 112–14
Veronique, 23
violence, 19, 50, 93–4, 134, 175
Virgin Mary, 127–9, 133–41, 146–7, 149–50
virginity, 89, 137, 141
visions, 135, 136
vivisection, 7, 83, 84, 125
voting rights, 7, 68, 175

Walker, Mary, 96
weakness, of men, 52–4
wealth, 72–3
Wells, H. G., *The Island of Dr Moreau*, 84
widows/widowhood, 45–6, 133–4, 136–8, 140
Williams, Bessie, 31–2
With Cupid's Eyes, 25

wives, 62–3, 68–9, 85–6, 147–8, 161–3, 168–9
Woman Against Woman, 3, 20
"Woman of the Future" (lecture), 173–5
women: gynocracy, 7, 173–5; suffrage, 7, 68, 175; bodies of, 8, 82, 105–6, 141, 158–9; education of, 15, 179 n.3; divorced, 24–5, 40–2; work of, 27, 74–8, 175–6; legal identity of, 36–7, 62–3, 68–9; single, 37, 38, 40–2, 75–6; agency of, 42, 103, 128, 136–40, 147; husbands, choice of, 43–4, 45–7; widows, 45–6, 133–4, 136–8, 140; autonomy of, 45–7, 51–3, 62–3, 71–2; lesbianism, 49, 54–5, 113–19, 141, 156–8, 167; strong, 52–4; and money, 61, 65–6, 70–3; married, 62–3, 68–9, 147–8, 161–3, 168–9; wives, 62–3, 68–9, 85–6, 147–8, 161–3, 168–9; masculine, 66, 98–9, 166; subjectivity of, 84–7, 89–91; doctors, 95–103; nurses, 100–1; sexuality of, 106–9, 111, 112–21, 126; spiritual power, 127, 128, 138; and religion, 130, 142–3, 149–50, 154–5, 160, 170–1; marriage, power in, 147–8, 161–3, 168–9; *see also* femininity; married women's property acts; property
Women's Printing Society, 75
Women's Union Journal, 75
Wood, Ellen (Mrs Henry Wood), 4; *St Martin's Eve*, 5; *East Lynne*, 40–1, 47, 48
work, of women, 27, 74–8, 175–6

www.ingramcontent.com/pod-product-compliance
Lightning Source LLC
Chambersburg PA
CBHW060952230426
43665CB00015B/2168